Family
Diversity
Continuity and Change in the Contemporary Family

Sage Sourcebooks for
SSHS
the Human Services

Pauline Irit Erera
University of Washington

Sage Publications
International Educational and Professional Publisher
Thousand Oaks ▪ London ▪ New Delhi

For information:

Sage Publications, Inc.
2455 Teller Road
Thousand Oaks, California 91320
E-mail: order@sagepub.com

Sage Publications Ltd.
6 Bonhill Street
London EC2A 4PU
United Kingdom

Sage Publications India Pvt. Ltd.
M-32 Market
Greater Kailash I
New Delhi 110 048 India

Printed in the United States of America

Library of Congress Cataloging-in-Publication Data

Erera, Pauline Irit.
  Family diversity: Continuity and change in the contemporary family/
By Pauline Irit Erera.
    p. cm. — (Sage sourcebooks for the human services series; v. 44)
  Includes bibliographical references and index.
  ISBN 0-7619-1292-4 (C : acid-free paper) — ISBN 0-7619-1293-2 (P :
acid-free paper)
    1. Family—United States. 2. Family services—United States. 3.
Family policy—United States. I. Title. II. Series.
  HQ536 .E73 2001
  306.85'0973—dc21   2001002217

This book is printed on acid-free paper.

01   02   03   04   05   10   9   8   7   6   5   4   3   2   1

Acquiring Editor:	Nancy S. Hale
Corwin Editorial Assistant:	Vonessa Vondera
Production Editor:	Diane S. Foster
Editorial Assistant:	Ester Marcelino
Typesetter/Designer:	Denyse Dunn
Copy Editor:	Stacey Shimizu
Proofreader:	Andrea Martin
Indexer:	Cristina Haley
Cover Designer:	Michelle Lee

CONTENTS

This book is dedicated with love to Richard Weatherley, without whom this book would have not been made possible.

ACKNOWLEDGMENTS

As this book is about families, it is my pleasure to start by expressing gratitude to my own families. First and foremost, I offer my profound gratefulness to my husband, Richard Weatherley, for his invaluable help, genuine and tireless support, and love. He extended his selfless and generous assistance from the early discussions about writing the book through the struggles and joy of writing it. His wealth of knowledge, guidance, and contribution are reflected throughout the book. Giving birth to this book was, in many ways, a family affair.

I wish to thank my sons, Doron and Liron Erera, who went along with me through the many transitions we experienced together, including the transitions from being a traditional family to becoming a single-parent family, a stepfamily, and more. Their trust, love, and respect throughout times of hardship and challenge made this book possible. I also wish to thank my parents, Ray and the late Alexander Kopelovitch. While raising me in a traditional family, they instilled in me an appreciation for diversity.

My deep gratitude to Catherine Keir for her wisdom, help, and friendship, and for being there for me from the very beginning of this project to its completion. Her perceptiveness, sensitivity, and depth helped me discover new ways of dealing with the challenges of authorship. She was instrumental in helping me turn the task of writing into a process of dialogue, self-discovery, and growth.

Boundless thanks to Yael Haft, who helped me to accept my own diversity and alternative lifestyle. Without her, this undertaking would not have been possible. She was there with me, as always, throughout the process.

I am grateful for the encouragement of James Whittaker and Ming Sum Tsui at the early stages of this project, and to Nancy Hooyman, Dean of the University of Washington School of Social Work, for her consideration and generosity in helping me find the time needed to complete the book.

I wish to express my appreciation to Christine DiStefano for bringing to my attention a feminist perspective on caregiving that has influenced this book.

My thanks to Professors Jean Kruzich, Peter Pecora, Cynthia Steel, and Steven Soifer, as well as to the anonymous reviewers who critiqued individual chapters of the book. Their helpful comments and suggestions, as well as their support, are greatly appreciated. I also wish to thank Peter Pecora and Jim Whittaker for sharing with me the revised edition of their book *The Child Welfare Challenge: Policy, Practice and Research* prior to its publication.

Chapter 1

WHAT IS A FAMILY?

Families have always come in various forms, reflecting social and economic conditions and the cultural norms of the times. However, since the 1960s, the increasing diversity among families in the United States and most other Western nations has been especially striking. At a dizzying pace, the traditional, two-parent, heterosexual family has given way to variety of family arrangements. Today, most adults no longer live in a coresident nuclear family (Hill, 1995). The first-married, heterosexual family we have cherished since at least Victorian times is but one of numerous alternative family structures (Csikszentmihalyi, 1997).

In 1998, just 26% of American households were composed of married couples with children. This was down from 45% in the early 1970s (University of Chicago National Opinion Research Center, 1999). Only half of American children live in families that the Census Bureau defines as the traditional nuclear family: a married couple living with their biological children and no one else (Vobejda, 1994). Furthermore, family arrangements differ considerably according to race and ethnicity. Although about 56% of white American children live in a traditional nuclear family, only about 26% of African American children and 38% of Hispanic children do (Vobejda, 1994).

In this chapter, I examine alternative constructions of what a family is. I trace the rise and decline of the traditional family, outline the subsequent increase in family diversity, and examine reactions to family diversity as expressed in the debate about "family values." I also discuss the continuing influence of the traditional family model. Finally, I consider the strengths and promise of family diversity, and set forth the perspectives that inform the analysis of the families in this book.

DEFINING FAMILIES

The family is not simply a social institution. It is an ideological construct laden with symbolism and with a history and politics of its own. As Jagger and Wright (1999) put it, "The groupings that are called families are socially constructed rather than naturally or biologically given" (p. 3). In studying families, we need to keep clear the distinctions between the institutionalized family, the ideology of the family, and the lives of actual families. Although social and economic forces shape family life, our understanding of family is shaped by the evolving patterns of the actual families around us. Furthermore, conceptions of what constitutes a family are necessarily rooted in time and place. White, Western, two-parent families have generally been regarded, explicitly or implicitly, as the model or template against which we compare all families, regardless of culture, ethnicity, race, or class. This parochial view distorts our understanding of diverse families by considering them deviations from the norm (Smith, 1995; Thorne, 1982).

One early definition of the family was that offered by the anthropologist George Peter Murdock (1949), based on his survey of 250 ethnographic reports:

> The family is a social group characterized by common residence, economic cooperation, and reproduction. It includes adults of both sexes, at least two of whom maintain a socially approved sexual relationship, and one or more children, own or adopted, of the sexually cohabiting adults. (p. 1)

Murdock identified the basic family unit found in about one quarter of the societies he surveyed as "a married man and woman with their offspring" (p. 1), which he termed a nuclear family. Another quarter of the societies were predominantly polygamous, with families based on plural marriages of a spouse, hence, in his view, constituting two or more nuclear families. In the remaining half surveyed, the families were extended in that the nuclear family resided with the bride's or the groom's parents and/or other relatives. Murdock, reflecting the prevailing orthodoxy of the times, concluded that the nuclear family was universal and inevitable, the basis for more complex family forms.

Given the diversity of families and the political debates about them, a single, all-encompassing definition of "family" is impossible to achieve. Families are defined in a variety of ways depending on the purposes and circumstances (Smith, 1995; Sprey, 1988). Although traditionalists have held blood ties or consanguinity to be a defining characteristic of the family, others argue that we should define families according to the attachments and intimacy that individuals have toward significant people in their lives. This latter definition shifts the focus from the family's structure or legal status to the nature and meaning of relationships (Dowd, 1997).

Diverse families challenge our definition and perceptions of what a family is. These families also "challenge gender roles and influence gender typing by what they say and what they do" (Dowd, 1997, p. 110). They force us to reconsider our conceptions of what a mother, father, parent, and sibling are. Is a family defined by genes and blood relationships? Shared residence? Is it a group of people who provide one another social, emotional, and physical support, caring, and love? Does a family necessarily involve two adults? Are these adults necessarily of the opposite sex? Must families be based on marriage? Can a child have two or more mothers or fathers? Is a parent more "real" by virtue of biological or legal status? Does a family have to share a common residence, economic cooperation, and reproduction to be a family? Such questions, highlighted throughout the book, are the subject of heated debates about the family and "family values."

THE RISE AND DECLINE OF
THE TRADITIONAL FAMILY

The Heyday of the Traditional Family

The 1950s saw a surge in family formation associated with the end of the depression and World War II. Although few Americans ever enjoyed family lives as harmonious, wholesome, or predictable as the ones portrayed in those beloved fifties television sitcoms, such programs symbolized a definition of ideal family life that was widely shared in that decade. Three fifths of U.S. households in that period fit the model of the nuclear family structure, with its breadwinner-husband and homemaker-wife, of their pop culture icons. The economy was booming and even many working-class men earned enough to support such families. Yet this upsurge in marriage and childbearing proved to be a short-lived experiment. Starting in the 1960s, fertility rates began to decline, and the trend to early marriage was reversed (Silverstein & Auerbach, 1999). Family life in the 1950s was hardly ideal. Families were not as well off economically as they would become by the end of the 1960s; African Americans in particular had higher rates of poverty than they do now. Women, minorities, lesbians, gays, and nonconforming groups were subject to discrimination, and family problems got little attention or social assistance (Coontz, 1997).

In some ways, the decline of the 1950s family grew out of the trends and contradictions of the fifties themselves. The main reason for family change was the breakdown of the postwar social compact between government, corporations, and workers. The 1950s were years of active government assistance to families. Government-backed home mortgages financed many of the new family homes, and the minimum wage was set high enough to support a family of three above the poverty level. Large numbers of workers joined unions, received pensions and health benefits, and worked a relatively short workweek. Corporations and the wealthy were taxed at high rates to support high levels of spending on veterans benefits and public works (Coontz, 1997).

Family Diversity in the 1960s and 1970s

The affluence and optimism that explains the family behavior of the postwar generation were challenged by America's new economic problems, whose impact was felt at the family level in the form of inflation and lower real earnings. Public policies aggravated these problems by cutting taxes for corporations and the wealthy while cutting spending for services, public works, and investments in human capital (Coontz, 1997). This meant that families had to modify the socially valued form of the family to try to protect their socially valued lifestyle: the standard of living to which they had become accustomed. Economic pressures made women's employment more a matter of necessity than of choice (Coontz, 1997). Today's politicians are being disingenuous when they advocate a return to the 1950s family while opposing the kinds of social and political supports that helped make it possible (Coontz, 1997).

Along with the economic shifts in the late 1950s and early 1960s came technological developments and social movements that also contributed to the stunning increase in family diversity. The example of African Americans' struggle to secure civil rights inspired other minorities and marginalized groups—women, gay men and lesbians, the disabled—to fight for their rights. The 1960s and 1970s became an era of diversity and identity politics as a host of "others" sought recognition and liberation from the constraints of discriminatory laws, social policies, and negative stereotypes. Foremost among those claiming their rights were women.

The struggle for women's liberation was advanced by the availability of the birth control pill and other methods that gave women control over reproduction. These changes generated an increased acceptance of sexual behavior not necessarily linked with marriage, for women as well as for men (Riley, 1997). While white feminists began to claim the right to control and limit their fertility through the use of contraception and abortion, women of color started claiming the right to have their fertility not be controlled by forced contraception and sterilization (Hargaden & Llewellin, 1996). By 1973, many women in the United States and other industrialized countries were able to prevent pregnancies, had access to legal abortion, and could end unwanted pregnancies before birth (Riley, 1997).

The movement for gender equality led to increased employment opportunities for women, while at the same time declining wage rates for unskilled male workers made them less desirable marriage partners. Although paid far less than their male counterparts, an increasing number of women were now employed and financially independent. Consequently, more women who were unhappy in their marriages were able to divorce (Coontz, 1997; Riley, 1997). The changing roles of women, their increasing participation in the labor force, and their economic independence had undercut the economic basis of marriage (Lichter & McLaughlin, 1997). With divorce becoming more available, community norms regarding divorce, single parenthood, and nonmarital childbearing began to change. More people were themselves the product of diverse families, and were more accepting of divorce, single parenthood, and women's right to live independently.

Single-parent families were in many respects the pioneers of family diversity, paving the way for the recognition of other families. The growing acceptance of divorced, single-parent families facilitated the emergence of yet another form of single parenthood: that resulting not from divorce, but from women electing to give birth while remaining single. Women increasingly saw motherhood without marriage as offering greater satisfaction and security than a marriage of questionable stability (Mann & Roseneil, 1999). Increasingly, women chose to cohabit rather than formally marry, to postpone marriage and childbearing, and to live alone. Still others chose to give birth, adopt, or foster children as single parents. Many women, defying the stigma attached to childless women, elected not to have children at all, thus creating a new family configuration: childless families by choice. With fewer unwanted pregnancies and fewer unwanted births, and with more white, single mothers keeping their babies as had African American mothers in the past, fewer white babies were available for adoption (Riley, 1997). The decline in the number of babies placed for adoption precipitated an increased interest in international adoptions as an alternative. Because these adoptions often involved children who were racially and/or ethnically different from their adoptive parents, the adoption could not be kept secret as had been the practice in the past. The growing acceptance of adoptive families, in turn, facilitated a greater acceptance of stepfamilies and other families not related by blood.

With the increasing numbers and visibility of single-parent, step-, and adoptive families, the gay liberation movement opened the way for the emergence of gay and lesbian families. Some gay men and lesbians were divorced and had custody of the children, becoming in the process single-parent families. Others chose to give birth to a child within the lesbian/gay relationship.

Another factor contributing to family diversity since the 1970s, and especially to foster families and grandmother-headed families, has been a dramatic increase in the imprisonment of women and mothers, a legacy of the war on drugs with its harsh sentencing policies. Most of the women in prison are there for drug-related offenses, often because of the activities of a male partner. This, together with the growing number of women, especially women of color, infected by HIV (the human immunodeficiency virus) has contributed to an increasing number of children whose mothers are not able to parent them. In addition, many children, and especially African American children, are removed from homes considered unfit and placed in foster care, sometimes with relatives. Increasingly, grandmothers are assuming responsibility for raising their grandchildren.

Finally, innovations in reproductive technology have vastly opened up the possibilities for people to create new kinds of families, further challenging conventional definitions of family. New reproductive technologies (NRTs) include donor insemination, embryo freezing and transfer, ovum extraction, and *in vitro* fertilization (IVF). The first test-tube baby, conceived through *in vitro* fertilization, was born in England in 1978, and the first surrogate birth, in which an embryo was transferred to a woman with no genetic connection to it, took place in 1986. In 1992, a postmenopausal grandmother gave birth to her own granddaughter in South Africa, having served as a surrogate for her daughter's embryo.

To protect marriages, the law in most jurisdictions recognizes husbands of inseminated women as the "real" fathers (Benkov, 1997) while denying parental rights to donors (Bartholet, 1993). Although NRTs reflect a preference for biological reproduction over social parenting through adoption, fostering, or informal care of relatives (McDaniel, 1988), social parenting has become a powerful force in family diversity. NRTs were originally administered to support traditional nuclear families, and were denied to unmarried women. However, as they became increasingly available through for-profit laboratories seeking to expand their markets, they were offered to single women, including lesbians. To date, about one million children have been conceived in laboratories in the United States (Benkov, 1997). The NRTs have undermined the cultural norm that blood relations are the *sine qua non* of families, and that nonbiological members are not "real" family members. Families created through reproductive technologies, similar to adoptive-foster families, and to some extent like stepfamilies, defy the notion that biological conception has to be the basis for family formation. This disjunction between reproduction and parenting, between the biological and social aspects of parenting, alters the meaning of parenthood, kinship, and family (Benkov, 1997; Gross, 1997; Stacey, 1996).

Families in the 1980s and 1990s: The Backlash Against Family Diversity

The 1980s and 1990s were, in many respects, a period of regression in the United States with respect to civil rights and policies supporting diversity. The family became, and continues to be, a battleground over contending visions of what a family ought to be. Voices on the right blame changes in the family for a wide range of social problems, while voices on the left look to the family to provide the basis for a more communitarian society. At one extreme, we hear claims that the family is obsolete, a reactionary institution destined to disappear. At the other, conservatives strive to uphold "family values," advocating a return to the conventional family arrangements enshrined in midcentury television sitcoms (Csikszentmihalyi, 1997). Across the political spectrum, invoking "family values" is a way of idealizing the traditional nuclear family to the exclusion of other family forms (Jagger & Wright, 1999).

Family values proponents offer a simple and dangerous misdiagnosis of what they consider wrong in America—the "family breakdown" thesis (Stacey, 1998). Family breakdown—namely the high divorce rates, the decline of the two-parent married family, and the increase in family diversity—has been blamed for everything from child poverty, declining educational standards, substance abuse, high homicide rates, AIDS (acquired immune deficiency syndrome), infertility, and teen pregnancy to narcissism and the Los Angeles riots (Coontz, 1997; Jagger & Wright, 1999; Wright & Jagger, 1999). Family breakdown is, in turn, attributed to a generalized decline in family values, which is often blamed on a lack of commitment to marriage, an acceptance of female-headed families as a way of life, feminism, the sexual revolution, and gay liberation (Beca Zinn, 1997; Coontz, 1997). Hence women's desire for personal fulfillment is described by conservatives as an egotistic abandonment of parental obligations that sacrifices the well-being of children (Council on Families in America, 1996). Ironically, the current emphasis on family self-sufficiency and the pressure on single mothers to be self-supporting are in direct conflict with conservatives' traditional preference for full-time mothers (Wright & Jagger, 1999).

In keeping with the family breakdown thesis, political discourse in the 1990s blamed single motherhood for the perpetuation of an "underclass" in British and American society. Although there is little consensus among scholars about the underclass, or whether it exists at all, under the label of the underclass debate, researchers returned to old questions about the relationship between family structure, race, and poverty. In the 1960s and early 1970s, the discussion focused on how poor families adapted to poverty; current discussions, in contrast, are primarily concerned with the failure of women-headed families to lift themselves and their children out of poverty (Jarrett, 1994). For example, American conservative Charles Murray, who played a prominent role in blaming single motherhood for poverty and violence, argued (in Wright & Jagger, 1999) that more young women were choosing unwed motherhood because the sexual revolution had destigmatized it and the welfare system was rewarding it. Though welfare costs have always been a very small portion of the federal budget, single-parent families were also held responsible for a "crisis" of the welfare state (Beca Zinn, 1997; Mann & Roseneil, 1999; Wright & Jagger, 1999).

Although single mothers were being attacked, they suffered high rates of poverty, a legacy of social policies that especially disadvantages women and children. Welfare benefits to impoverished single mothers and their children in the United States declined markedly from the 1970s to the 1990s, and in 1996, the federal welfare entitlement was abolished in favor of a drastically limited employment-based program. The attacks on welfare were, in effect, attacks against struggling and vulnerable families (Stacey, 1996).

The attack on single mothers is partly a backlash against feminism, an attempt to restore fathers to their "rightful role." It is also motivated by concerns over how women are exercising their agency and their freedom of choice to become mothers or not. Instead of viewing disadvantaged women as committed, responsible mothers who assume custody and care of their children, the rhetoric portrays them as oppressors of the fathers. The fathers, on the other hand, who are at least as responsible for the creation of poor single-parent families, are often viewed as the victims. If they pay child support, they are heralded as responsible fathers, even though the child support is usually insufficient to meet the expense of raising the children, and even though they generally forgo the daily responsibilities of caring for the children. This rhetoric justifies reductions in government assistance to single mothers and their children, making their situations even worse (Mann & Roseneil, 1999).

THE FAMILY VALUES AGENDA

Family values proponents define the family as an institution comprising people related by blood and marriage that performs specific social functions. The majority of family values advocates use "the family" to mean a heterosexual, conjugal, nuclear, domestic unit, ideally one with a male breadwinner, female homemaker, and their dependent offspring—a version of the 1950s television Ozzie-and-Harriet family, sometimes updated to include employed wives and mothers (Stacey, 1998). This prescriptive definition of what constitutes a proper family obscures racial, class, and sexual diversity in domestic arrangements, as well as masking the inequities within the traditional family (Stacey, 1998). Pluralism, so commonly recognized in other aspects of American society, has yet to be fully accepted when it comes to the family (Klee, Schmidt, & Johnson, 1989).

A striking feature of our contemporary family politics is the chasm between behavior and ideology. Most family values enthusiasts still judge our "brave new families" by a fifties standard to which only a minority of citizens would wish to return (Stacey, 1998). In a 1999 national survey, for example, only a third of the respondents thought that parents should stay together just because they have children (University of Chicago National Opinion Research Center, 1999). Support for "traditional family values" serves political purposes. It provides a rationale for family surveillance and intervention, focuses attention on individual moral solutions to social problems rather than costly public solutions, and offers a simple alternative to dealing with the real complexities of social change. The new call for family values represents an effort to reduce collective responsibility and increase the dependency of family members on one another (Wright & Jagger, 1999).

Pro–family values stories are appearing in the press, in popular magazines, on radio and television talk shows, and in scholarly journals. During the late 1980s, a network of research and policy institutes, think tanks and commissions, began mobilizing to forge a national consensus on family values and to shape the family politics of the "new" Democratic Party. Central players were the Institute for American Values and the Council on Families in America, whose goal is to restore the privileged status of lifelong, heterosexual marriage.

The Council on Families in America (1996) urges marriage counselors, family therapists, and family life educators to approach their work "with a bias in favor of" marriage" and to "link advocacy for children to advocacy for marriage" (p. 311). It advocates a revision of the federal tax code "to provide more favorable treatment for married couples with children" (p. 313), and advocates a "bias in favor of marriage-with-children in the allocation of subsidized housing loans and public housing" (p. 314).

Marriage has become increasingly fragile with the increase in women's employment and their reduced economic dependency on men. It has also become less obligatory, particularly for women. In all cultures and eras, stable marriage systems have rested upon coercion—overt or veiled—and on inequality. Proposals to restrict access to divorce and parenting implicitly recognize this. Without coercion, divorce and single motherhood will remain commonplace. It seems a poignant commentary on the benefits to women of modern marriage that even when women retain chief responsibility for supporting children, raising them and caring for them, when they earn much less than men with similar "cultural capital," and when they and their children suffer major economic loss after divorce, so many regard divorce as the lesser evil.

Rather than examining and solving the problems of traditional marriages that so often end up in divorce, advocates of family values aim to coerce women to stay in marriages by erecting barriers to divorce. They wish to restore fault criteria to divorce proceedings and impose new restrictions, like mandatory waiting periods and compulsory counseling. Claiming that divorce and unwed motherhood inflict devastating harm on children, they seek to revive the social stigma that once marked these "selfish" practices. They advocate restricting adoption to married couples, and they oppose welfare payments to unmarried mothers. However, in their staunch advocacy of marriage, they avoid examining what might be lacking in a traditional marriage, especially for women, or questioning why so many women choose to divorce or not to marry.

What is primarily at stake in the debate over the family is the relationship between the sexes. Advocates of family values assign responsibilities to families without explicitly acknowledging the burdens that family life places on women or the gender conflicts resulting from unequal roles. At the same time, they place most of the blame for family problems on "deviant" women, especially those who raise children alone.

The Significance of Family Structure

Contrary to the claims of family values advocates, there is no empirical basis for granting privileged status to the heterosexual, nuclear, two-parent family (Acock & Demo, 1994; Dowd, 1997; Silverstein & Auerbach, 1999). Few social scientists would agree that a family's structure is more important than the quality of the relationships between parents and children. Revisionists employ academic sleights of hand to evade this consensus. For example, they rest claims on misleading comparison groups and on studies that do not use any comparison groups at all. In fact, most children from both divorced or nondivorced families turn out reasonably well; and when other parental resources—like income, education, self-esteem, and a supportive social environment—are roughly similar, signs of two-parent privilege largely disappear. Most research indicates that a stable, intimate relationship with one responsible, nurturing adult is a child's surest path to becoming a nurturing adult as well (Furstenberg & Cherlin, 1991). As Dowd (1997) points out, "Dysfunctional families come in all shapes and sizes; so do healthy families" (p. xv). There is no question that two responsible, loving parents generally can offer children more than one parent can. However, three or four might prove even better. Putting the case against the essential significance of structure, Dowd (1997) concludes,

Children need love, care, and parenting. Structure neither produces nor insures that those things will be present. We need to put children first, structure second. It makes no sense to punish children or separate them from their families as the consequence of structure that they had no hand in creating and that are unconnected to their well-being. (p. xix)

The "Essential Father"

With many mothers no longer at home full time, and in the absence of universal child care and policies to help families integrate work and caregiving, the conservative stance taps into widespread anxiety about "who will raise the children" (Silverstein & Auerbach, 1999). Attacks on single-parent families are also based on claims that families without fathers cannot socialize sons into civilized manhood (Charles Murray, in Wright & Jagger, 1997). These concerns about the well-being of children, and especially boys, represent a reaction against the women's movement, the perceived loss of male privilege, and the gay liberation movement (Silverstein & Auerbach, 1999). As expressed by the Council on Families in America (1996), "The explosion of never-married motherhood in our society means that fathers are increasingly viewed as superfluous, unnecessary, and irrelevant" (pp. 302–303). Men have lost their position at the center of family life. With marriage losing its normative force and with increasing numbers of women working, men have seen their economic ascendancy over the family being eroded, and most are expected to share at least some of the domestic tasks. The conservative concern about the necessity of the "essential father" can be seen as an effort to reestablish male dominance by rescuing the traditional family based on traditional gender roles (Silverstein & Auerbach, 1999).

Conservatives have it backward when they argue that the collapse of traditional family values is at the heart of our social decay. The losses in real earnings and in breadwinner jobs, the persistence of low-wage work for women, global economic restructuring, and corporate greed have wreaked far more havoc on Ozzie-and-Harriet land than have the combined effects of feminism, the sexual revolution, gay liberation, the counterculture, narcissism, and every other value flip of the past half-century. There is no going back to the "good old 1950s," when breadwinner husbands had unpaid homemaker wives who tended dependent children and the household full time. The modern family has been decisively replaced by the postmodern family of working mothers, high divorce rates, and diverse family arrangements (Coontz, 1997; Stacey, 1998).

Nevertheless, the traditional family continues to cast its shadow over other family forms.

THE HEGEMONY OF THE
TRADITIONAL FAMILY

The overpowering strength of the paradigm of the first-married, heterosexual family lingers even though this family style has long since lost its place as the most prevalent (Glick, 1989). Despite the diversity, society's institutions continue to support a single family structure that is no longer applicable to the majority of families. As Dowd (1997) states,

> We as a society, through law, support nuclear marital families in significant material and ideological ways. We provide resources including financial support, fringe benefits, tax breaks, and housing. We facilitate the use of reproductive technology or adoption for favored families. We define our vision of family, ideologically and practically . . . by limiting recognition of non-marital families. (p. 4)

The supremacy and the idealization of the traditional family model are expressed in laws, policies, and institutional practices, attitudes, and behaviors. Nuclear families have historically provided a model of normalcy for which family specialists, such as psychologists, social workers, family researchers and theorists, have based their ideals (Adams & Steinmetz, 1993). Increased social tolerance for diversity has, to some extent, modified the notion that nuclear families offer an exemplary family structure. Nevertheless, social policies and attitudes still favor the traditional family. This puts enormous pressures on diverse families to play down their uniqueness and to act like the traditional family, as if this is the only "right" kind of family, irrespective of the differences in structure and style. Despite its demographic decline, "The image of this idealized form [of the traditional nuclear family] persists in the social consciousness and remains the standard against which all other configurations are compared" (Allen & Baber, 1992, p. 379).

Viewed against a template of the first-married, heterosexual family, other family structures tend to fall into two broad stereotypical categories: the deviant and the variant. A deviant stereotype is assigned to families that seem much too different to be regarded as a variation of the first-married, heterosexual family. In the past, this included the single-parent family, and now includes lesbian and gay families, teenage single-parent families, and childless families, among others. Deviant implies not only that these families are different, but that they are bad or wrong in some way. Therefore, "deviant" families need somehow to prove their legitimacy. The variant family stereotype views diverse families more positively, considering them more or less like first-married, heterosexual families, but with a difference. Families considered variant usually have two parents of the opposite sex who reside with children in the same household; notable examples are adoptive and stepfamilies. Although lacking the negative connotation of deviance, this positive stereotype is also problematic. It establishes unrealistic expectations based on the model of the traditional nuclear family. Because such families are not quite the same when measured against the template, they may be left feeling that they are falling short in some respects. The stereotypes exert pressures on families to try to function in the same mold as the traditional family, or to "pass" in order to gain the legitimacy and resources reserved for traditional families. The appeal of assimilation is especially attractive for those families that most resemble a traditional family. "Passing," however, creates tensions between the actual and idealized lifestyles of family members. As Eheart and Power (1995) found in their study of adoptive families, "failure occurs when families live stories that differ in acceptable ways from their expectations of what their family life should be like" (p. 211). It engenders a falsehood that may lead family members to experience a sense of failure, shame, and identity confusion. At the same time, it restricts their creativity, flexibility, and uniqueness (Biddle, Kaplan, & Silverstein, 1998). In contrast, when families manage to let go of myths of the ideal family life, their lives are experienced as appropriate and fitting.

It is therefore not surprising that with the exception of stepfamilies and single-parent families, the families discussed in this book have rarely been examined as family structures in their own right. To the extent that they have been considered at all, it has been from a particular academic or practice perspective. Foster families, viewed as nuclear families temporarily hosting an additional child, are examined from the standpoint of child welfare; gay and lesbian families, under gender or women's studies; and grandmother-headed families, within gerontology or race and gender studies. Furthermore, these families are often characterized as lacking something. Single-parent families are deemed deficient for lack of a father. Grandparents raising grandchildren are discounted because they are old, are not the parents, and are frequently people of color and poor. Gay and lesbian families are not considered as families at all because the partners are of the same sex and because they are not married. The refusal to acknowledge them as families is a denial that their relationships count, regardless of their stability, duration, or quality.

Family theories do not sufficiently account for families in their diversity. New perspectives are needed that value family plurality and resilience (Demo & Allen, 1996; McAdoo, 1998). As Weitzman (1975) noted a quarter of a century ago, in a diverse society, a single family form cannot fit the needs of all. Rather than shaping concepts of the family from a single mold, we must recognize the diversity and fluidity of family and household arrangements, and acknowledge change in families as a sign of strength.

NEW ALTERNATIVES AND PERSPECTIVES
FROM DIVERSE FAMILIES

Changes in the family are a necessary part of the transformation of society that allows women access to employment, alternative roles, and greater freedom outside the domestic sphere (Gross, 1992). As Coontz (1997) persuasively argues, "It is the lag in adjusting values, behaviors, and institutions to new realities that creates problems in contemporary families" (p. 109). For example, the highest rates of violence against women are found in states where women's status has improved the least (Coontz, 1997). Because the gender structures supporting inequality exist on the institutional, interactional, and individual levels, it must be attacked on all those levels (Risman, 1998). Risman invites us to go ahead and violate these inequitable gender rules, to "dare a moment of gender vertigo," as a necessary collective step toward constructing a more equal society (p. 162).

The continuing bias against diverse families perpetuates a system of patriarchal domination. This domination, however, can be challenged through the reinterpretation of difference, recognizing family diversity as a strength and a resource rather than a deficit. By valuing the differences among families, we affirm the liberating benefits of a multicultural society. Although the eclipse of the traditional family by a diversity of other family styles is unsettling to many, it also brings hope for greater democracy and equality in family relations, especially for women and members of sexual minorities. Instead of resisting change and trying to revive the patriarchal structures of the past, we should accept the changes that are already well under way, with grace, wisdom, and tolerance (Stacey, 1998).

ORGANIZATION AND
PERSPECTIVE OF THIS BOOK

The conservative Council on Families in America (1996) has urged family scholars to "re-write educational textbooks and family life education curricula so that marriage-with-children is portrayed as a desirable social good rather than as just one of many equally desirable lifestyle alternatives" (p. 312). In contrast, this book seeks to portray and celebrate the whole panoply of family structures and lifestyles that are evolving in our society, highlighting these families' strengths and adaptability.

When I began this project, the working title was *Understanding Nontraditional Families*. However, the conventional terminology describing diverse families as "nontraditional" implicitly affirms the preeminence of the traditional family as the one appropriate template against which all other families are to be judged. My aim, however, is to shift the focus, allowing diverse families to take their natural place at center stage alongside the traditional nuclear family, hence liberating diverse families from the tyranny of the traditional family model. Although I have not totally banished the term *nontraditional family,* my struggles to find alternative terminology served as yet another reminder of how firmly entrenched the traditional family model is in our thinking and language.

Four key perspectives inform the analysis of the families in this book. First, in addition to examining family structure and dynamics, each family is considered within its unique social, legal, and historical environment. Families exist and can be understood only within a broader context. Different families have different histories and are viewed quite differently by society.

Second, the families are examined from a feminist perspective. That is, rather than viewing daily family life as personal, the assumption is that the personal is public and that family lives are a microcosm of the society at large. Interpersonal relations within families, and especially gender relations, represent issues of power and domination, reflecting social structures and institutions. Men and women's experiences in families differ considerably. Although not at all neglecting the role of men, I focus more on women who are, in most cases, the principal caretakers within these families.

Third, I consider how race, ethnicity, age, sexual orientation, and gender intersect in diverse families. Irrespective of where they fit within these categories, nontraditional families, like minority groups, tend to be viewed by the dominant society as "other." In this sense, an exploration of family diversity can also enhance our understanding of diversity and multiculturalism in the larger society.

Finally, I consider diverse families from a strengths perspective, acknowledging their capacities, competence, and resilience. Each family is analyzed as a family structure in its own right, rather than as a variant of the traditional family. The stresses and difficulties are by no means ignored, but are considered from the standpoint of these particular families. Furthermore, as this book shows, diverse families can teach us valuable lessons about family relationships, lessons that apply to all families, including the traditional family. They can teach us about resilience and creativity, gender equality, and the benefits of an egalitarian division of labor within the family.

Although this book does not directly address the traditional nuclear family, it is constantly present by implication and by contrast, and in that sense, the book is as much about the traditional family as it is about family diversity. However, instead of viewing diverse families through a traditional family lens, I view the traditional family from the standpoint of what diverse families can teach us. In so doing, the experience of diverse families sheds light on both the traditional family and the social structures that sustain it. Far from being a private haven of unconditional love, support, and nurturance, the traditional family is revealed as an arena where societal issues of power, gender, and otherness are played out on a daily basis. After all, if the traditional family were as ideal as it is portrayed by its proponents, there would not be so many diverse families.

Furthermore, traditional families have much to learn from members of diverse families about such basic assumptions as the importance of blood relationships and formal marriage for family life, or about the need to share residence with family members in order to feel that we are a family and to be accepted as one. In reading about the individual families, the reader is invited to ask herself or himself about these and other assumptions we have about family life. For example, is one family better than others are? Does one family style suit everyone? Although these issues are addressed throughout the book, I will revisit them in the concluding chapter (Chapter 8).

These questions posed by diverse families are neither trivial nor minor. They challenge the core premises on which the traditional family is based, and in that sense, they undermine the traditional family. Yet questioning the seemingly unquestionable assumptions about the traditional family can also inform people who choose to live in such families how to improve their lives and strengthen their families. If we care about families, we should learn from them why they chose a different path and what solutions they have to the problems of the traditional family. In that sense, to understand the traditional family better, and in order to help it change, we should heed diversity. And although we learn from diverse families, we ought to listen carefully to the lessons taught also by members of minority groups, including women, people of color, persons from diverse ethnicities and cultures, immigrants, and lesbians and gays, as well as people with disabilities, the homeless, and the elderly. I believe that drastic change in existing gender relations in families, especially in the traditional family, will result in greater happiness for women and men. Although enhancing a sense of well-being, egalitarianism, and cooperation between the couple, it will also serve as a model for children about fairness, mutual respect, and justice. This learning within the family can then be extended beyond its confines to bolster all aspects of our social and political structures with newfound respect for nonconformity, diversity, and innovation as principles of societal organization.

This book examines six different families: adoptive, foster, single-parent, step-, gay and lesbian, and grandmother-headed families. I selected these families primarily because their unique structures set them apart from traditional, nuclear, heterosexual families. There are, of course, many other family types that could also claim inclusion in a book about family diversity, such as cohabiting families, childless families, and extended and multiple generation families, to name a few. Although necessarily focusing on just some families, many of the observations about the families in this book apply to other families as well.

The families addressed in this book often intersect. For example, a stepfamily may be also an adoptive or gay family, and a grandparent-headed family may also be a foster, single-parent family. Furthermore, like all families, diverse families are dynamic and changing. For example, a foster family may become an adoptive family, a single-parent family may become a stepfamily, and an adoptive family may give birth to biological children. Though each family chapter may be read on its own, a reading of several or all chapters will reinforce the general observations about family diversity that are summarized in this and in the concluding chapter.

DISCUSSION QUESTIONS

1. How are families depicted in the media today? How well do these portrayals capture the reality of family diversity?

2. Are some families and some family relationships more "real" than others? Are some family styles better than others are? What criteria do you think are most appropriate for assessing family styles?

3. What changes in the family would you expect to see in the next 10 years? The next 25 years? Why would you expect these changes to occur?

4. Why do you suppose the United States lags so far behind other industrialized countries in its policies to support children and families? What would it take for the United States to start to catch up and to adopt more family-friendly policies?

5. A number of social and economic developments since the 1960s have contributed to a dramatic increase in family diversity. How might families be affected by globalization and corporate restructuring?

6. What are the influences that drive the family debate? Is it likely to continue? Why or why not?

7. Should there be any restrictions placed on the availability of NRTs? Or should they all be available to anyone who can afford them? Is it fair to deny them to those who cannot afford the cost?

SUGGESTIONS FOR FURTHER READING

Acock, A. C., & Demo, D. H. (1994). *Family diversity and well-being.* Thousand Oaks, CA: Sage.

Coontz, S. (1997). *The way we really are: Coming to terms with America's changing families.* New York: Basic Books.

Jagger, G., & Wright, C. (Eds.). (1999). *Changing family values.* London: Routledge.

McDaniel, S. A. (1988). Women's roles, reproduction, and the new reproductive technologies: A new stork rising. In N. Mandell & A. Duffy (Eds.), *Reconstructing the Canadian family: Feminist perspectives* (pp. 175–206). Toronto, Ontario: Butterworths.

Stacey, J. (1996). *In the name of the family: Rethinking family values in the postmodern age.* Boston: Beacon.

Stacey, J. (1998). *Brave new families: Stories of domestic upheaval in late twentieth century America* (Rev. ed.). New York: Basic Books.

Chapter 2

FOSTER FAMILIES

Foster care is a temporary arrangement, usually made by a state or municipal child welfare agency, that places a child from an abusive or poverty-stricken home in the care of a foster family. Foster care is the nation's leading form of substitute care (Denby & Rindfleisch, 1996). There were 568,000 children in foster homes as of September 1999 (U.S. Department of Health and Human Services, 2000).

Foster and substitute care are regarded as the last resort for troubled families. The Adoption Assistance and Child Welfare Act of 1980 (Public Law 96-272) and the Adoption and Safe Families Act of 1997 (Public Law 105-89) require caseworkers to make reasonable efforts to prevent unnecessary removal of children from their birth families and help preserve the birth family. Children are removed from their homes not only because of abuse and neglect, but also in many instances because the families are poor and lack the means to provide for their basic needs (Anderson, 1997; Courtney, 1994; Courtney & Barth, 1996; Gustafson & MacEachron, 1997; Nelson, 1992; Nissim, 1997). As poverty is associated with race in the United States, there is a disproportionate number of children of color in out-of-home care (Anderson, 1997).

Contrary to what many assume, foster families have a distinct family structure. Rather than being examined as a family structure in its own right, the foster family has been considered primarily in the context of child welfare. From that perspective, foster families are seen as nuclear families temporarily hosting an additional child. The fact that this "temporary hosting" significantly alters the foster family's structure has been overlooked by child welfare and family studies scholars alike.

There are several reasons for this lack of attention to the structure of foster families. The central concern of child welfare professionals is the foster child, not the host family. The foster family is regarded as a temporary means for promoting the child's well-being. This view of the foster family as a temporary residence reflects the strong belief—supported by studies on human development and attachment—that the birth family is the child's true family. It is consistent with the current thrust of child welfare policy toward family preservation, reunification, and permanency planning. However, foster families are not always "temporary." Foster placements may continue for years, and some foster families adopt the foster children. In those instances where placements are short term, the foster family may have a succession of foster children, rendering their status as foster families permanent. Furthermore, with 60% of nuclear families divorcing, one can argue that they, too, are "temporary."

This chapter examines the foster family, its prevalence, structure, variability, and dynamics. Perhaps more than any other family type, it is shaped by laws, policies, and practice approaches that are often in contention from differing ideological perspectives.

PREVALENCE AND DEMOGRAPHIC CHARACTERISTICS OF THE FOSTER FAMILY

Until recently, the primary source of national data on children in foster care has been a voluntary survey of states, conducted annually since 1982 by the American Public Welfare Association (APWA). This survey is known as the Voluntary Cooperative Information System (VCIS). Because the survey is voluntary, not all states participate or respond to all questions, and reporting periods and definitions are not consistent for all states. The Department of Health and Human Services (HHS) has since implemented a mandatory data collection system, known as the Adoption and Foster Care Analysis and Reporting System (AFCARS), in which all states are required to participate. The first AFCARS data became available for 1994.

About half of the children in foster homes are male (51%) and half female (49%). The median age of children in foster care in 1999 was 10.1, as compared to a median age of 12.6 at the end of 1982. Of children in foster care at the end of 1999, 29% were under age 6, 26% were ages 6–10, 28% were 11–15, and 16% were 16–18. Two percent were over 18 years of age (U.S. Department of Health and Human Services, 2000).

Numerous studies document the lack of stability in foster care, showing that children frequently move in and out of care (Courtney & Barth,

1996; Dumaret, Coppel-Batsch, & Couraud, 1997; Palmer, 1996; Walsh & Walsh, 1990). At the same time, many children in foster care remain in care longer than is desirable. This occurs because of the unclear or unachievable expectations of birth families, or the lack of requisite support services to facilitate reunification (Burton & Showell, 1997). Of children in 1999, 19% had been in care for less than 6 months, 14% for 6–11 months, 34% for 1–3 years, 15% for 4–5 years, and 18% for 5 years or more. The median length of stay in foster care in 1999 was 22 months (U.S. Department of Health and Human Services, 2000). In July 2000, a group of 13 foster children filed a class action lawsuit against the California Department of Social and Health Services (DSHS) over the frequent moving in and out of care. Their goal was to force changes in the way the state decides to move children from one foster home to another and to give children a more formal voice in those decisions (Barker, 2000).

About a third (36%) of the children in foster care in 1999 were white, non-Hispanic; 42% were black, non-Hispanic; 15% were of Hispanic origin; 2% were American Indian or Alaskan Native; and the rest were of unknown or other racial/ethnic background (U.S. Department of Health and Human Services, 2000).

Foster children exit foster care via one of three routes: (a) by reaching the age of majority while still in care, or being legally emancipated to independent living; (b) by family reunification, placement with a relative or guardian, or adoption; or (c) by an "unsuccessful" exit from care (i.e., leaving before they were supposed to leave, usually to another foster family or to residential care). Most children eventually return to their birth families following their exit from care even if they have spent a long time in foster care (Courtney & Barth, 1996). Of children exiting foster care during the period of October 1998 through March 1999, 59% were reunified with their parents or primary caretakers, and 9% were living with other relatives (U.S. Department of Health and Human Services, 2000).

Many children in foster care are adopted by former foster parents, relatives, and unrelated families. Of the 46,000 children adopted from the public foster care system in 1999, 64% were adopted by their foster parents, 16% by relatives, and 20% by nonrelatives. Thirty-nine percent of the adoptees were white, non-Hispanic; 43% were black, non-Hispanic; and 2% were Asian/Pacific Islanders or American Indian/Alaskan Native (U.S. Department of Health and Human Services, 2000). There is no definitive source of information on the number of transracial adoptions of children in foster care. Estimates range from 1% (Stolley, 1993) to 4% of all adoptions of children in foster care (Child Welfare League of America, 1995).

HISTORICAL BACKGROUND AND THE SOCIAL-CULTURAL CONTEXT

Children have been placed in families other than their own birth families throughout history, fostered by relative and nonrelative families. American child welfare has its roots in the Elizabethan English Poor Law designed to protect society from the poor rather than to protect the poor. Children who were homeless or whose families could not adequately care for them were forced to become self-supporting at an early age. The early "services," consisting mostly of apprenticeships, workhouses, and sometimes almshouses, were carried over to the American colonies.

In the late 19th and early 20th centuries, neglected and abandoned children in orphanages or on the streets of New York were shipped on "orphan trains" to farms in the west. The orphan trains, the first extensive and systematic child placement in the United States and a precursor to today's foster care, were conceived and implemented by Rev. Charles Loring Brace and the Children's Aid Society. Only healthy white children were selected. Although some of the children were accepted as members of the families, others were exploited as unpaid laborers. Many were adopted and some were kept indefinitely, in what we today call foster care. Between 1854 and 1929, over 150,000 children were placed through the orphan trains (Cook, 1995; McFadden, 1996).

In 1909, the White House Conference on Children affirmed that children need families and that families are better for children than orphanages and institutions. This reflected the shifting attitudes toward children as needing special protection and care. This change in attitudes led to the passage of laws prohibiting child labor, and to establishment of the juvenile court and other special, separate services for children. Although orphanages continued to exist, the goal was to provide children with a substitute family. Especially since the 1950s, the deinstitutionalization of children has been a public policy priority.

Until the 1970s, the focus of child welfare was on "saving the children" rather than treating their families. This gained impetus with the recognition of what the medical establishment termed *the battered child syndrome* in 1961, eventually leading to the passage, in 1974, of the Child Abuse Prevention and Treatment Act (Public Law 93-247). This legislation prescribed state reporting laws, and encouraged states to develop programs to deal with abuse and neglect. Children deemed to be at risk were removed from their families. However, though the law mandated state reporting, it did not clearly define child abuse, nor did it do much to provide for treatment or prevention. Consequently, as noted by McGowan,

> This law has had the effect of greatly enlarging the pool of children coming to the attention of public authorities as potentially in need of care and protection, without providing the resources or guidelines necessary to enable states to deal more effectively with this population. (as cited in Pecora, Whittaker, & Maluccio, 1992, p. 13)

By 1977, more than 520,000 children were in foster families. It soon became apparent that once placed in foster families, children would usually be left there for many years. It was far easier to place them in care than to get them out (see, for example, Fanshel, 1982; Fanshel & Shinn, 1978). This realization gave rise to the concept of permanency planning, which has been a guiding principle in child welfare since the mid-1970s. With the passage of the federal Adoption Assistance and Child Welfare Act of 1980, permanency planning was enacted into law (McFadden, 1996).

The Adoption Assistance and Child Welfare Act of 1980 offered financial incentives to states to limit foster care, and it encouraged a variety of services to prevent out-of-home placement. These included emergency shelters, day care, homemaker services, counseling, and limited emergency financial assistance. It provided an adoption subsidy program for hard-to-place children (i.e., minority children, handicapped children, siblings, and children over age 12). It further required that child welfare agencies make "reasonable efforts" to prevent child placement (Pecora et al., 1992, p. 22).

Following the passage of the Adoption Assistance and Child Welfare Act of 1980, there was a temporary reduction in the number of children in foster care, from about 520,000 children in 1977, to 275,000 in 1984. Between 1986 and 1990, however, the number of children in foster care nationwide increased by 57% (Denby & Rindfleisch, 1996), a rate of increase 33 times faster than that for the child population as a whole (Craig, 1995).

Infants and very young children are entering foster care at a growing rate, and relatives are playing a larger role as foster parents for the children of their kin. African American children are disproportionately represented in foster care, and are more likely to be waiting for adoption than to have been adopted. Of foster children with established "permanency goals" of adoption, fewer than one third are legally available to be adopted; of children who are legally available for adoption, almost half wait two or more years for an adoptive home.

The goals of permanency planning are to prevent children's placement outside their families and to ensure that they have a permanent home. When necessary to place children outside the home, the aim is to limit the time they spend in out-of-home care and to place them in the least intrusive setting. Long-term goals for permanency should either facilitate reunification with the birth family or, alternatively, facilitate their adoption or permanent stay with a foster family (Maluccio, Fein, Hamilton, Klier, & Ward, 1980; Pecora et al., 1992).

Until the 1980s, foster families were regarded as volunteers and quasi clients. The Adoption Assistance and Child Welfare Act of 1980 and the permanency planning principle provided an impetus for the growing professionalization of child welfare services and for redefining foster parent roles (McFadden, 1996). Since then, foster parents have increasingly been regarded as paraprofessionals who require training and who work with the caseworker to help children attain permanency (Maluccio & Fein, 1983; Ryan, McFadden, & Warren, 1981; Shaw & Hipgrave, 1983).

A major criticism of the foster care system is that children are often separated from the parents only because their parents are poor and lack the means to provide for the children's basic needs (Gustafson & MacEachron, 1997; Nelson, 1992). Families with incomes below $15,000 are 4.5 times more likely to be reported for child maltreatment than families with higher incomes. African American and Native American children are especially at risk, because many are raised in poor families (Anderson, 1997). However, the shockingly high rate of child poverty in the United States has not been addressed by public policy. Instead, attention has been focused on the foster care system itself, rather than on the conditions that result in the removal of children from their parents. As Pecora, Whittaker, and Maluccio (1992) have noted, "A significant number of children would be prevented from being placed if sufficient resources were available for family income assistance, housing, health care, and crisis intervention support" (p. 27).

The court referral system is itself often a source of ethnic bias in service provision to children in foster care. Compared with African Americans and Hispanics, Caucasian children are more likely to receive orders for mental health services, particularly psychotherapy and counseling, and to receive significantly more services both prior and subsequent to removal from their homes (Courtney et al., 1996; Garland & Besinger, 1997). They are also more likely to be adopted.

As the child welfare system has changed, so have the needs of the children in care, and this has placed new strains on the foster care system. Prior to permanency planning, the majority of the children in foster care were poor. Currently, poverty is only one of the reasons for placing children outside their birth families, because many children in care have a variety of special needs. These include being affected by parents' substance abuse, being HIV positive, or being the victims of physical and sexual abuse (Eastman, 1982; Hartman, 1993; McFadden, 1996; Smith & Merkel-Holguin, 1995). To provide them with appropriate care requires that foster parents receive more support and supervision. The need to provide special care, the low pay and limited support the families receive, and the increased employment of women outside the home have contributed to a steady decrease in the supply of foster families (Pecora, Whittaker, Maluccio, & Barth, 2000).

Although the goal of permanency planning is to limit the time children spend in out-of-home care, the implementation has fallen short of expectations, especially for minority children (Anderson, 1997). As Fein and Maluccio (1992) put it, permanency planning became a kind of dogma among child welfare workers. Rather than enhancing family stability, the system results in a disproportionate number of minority children being placed in out-of-home care, staying in the system longer, having more undesirable experiences, receiving fewer in-home services, and being less likely to be placed in adoptive families than Caucasian children (Anderson, 1997; Courtney, 1994).

Against the background of the increasingly apparent limitations and disappointing results of the Adoption Assistance and Child Welfare Act of 1980, new legislation was enacted. The Omnibus Budget Reconciliation Act (Public Law 97-35), and Family Preservation and Support Services Act of 1993 (Public Law 103-66) required states to implement family support and family preservation strategies (Maluccio, Abramczyk, & Thomlison, 1996). The Adoption and Safe Families Act of 1997 changed and clarified many of the provisions of the 1980 Adoption Assistance and Child Welfare Act.

Family Preservation

Family preservation is a model of social service intervention for families whose children are at risk of placement in foster homes. The model applies concepts of crisis intervention, family systems, life-space intervention, and other cognitive behavioral theories to provide full-service intervention within a limited time frame. Family preservation, however, is not appropriate for all families, limiting its applicability. To achieve its goal, family preservation requires adequate economic, social, community, and health care resources, including a drastic reduction in caseworkers' caseloads (Alexander & Alexander, 1995; Hartman, 1993). Though it can mobilize needed services and resources, it cannot substitute for such resources (Hartman, 1993). As resources are severely limited, the success of family preservation has been modest.

LEGAL AND POLICY ISSUES

Among the laws most pertinent for foster care as well as adoption are the Adoption Assistance and Child Welfare Act of 1980, the Adoption and Safe Families Act of 1997, the Indian Child Welfare Act of 1978 (ICWA, Public Law 95-608), and the Multiethnic Placement Act of 1994 (MEPA, Public Law 103-382). The first two define the thrust of out-of-home placement and philosophy, and the last two attempt to deal with difficult issues related to the removal from their homes of children of color.

The Adoption Assistance and Child Welfare Act of 1980

This landmark legislation was designed to prevent the unnecessary removal of children from their families and to promote reunification if foster placement has occurred. Both the Adoption Assistance and Child Welfare Act of 1980 and permanency planning philosophy expressed a preference for adoption over long-term, out-of-home care when children cannot be reunified with their families. The legislation encouraged the adoption of children in foster care by providing foster families with maintenance payments and Medicaid when they adopted. Under previous regulations, if the foster family adopted, maintenance payments were cut off. This legislation recognized the essential failure of the foster care system, which since the 1960s had provided federal subsidies for placing children with foster families while neglecting to subsidize attempts either to rehabilitate birth families or to find some means whereby children could remain with one set of foster parents rather than being shifted from family to family.

The law provided for states to implement information systems documenting the status of children in care and preplacement services aimed at preventing placement. These could include 24-hour emergency caretaker and homemaker services, emergency shelters, and counseling. It encouraged states to establish procedural safeguards for removal of children from the home, and it provided adoption subsidies for children with special needs or from low-income families irrespective of the adoptive family's income (Pecora et al., 2000).

Unfortunately, the law has failed to live up to its promise, primarily because the federal funding has been grossly insufficient to induce states to improve their services.

The number of finalized adoptions for children in foster care has only recently begun to increase, despite the fact that the number of children in foster care continues to grow. In 1999, there were only 19,222 finalized adoptions of children in foster care—3.4% of the total number of children in care that year and only about 18% of the children whose plan called for adoption (U.S. Department of Health and Human Services, 2000).

The Adoption and Safe Families Act of 1997

The Adoption and Safe Families Act of 1997 was enacted amidst concerns that the Adoption Assistance and Child Welfare Act of 1980 had gone much too far in safeguarding parental rights at the risk of children's safety. The pendulum had swung from an emphasis on keeping children together with their birth families to speeding up the process of removal and termination of parental rights. The safety of children was now the paramount concern.

The law establishes time lines for termination of parental rights. Whereas the previous law did not stipulate any time lines, the new legislation requires states to file for the termination of parental rights and concurrently to process an adoptive placement for any child who has been in foster care for 15 of the most recent 22 months (Pecora et al., 2000). Permanency hearings to determine if and when a child will be returned to the home must be held within 12 months of out-of-home placement instead of the 18 months required under previous law. Although states are still required to make "reasonable efforts" to reunify and preserve families, this does not apply in cases where a court has found that the parent has committed felony assault against the child or sibling, has conspired with or aided another person to do so, or has subjected the child to sexual abuse, abandonment, torture, or chronic abuse (Pecora et al., 2000).

Although welcoming provisions that expand health care coverage for adopted children with special needs, improved coordination with substance abuse treatment programs, and requirements that states be assessed according to their performance on outcome measures tied to the AFCARS, child welfare experts have raised concerns about the more stringent time limits. They point out that treatment regimes, especially for substance abuse, normally extend beyond the 12-month family reunification limit. Furthermore, the performance indicators, though addressing child safety and permanence, do not include any direct measures of child and family well-being (Pecora et al., 2000).

The Indian Child Welfare Act of 1978

The 1978 ICWA was enacted to prevent unnecessary removal of Native American children from their families. It requires states to present evidence "beyond a reasonable doubt" that continued parental custody would cause the child serious emotional or physical damage. This act was an attempt to end the practice of sending Native American children away from their families in order to "civilize" and educate them, thereby destroying Indian culture and tribal integrity (Bakeis, 1996). It represents a break with the assimilationist social welfare policies of the boarding school era (1880s–1950s) and the Indian adoption era (1950s–1970s). It seeks to protect tribal self-determination and heritage and to promote family preservation (George, 1997). Recognizing Indian tribes as sovereign governments, the ICWA acknowledges that the tribe has exclusive jurisdiction over child custody proceedings. In cases involving children not living on the reservation, jurisdiction can be transferred to a tribal court at the request of the parent or the tribe. If Indian children are considered for out-of-home placement, preference must be given to placing them with the child's relatives or other tribal members. A key provision of the law requires a higher standard of proof for custody proceedings. In place of the less stringent standard requiring "clear and convincing evidence," parental rights can be terminated only if there is evidence "beyond a reasonable doubt" that the child risks serious emotional or physical harm by remaining with the parents. Though the law provided for grants to tribes and Indian organizations to establish prevention services, this has been hampered by a lack of funding.

Studies show that the ICWA gave substantial control to Indian tribes over the placement of Indian children in foster and adoptive families. Between 1975 and 1986, the rates of foster care and especially adoption have decreased substantially (MacEachron, Gustavsson, Cross, & Lewis, 1996). At the same time, implementation has lagged because of unfamiliarity with its provisions as well as resistance. A case review in four states found that 53% of Indian children had been placed in non-Indian homes (Planz et al., cited in Pecora et al., 1992, p. 21). Furthermore, the ICWA applies only to children in tribes recognized by the Bureau of Indian Affairs.

Bakeis (1996) argues that by enforcing this higher standard of proof (i.e., "beyond a reasonable doubt") in abuse and neglect termination cases the ICWA infringes on the rights of both Native American parents and the abused and neglected children. With respect to adoption, Native American parents may not choose the adoptive parents and are not afforded the same anonymity that other parents receive. To achieve the goals of the ICWA, Congress should enact an amendment stipulating that the ICWA apply only to those children who are part of an existing Native American family, and that the adoption placement preference apply only where the child has been removed by the state from an existing Native American family and when a parent of such a child makes the request.

The Multiethnic Placement Act of 1994 and the Interethnic Adoption Provisions Act of 1996

Interracial placements have long been subject to debate. In 1972, the National Association of Black Social Workers (NABSW) adopted a resolution opposing the placement of African American children in white families and encouraging same-race adoptions and foster placement. Though the Association continues to assert this position, it has not been realized in public policy.

The 1994 MEPA (Public Law 103-382) forbade federally funded agencies from solely considering race, culture, and ethnicity in making foster care and adoption placement decisions (Curtis & Alexander, 1996). Proponents of the law cited concerns about the delays in placing minority children for adoption, and questioned the constitutionality of denying white parents the opportunity to foster or adopt an African American child on grounds of race. Under the MEPA, placement agencies could consider the cultural, ethnic, or racial background of the child as well as the ability of the prospective adoptive or foster parents to meet the needs of children of such backgrounds. However, ethnicity and race could be only one of a number of factors used in making the placement decisions. The law was amended in 1996 with enactment of the Small Business and Job Protection Act of 1996 (Public Law 104-188). The amendment, Section 1808, Removal of Barriers to Interethnic Adoption— also known as the Interethnic Adoption Provisions Act (IEAP)— removed language from the MEPA allowing race and ethnicity to be considered at all in determining the best interests of the child in a placement decision. The rationale for the amendment was the large number of African American children in foster homes waiting for adoption, though, as discussed in Chapter 5, this remains in dispute. Minority children, who constituted about 60% of those in foster care in 1994, wait about twice as long as other children for a permanent home (Pecora et al., 2000). The delays in placement of minority children are related to their families' higher rates of poverty, lack of substance abuse treatment programs, and racial discrimination (Pecora et al., 2000).

STIGMA AND STEREOTYPES
OF THE FOSTER FAMILY

As a nontraditional family, foster families are subject to stereotypes reflecting confusion and ignorance about foster care. The most thorough documentation is Molin's (1994) study, based on numerous workshops with foster parents.

According to Molin, the positive stereotype views foster parents as saints and martyrs, dedicated, altruistic, and idealized parent figures who are able to handle burdens that ordinary parents are not capable of bearing. This idealization also reflects a stereotype of foster children as difficult to care for and requiring the selfless dedication of foster parents. The positive stereotype has the effect of isolating foster parents from the larger community, because if they are so gifted and giving, then they do not need support and nurturance. There is an expectation that they will somehow resolve all the child's problems, expending unusual effort in tutoring, mentoring, and helping the child function in school and interpersonal relations. They are not expected to voice their own needs or complain about the children, like other parents do. Thus, foster parents feel that people are disappointed in or angry with them when they "come off their pedestals" and behave like other parents. Molin (1994) suggests that this idealized stereotype serves as a social defense. It allows the larger society to avoid responsibility or guilt for the pain of the children who were removed from their birth families. Instead, the responsibility is projected on to individuals who are defined as uniquely suited for caring for these children.

Negative stereotypes are the "split-off aspects of this idealized parent image" (Molin, 1994, p. 21). With this stereotype, foster parents are viewed as motivated by financial gain, or as seeking to adopt the children through the back door. Like the stereotype of the wicked stepmother, foster parents are also viewed as exploiters of children, using them for domestic chores and labor, and even molesting and abusing them. Viewed as neglectful or abusive caregivers, they are also suspected of causing or contributing to the child's problems. In both object-relations terms and in Jungian psychology, this reflects the splitting between the good (birth) mother and the bad (foster) mother who is disowned as a parent. Conversely, when the foster mother is idealized, the birth mother is stigmatized, pathologized, and discredited (Meyer, 1985; Molin, 1994).

The foster children are also stereotyped. The positive image is that they are victims of neglectful and abusive parents, or are needy and abandoned waifs who deserve sympathy and will respond with gratitude and love. Molin (1994) suggests that the image of the child as an orphan reflects the society's difficulty in dealing with children who are attached to parents who arouse strong negative feelings. The negative stereotype holds foster children to be deficient, damaged, deliberately destructive, and emotionally disturbed. This stereotype leads to suspicion and the scapegoating of foster children in the community, reflecting the sense of threat and uneasiness about the alien. As foster children may be different from their classmates, neighbors, and foster family in terms of ethnicity, race, and socioeconomic class, and as they are regarded as transient members of the family and community, they are considered different and as "others." Some may question the children's entitlement to education and other community resources. The stigmatization of foster children also reflects negative feelings toward the children's parents extended to the child. Even as adults, regardless of how well they are doing, former foster children tend to experience this sense of stigma (Festinger, 1983; Molin, 1994).

FAMILY STRUCTURE

The assumption that foster families are essentially nuclear families is inaccurate on two grounds. First, with the addition of the foster child, it becomes a unique form of a binuclear extended family. Second, the foster family was not necessarily a nuclear family even before the joining of the foster child. Foster families come in all varieties, including kin families (relative foster families), single-parent families, stepfamilies, and gay and lesbian families.

This section considers the structure of foster families and the implications of accepting new members. It discusses the following structural characteristics of the foster family: (a) families created by the joining of an additional family member, (b) families created by the disruption of previous families, (c) residential and nonresidential family members, (d) multiple parental figures, (e) role ambiguity, (f) divided loyalties, and (g) payment for raising children.

Families Created by the Joining of an Additional Family Member

Although first-married, "normative" families are created by the formation of the couple, followed by the birth of their children, the foster family is a well-established system that is transformed and re-created into a "foster family" by the joining of a foster child. Both the joining child and the "absorbing" family have their own family connections, rituals, and habits. Foster families constitute, at least in their early stages, distinct subsystems: the "veteran" or absorbing family members, and the "newcomer"—a separate subsystem. As in any system, when a new member joins, all members need to make adjustments, and the relationships within the family become more complex (Seaberg & Harrigan, 1997). Furthermore, as the child is not expected to be a permanent member of the foster family, he or she may be regarded as an outsider. This, in turn, may create instability and disequilibrium in the family, especially in the early stages (Seaberg & Harrigan, 1997).

As the foster child is the newcomer, who is lacking the support and backing of birth parents, he or she is relatively marginal. This marginality is reinforced by the labeling of the foster child's birth parents as dysfunctional and by the fact that the relationship between the foster family and the foster child is defined as temporary; the love and caring for the child are expected to be conditional. Consequently, the joining foster child might be excluded from the foster family while feeling deeply connected to his or her nonresidential birth family. In addition, there is the expectation that the child will adjust to the foster family rather than the family adjusting to the child (Kadushin & Martin, 1988).

Although Seaberg and Harrigan (1997) found that the impact of having a foster child on the family is minimal and that the impact tended to be viewed as more positive than negative for both white and African American foster families, other studies found that foster care had a negative impact both on the foster parents' marriage and on the family as a whole (Grigsby, 1994; Kadushin & Martin, 1988; McFadden & Ryan, 1991). These inconsistent findings could reflect differences in family functioning at different stages of the family's life cycle. In the initial stages, the foster family may experience disequilibrium; with time, the family tends to adjust, establishing a new equilibrium.

Families Created by the Disruption of Previous Families

Foster families are created on the basis of the disruption of the birth family and a loss of family members, which set them apart from nuclear families. The literature addresses this history of loss and separation both from the birth parents' perspective (Hess & Proch, 1993; Kadushin & Martin, 1988; Pecora et al., 2000) and from the child's perspective, explaining the child's sense of loss according to theories of attachment and bonding (Grigsby, 1994; Kadushin & Martin, 1988; Urquhart, 1989). It is also likely that the loss experienced by the foster child, who is usually cut off from his or her birth family, affects in some way the entire foster family.

Parallel to the loss experienced by the foster child, foster families, too, are subject to loss and disruption when the foster children are reunited with their birth families. The multiple experiences of loss are often emotionally draining and stressful for foster families, and contribute to their decisions to opt for a long-term placement or to cease functioning as foster families (McFadden, 1996). Urquhart (1989) observed that the foster family does not receive the needed legitimacy and support to grieve for the child who left their care; and if they express grief, they are viewed as inappropriate or neurotic. Grieving may be especially complicated when the relationship with the child was ambivalent; when the foster family either does not know how the child is doing after leaving their home or learns that the child is not doing well; or when the child is returned to the same or even worse family circumstance (McCoy, 1962; Urquhart, 1989).

The entry and the leave-taking of the foster child are significant transition events that influence the foster family structure (Molin, 1994). Such changes often happen with short notice (Urquhart, 1989; Wells & D'Angelo, 1994). From the perspective of crisis and systems theories, the departure of the child is a crisis of dismemberment for the family system (McFadden, 1996). The child, along with his or her history and ties to the birth family, transforms the structure of the foster family, and in some ways the newly formed foster family replaces the previous family structure (Eastman, 1979, 1982; Molin, 1994).

Residential and Nonresidential Family Members

Foster families comprise residential and nonresidential family members. The residential members include one or two foster parents who are not the birth parents of the foster child, their birth children, and one or more foster children. The nonresidential family members are one or two parents (the foster child's birth parents) and the foster child's biological siblings. This constellation is represented in the issue of names used in the foster family. First, the last names used by the different family members do not all match their residency. Although the foster child has a different surname from the other residential family members, he or she shares the same surname with nonresidential family members. This reflects the separate identities and loyalties of the family members. In some long-term foster placements, children may change their last name to that of the foster parents even though an adoption is not likely. Second, foster children may refer to their foster parents as "mom" and "dad," use their first names, or use other names (McFadden, 1996; Wells & D'Angelo, 1994). Furthermore, although foster children refer to their nonresidential birth parents as "mom" and "dad," the birth children of the foster parents refer to their residential parents as "mom" and "dad" at the same time.

Because of the losses foster children experience, they may experience confusion about who is in or out of their family. Foster children tend to exclude their birth parents from the description of their family, and they make no distinction between their foster siblings and their biological siblings (Gardner, 1998).

The presence of residential and nonresidential family members extends the membership of a foster family beyond the family's household. The physical boundaries of these families are incongruent with their psychological boundaries (Pasley & Ihinger-Tallman, 1989). Family theorists have defined this situation as family boundary ambiguity (Boss & Greenberg, 1984; Pasley & Ihinger-Tallman, 1989). Molin (1994) found that families with more open and flexible family boundaries had less conflict, ambivalence, and concerns regarding the relationship with both the foster child and his or her birth family, and with their own extended families. Nevertheless, from a systems perspective, when the family's boundaries are too open and flexible, the family is in danger of entropy through losing its identity (Eastman, 1979). Thus, maintaining open family boundaries requires finding the right balance of family cohesion and integrity (McFadden, 1996; Pasley & Ihinger-Tallman, 1989). Relative foster families also need to redefine their relationships with their extended family (McFadden, 1996; Molin, 1994).

The issue of family boundaries also affects the foster parents as a couple. Focusing on the foster family as the provider of care (expressed in the often used term *foster care*) may blur the fact that this care is given within a family context and that the parents are also a couple. Hence a critical boundary issue is the need to maintain the marital subsystem, taking care that the couple has some privacy and time to nurture their intimate relationship (McFadden, 1996).

Multiple Parental Figures

Foster families usually include more than two parental figures: There are two residential foster parents, who perform their parental role on an everyday basis, and at least one nonresidential parent, who performs as a parent on a partial basis. In addition, the caseworker is also involved as a kind of parental figure. It is the caseworker who removes and places the child and who is ultimately responsible for the foster child's well-being (McCoy, 1962). Though acting as the child's parents on a daily bias, foster parents are partial parents. As such, their parental role is both difficult to define and difficult to perform (McCoy, 1962; Wells & D'Angelo, 1994).

The presence of nonresidential parents, especially if they are involved in their children's lives, means that residential parents need to share parental responsibilities and authority. This may lead to conflict, especially if the parental figures have different goals or priorities (Eastman, 1982; Wells & D'Angelo, 1994). Indeed, foster care studies suggest that the relationship between foster and birth parents is inherently conflicted (Kadushin & Martin, 1988; Seaberg, 1981). Visitation is the most prevalent arena for this mutual tension, and is regarded by foster parents as undesirable (Kadushin & Martin, 1988; Simms & Bolden, 1991). The nonresidential birth parents may also contribute to this problematic relationship. They tend to dislike foster parents and be jealous of them, and they may compete with foster parents for the affection and loyalty of the child (Kadushin & Martin, 1988; Simms & Bolden, 1991). When collaboration between foster and birth parents is discussed, it is presented as an ideal-role prescription, in which the foster parents serve as helpers to the birth parents, providing them with information and emotional support, and teaching them parenting skills (Maluccio, Warsh, & Pine, 1993; Pecora et al., 1992; Ryan, McFadden, Rice, & Warren, 1988; Seaberg, 1981). Similarly, although the parental authority in foster care is shared with the caseworker, collaboration between foster parents and caseworkers is usually not the norm (Hess & Proch, 1993; Maluccio et al., 1993; Pecora et al., 2000; Pine, Warsh, & Maluccio, 1993). The research literature suggests that although expected to coordinate with caseworkers and birth parents, foster families basically are independent of the birth parents. Rather than a "complementary family," foster families are essentially a "substitute family" that in the process of rearing the foster child "forgets" that it is not the birth family (Hess, 1988; Smith & Smith, 1990).

The existence of multiple parental figures is dramatically shown when two or even more families contend for custody of the child. This may occur when (a) the birth parents wish to have the child returned and the foster family fights to continue custody, often with the hope of adopting the child, (b) both the relatives of the child and the foster parents wish to have custody, and (c) the foster parents wish to adopt the child, but the caseworker prefers that another family adopt the child. This latter case is most likely to happen in transracial adoptions (Stokes & Strothman, 1996).

Role Ambiguity

Foster families are asked to fulfill an ill-defined role that lacks clearly defined norms (Eastman, 1979, 1982; McCoy, 1962; McFadden, 1996; Meyer, 1985; Wells & D'Angelo, 1994). This ambiguity may affect their relationships with the foster child, the child's birth family, their own family (i.e., relations between the siblings and with the extended family), and systems outside their family, including social service agencies, schools, the neighborhood, and the community. Foster parents are unclear as to the extent to which they are professionals, volunteers, baby-sitters, or the equivalent of birth or adoptive parents (McFadden, 1996; Meyer, 1985; Molin, 1994; Wells & D'Angelo, 1994). Little is mentioned in the literature about parenting ambiguity, suggesting that foster parents are expected to follow the parenting models of nuclear families. Doing so, however, may place them in a bind. If foster parents act as if they were the birth parents, they are likely to experience conflicts with the child. If they do not, they are without clear guidelines (Erera, 1997a). As Eastman (1979) suggests, foster families "often find it difficult to know how fully to integrate a [foster] child into the family system" (p. 565), because the child does not, and never will, belong to the foster family. The challenge is to find an appropriate balance between separateness and connectedness.

This ambiguity about the foster parents' role is reflected in the characterization of foster families as substitute or replacement families. This representation, expressed by policy makers, researchers, caseworkers, and foster families themselves, reflects both an assumption that foster families act as substitute nuclear families and a stigmatizing view of the birth families for which a substitute must be found (Hess, 1988; Smith & Smith, 1990).

An additional source of ambiguity is the fact that although caring is provided in the private domain of the family, it is done under the aegis of a public agency and judicial system and so is circumscribed by federal and state policies (Wells & D'Angelo, 1994). This sets the stage for conflict between private and public expectations and demands (Molin, 1994). On the one hand, family life and caregiving are conceived of as a private matter, taking place in the home. On the other hand, foster parents are expected to be professionals who are paid for their knowledge, skills, and hard work, and their jobs are defined by public policies (Molin, 1994; Smith & Smith, 1990; Wells & D'Angelo, 1994). Whereas the private role implies that caring for the foster children should not differ from parenting birth children and should be done as a private affair, the public role implies cooperation and the sharing of authority with caseworkers and the foster child's birth family. Foster parents report a sense of frustration at the discrepancy between their own identities as foster parents and the images of foster families they encounter when interacting with other systems (Molin, 1994). The low pay for foster care, which reflects the society's devaluation of caring, caregivers, and "women's work" (Smith & Smith, 1990; Tronto, 1993), contributes to this confusion about the foster mother's role. Meyer (1985) places the predicament of foster mothers at the intersection of gender, social class, and racial oppression:

> To be a woman, to be a mother, to be lower class or poor, to be in a minority group, to work for (with? under?) a child welfare agency, to be paid a pit-tance, to be asked to parent a child whom no one else is able to parent, to try to love a child and to lose him or her when loving has been achieved, to be supervised by a 22-year-old social worker, to have to deal with school teachers, police, courts, medical appointments, angry biological parents, and the impact of all of this upon one's own family—that is the lot and life of a typical foster mother in America. (p. 252)

The ambiguous boundaries between the private and the public domains are also manifested in the attitude of neighbors who inquire about the foster child's background and family history (Molin, 1994). Foster parents need to assert the boundaries of privacy that would other-wise be extended without question to birth children and parents in intact families.

Uncertainty about the role of foster parents is also reflected in the atti-tudes of medical professionals. Some may reject the right of foster par-ents to function as custodial parents, questioning their authority to make decisions on the children's behalf. Foster parents, for example, are fre-quently denied access to the foster child's medical records. Such atti-tudes undermine the foster parents' status and identity, delegitimizing and disempowering them. Consequently, foster parents find themselves having to justify and assert their role and legitimacy (Molin, 1994).

The ambiguous status of foster parents goes along with their being a nontraditional family (Eastman, 1982; McFadden, 1996). As Molin (1994) observes, "Supporting foster families involves confronting the ambiguity and ambivalence about their status, including the question whether they are to be regarded in fact as a category of family" (p. 26). It seems that the more the foster parents are viewed, and view themselves, as professionals who work hand-in-hand with caseworkers and who are trained and supported by caseworkers, the less they view themselves as parents.

Divided Loyalties

From the foster children's perspective, being raised by substitute parents, while at least one of their birth parents lives elsewhere, may pose several difficulties. These include the necessity of blending into new families, neighborhoods, and schools (Johnson, Yoken, & Voss, 1995); feeling rejected and abandoned (Festinger, 1983; Palmer, 1996); and feeling confusion about establishing a sense of identity, belonging, and personal significance (Burton & Showell, 1997; Fanshel & Shinn, 1978; Kadushin & Martin, 1988; Maluccio, Fein, & Olmstead, 1986). They may idealize the nonresidential birth parents (Kompara, 1980) and experience a sense of loss, grief, and longing, which are further related to the child's ability to develop attachment and bonding (Grigsby, 1994; Kadushin & Martin, 1988; Maluccio et al., 1986; Twigg, 1995). The sense of loss may be especially intense if the child is older and has experienced several placements (Courtney & Barth, 1996). Foster children also need to cope with fantasies of a preplacement ideal and with blaming themselves for their removal from the home (Kadushin & Martin, 1988; Maluccio et al., 1986). Finally, foster children often feel powerless at not participating in the decisions about their removal from their families, their placement in foster care, and their return to their families. Some children, especially the younger ones, do not fully comprehend the reasons for their placement (Johnson et al., 1995).

Living with foster families can generate a sense of divided loyalty. Children tend to view loyalty to the foster parents as disloyalty to the birth parents (Erera, 1997b; Kadushin & Martin, 1988; Maluccio et al., 1986; Mech, 1985). As it is difficult psychologically to maintain dual loyalties, children tend to identify with one family. In one study, foster children in long-term care consistently related to their foster family rather than their birth kin as family. These children expressed no preference living with their birth families, a reflection of the numerous losses the children had experienced and their confusion about who was in or out of their families (Gardner, 1998).

In addition to living apart from their birth parents, foster children are frequently separated from their siblings (Kosonen, 1996). Children are most likely to be placed with siblings in temporary and relative foster placements. Fewer white siblings are placed together than siblings of other races (Fein & Staff, 1992). A major reason for failing to place siblings together is that social workers lack complete information about the family composition, especially when contact with parents has been lost or siblings have moved from the area (Kosonen, 1996).

Payment for Raising Children

Foster care is conditional on the foster parents receiving payment. This sets foster families apart from nuclear families that are expected to raise their children without direct public reimbursement. Receiving public funds, foster families undertake a general societal responsibility.

The actual payment for raising foster children is alarmingly low. In Santa Clara County, California, for example, the monthly rate for fostering a child who is not a relative ranges between $393 and $553, depending on the child's age. In Washington State, the rate ranges between $351 and $500 (C. Gerring, personal communication, August 2000). In addition, children in both relative and nonrelative foster families are covered by Medicaid and receive a one-time yearly allowance for clothing (around $250). Foster children are also entitled to subsidized or free lunch at school, summer camps, and fees for extracurricular school activities (C. Shaffar, personal communication, August 2000). The current rate for fostering children with special needs in Santa Clara County, California, ranges between $31 and $1,326, paid in addition to the regular rates and depending on the child's needs (C. Gerring, personal communication, August 2000). In Washington State, the rate for fostering children with special needs is entirely flexible, depending on the child's needs. A large number of foster families, and especially relative foster families and single-parent foster families, are themselves poor and have frequently depended on Aid to Families with Dependent Children (AFDC) funds to support the children in their care (Fein, Maluccio, Hamilton, & Ward, 1983; Gebel, 1996; McLean & Thomas, 1996). With the passage of the 1996 Personal Responsibility and Work Opportunity Reconciliation Act (PRWORA, Public Law 104-193), public welfare entitlements were ended, placing poor foster families in an even more precarious situation. The failure to provide sufficient economic support for foster families is yet another example of the low priority this society places on the well-being of children (Fein, 1991).

FAMILY DYNAMICS

This section on family dynamics considers three key areas: (a) visitation and the relationship between foster and birth families, (b) relationship with caseworkers, and (c) relationship with the children.

Visitation and the Relationship Between Foster and Birth Families

In the past, the relationship between foster parents and birth parents was assumed to be inherently conflictual. This was based, in part, on the presumption that these families vie for the child's affection and on the tendency to split the "good" (foster) mother and the "bad" (birth) mother. Such notions reinforced competition between foster and birth mothers, while overlooking their common interests (Smith & Smith, 1990). They constrained the interactions between foster and birth parents, as well as interactions between the birth families and their children (Goerge, 1970). With the introduction of permanency planning in the 1980s, however, contact between birth parents and their children has been increasingly encouraged.

The relationship between foster and birth parents has been described as an interaction between women of different social classes. Smith and Smith (1990) note that the majority of the children come from the most disadvantaged and stigmatized families, particularly those headed by single mothers; are cared for by upper working-class foster mothers; and are supervised by middle-class, usually female, caseworkers. Women do the caretaking as birth mothers, foster mothers, or caseworkers (Smith & Smith, 1990).

Regular contact between the foster children and their birth parents is a necessary condition for realizing reunification (Folaron, 1993; Hess & Proch, 1993; Maluccio et al., 1986; Pecora et al., 2000). Foster children who are visited by their birth parents are more likely to be returned to their homes (Fanshel, 1982; Fanshel & Shinn, 1978; Milner, 1987; Seaberg & Tolley, 1986). Regular visits enable foster children to maintain their attachment to birth parents (Grigsby, 1994), maintain their own sense of identity and personal significance (Burton & Showell, 1997; Fanshel & Shinn, 1978; Kadushin & Martin, 1988; Maluccio et al., 1986), and retain a realistic picture of the birth parents, avoiding both fantasies of a preplacement ideal and blaming themselves for their removal from the home (Kadushin & Martin, 1988; Maluccio et al.,

1986). Children who were regularly visited were found to have better emotional adjustment and better school adjustment, and showed greater gains in intelligence scores (Fanshel & Shinn, 1978). Such children also exhibited fewer behavior problems (Cantos, Gries, & Slis, 1997), including less abusive language and less immature behavior with peers (Borgman, 1985). In addition, independent of parental visiting, kin visiting was found to affect the children's family attachment (Poulin, 1992).

There is compelling evidence that regardless of whether or not reunification is planned, visitation is in the best interests of the child and is the key means of accomplishing both the preservation of family ties and family reunification (Cantos et al., 1997; Davis, Landsverk, Newton, & Ganger, 1996; Folaron, 1993; Hess & Proch, 1993; Maluccio et al., 1986; Pecora et al., 1992; Seaberg & Tolley, 1986). Foster parents need to have regular contact with both birth parents and caseworkers to facilitate visitation and reunification. In most cases, however, contact between foster parents and birth parents is limited, and birth parents visit their children infrequently (see, for example, Erera, 1997a; Palmer, 1996; Pecora et al., 2000; Poulin, 1992). As Smith and Smith (1990) describe it, "The official policy of maintaining links to the child's family tends to be honored more in the breach than in practice" (p. 68).

Despite legislative mandates, many agencies lack a visitation policy or explicit family preservation, visitation, and reunification objectives (Fein & Maluccio, 1992; Hess, 1988; Proch & Howard, 1986). In addition, foster parents receive insufficient training and support from the social service agency (Urquhart, 1989), and see their caseworkers infrequently (Simms & Bolden, 1991; Strover, 1997). The insufficient contact with caseworkers is due, at least in part, to caseworker turnover and excessive caseloads (Hess & Folaron, 1991; Maluccio et al., 1986). Furthermore, foster parents may distance themselves from caseworkers because they perceive them as allied with the birth parents and as intruders whose involvement undermines their own authority in the family (Eastman, 1982; Erera, 1997a; McFadden, 1996; Wells & D'Angelo, 1994).

The foster parents' detachment from birth parents may also reflect the wishes of the birth parents. Birth parents tend to refrain from regular contact with their children who are in foster care, and thus from foster parents. This avoidance has been attributed to feelings of shame and to hostility arising from the removal of their children (Kadushin & Martin, 1988). Birth parents may convert their guilt about inadequate parenting to hostility toward foster parents, who symbolize success in this area (Kadushin & Martin, 1988).

The foster parents may also avoid contact to protect their foster children from what they perceive as potentially dangerous birth parents. Despite the generally positive attitudes toward birth parents, about one fifth of the foster parents in Erera's (1997a) study thought that birth parents have a negative influence on the child. The very removal of children from their birth parents may reinforce the foster parents' conviction that birth parents are unfit (Kadushin & Martin, 1988). The literature suggests that foster parents look down on the birth parents, perceiving them as neglectful or abusive (Seaberg, 1981) and as morally and behaviorally repulsive (Kadushin & Martin, 1988). Foster parents often regard birth parents' visitation as a threat to the foster child (Kadushin & Martin, 1988; Mech, 1985; Ryan et al., 1988), and attempt to discourage it (Simms & Bolden, 1991).

Even if the major responsibility for realizing regular visitation is placed on the caseworkers, the foster parents' cooperation has been found to influence the frequency of birth parents' visits (Gean, Gillmore, & Dowler, 1985; Hess, 1988; Hubbell, 1981; Oyserman & Benbenishty, 1992; Simms & Bolden, 1991). Their attitudes and behaviors toward birth parents are critical (Hubbell, 1981).

The relationship between the children and their foster family may also be influenced by the bond between the children and their birth parents. Although this has not been examined in the foster care literature, research on stepfamilies suggests that good relations with the birth parents may enhance the bond between the child and the foster family, and may reduce the child's fears that the foster family is a permanent replacement of their birth family (Ahrons & Wallisch, 1987; Santrock & Sitterle, 1987). On the other hand, frequent and positive contact with the birth family can confuse the foster parents and inhibit their intimacy with the foster children (Clingempeel, Brand, & Segal, 1987).

Relationship With Caseworkers

Under permanency planning and reunification policies, foster parents are expected to (a) promote mutual visitation and contact between foster children and their birth parents, (b) engage birth parents in important decisions concerning the upbringing of their children, (c) enhance the parental skills of birth parents, whenever possible, and (d) hold regular conferences with caseworkers, and be supervised and consulted by them (Maluccio & Fein, 1983; Ryan et al., 1981; Shaw & Hipgrave, 1983).

To ensure that birth parents maintain regular contact with their children, several conditions must be met. These include developing a permanency plan, establishing a clear schedule for parental visitation, and providing foster parents with supervision and training (Maluccio et al., 1986).

Traditionally, it has been the caseworkers' responsibility to see that these conditions are met, especially visitations and the birth parents' parental skills training. Some advocate that these responsibilities be handled directly by foster parents. According to this view, foster parents are in the best position to assess the children's needs. Foster parents should promote mutual visitation and serve as parent aides, modeling parenting skills and healthy family relationships. They should provide the birth parents with information about community resources, as well as offering direct help (Maluccio et al., 1986; Pasztor, 1985; Ryan et al., 1981). The foster parents are, in this model, paraprofessionals who work hand in hand with caseworkers in the best interest of the foster children and of family preservation (Burton & Showell, 1997; Maluccio et al., 1993; Pecora et al., 1992; Pine et al., 1993). Several programs have applied this approach, including Casey Family Services and Lighthouse Youth Services (an Ohio-based, not-for-profit organization), as have therapeutic foster home programs. Some programs have extended "partnership parenting" to include whole-family foster care (see, for example, Becvar, Ray, & Becvar, 1996). In this approach, the foster family is viewed as an extended family that provides tangible and emotional resources and support. One program even places the entire birth family with the foster family (Nelson, 1992). Nonetheless, such programs are relatively rare.

Relationship With the Children

Few studies have examined the relationship between foster parents and the children they foster; and because of the methodological limitations of these studies, the results should be regarded as tentative. Nevertheless, the findings are not encouraging. Most document problematic parenting. Simms and Horwitz (1996) reported limited interaction between the foster parents and foster children, and found that the foster families lacked adequate play materials for the foster children. Blome

(1997) found that foster parents gave the foster children significantly less financial assistance for education and were significantly less likely to monitor the children's homework than parents of non–foster children. In some instances, foster parents, like birth parents, do abuse and neglect their foster children. Several studies address the policies and procedures on abuse allegations involving foster families (Carbino, 1992; Nixon, 1997).

IMPLICATIONS FOR
CHILD DEVELOPMENT

Several studies have reported positive outcomes from foster care, with the children overcoming childhood adversities to become socially well integrated (Dumaret et al., 1997), functioning adequately (Fanshel & Shin, 1978; Fein et al., 1983), and having developmental outcomes equal to or better than those who were returned to their birth families (Fanshel & Shin, 1978). Children (aged 6.5–15 years) with mentally ill parents and living with relative or nonrelative foster families displayed fewer behavior problems than children living with two birth parents, a single birth parent, or a birth and a stepparent (Stiffman, Jung, & Feldman, 1987–1988).

Most studies, however, find that children in foster care do not do well. They have low educational attainment (Blome, 1997; Colton, Heath, & Aldgate, 1995; Heath, Colton, & Aldgate, 1994), have a higher dropout rate, and are significantly less likely to have completed a general equivalency diploma (GED) or be in a college preparatory track than non–foster care youth (Blome, 1997). Foster youth also have more discipline problems in school and experience more educational disruption as a result of changing schools (Blome, 1997). Two studies in England found that even when foster children were placed in long-term care with middle-class families, they performed below average in reading, vocabulary, and math skills (Colton et al., 1995; Heath et al., 1994). In addition, half of the foster children aged from birth to 3 years old rated below normal on mental and psychomotor development, with two thirds below normal on emotional regulation and motor quality (Klee, Kronstadt, & Zlotnick, 1997).

The negative outcomes associated with placement in foster families persist through adulthood, with those leaving foster care being significantly more likely to be in prison, be homeless, use drugs and alcohol, and manifest mental health problems (Nissim, 1997). The transition out of foster care can be problematic. In nuclear families, youth reaching their eighteenth birthday are not normally expected to live on their own without the financial and emotional support of the family. However, there is little available to support independent living for youth leaving foster care who may need help with housing, independent living skills, securing employment, or higher education (Biehal & Wade, 1996; Fein, 1991; Iglehart, 1995).

One should regard the research findings, both positive and negative, with some caution, because the methodology, measurement, and sampling may not be sophisticated enough to isolate the effects of foster care (Fein, 1991). The studies do not control for the impact of the children's prior history, including the aftermath of child abuse or neglect experienced before entering foster care (see, for example, Colton et al., 1995; Fanshel, Finch, & Grundy, 1989; Heath et al., 1994). Neither have they controlled for the transition from one family to another, the repeated removals and placements in different families, and the losses the children experience with each such removal. We do not know what would have happened with these children had they stayed with their birth families, especially if intensive prevention services had been available.

VARIATIONS AMONG FOSTER FAMILIES

Foster families vary considerably, and can be classified according to the duration and type of care they provide, as well as by the characteristics of the foster parents. In this section, I consider some of the most significant kinds of foster families. These include long-term foster families, specialized foster care families, transracial foster families, relative foster families, adoptive-foster families, and single-parent, gay, and lesbian foster families.

Long-Term Foster Families

Long-term foster families, also called permanent foster families, are intended to provide foster children with a home until they reach maturity. In the past, this was the most prevalent type of foster family; today, it is much less frequent. Still, following a review of the success rates of adoption, family preservation, and family reunification programs, Fenster (1997) argues that permanent foster care should be maintained as an option and cites several advantages of permanent foster care: (a) It is federally funded; (b) it can lead to increased supervision of foster parents; (c) it increases permanence for more children; and (d) it promotes attachment by ensuring both child and foster parent stability.

Specialized Foster Families

Specialized foster care, also known as therapeutic or treatment foster care (Hudson, Nutter, & Galaway, 1994; Wells & D'Angelo, 1994), offers intensive care for emotionally disturbed children and adolescents; sexually abused children; children with a physical disability, including HIV infection; autistic children; and mentally disabled children (Hudson & Galaway, 1989; Kaplan & Fein, 1989).

Specialized foster families can implement treatment plans adapted to the child's needs, preventing, at least in some cases, institutionalization of the child (McFadden, 1996; Wells & D'Angelo, 1994). Some scholars argue that all foster families should be considered treatment homes, not just those for children with special needs (Pecora et al., 1992). Specialized foster families have been established mostly in the past decade, and so there are few studies documenting their effects. They have been found to produce positive effects on children's social skills, but had less success in reducing behavior problems, in improving psychological adjustment, and in reducing the degree of restrictiveness of postdischarge placement (Reddy & Pfeiffer, 1997).

One study found that specialized foster parents felt that their birth children had difficulty responding to the foster children's problems (Wells & D'Angelo, 1994), but another study found that the birth children were highly involved and attached to foster children with disabilities in their families (Reed, 1994). Wells and D'Angelo (1994) found that foster parents of children with disabilities experienced uncertainty and doubt about their roles as parents and as agency employees, their relationship with the birth mother and the caseworker, the nature of the care they should provide, and the transitions caused by the often abrupt removal of the child from their care. Wells and D'Angelo conclude that "being a specialized foster care parent is an intense experience for which we found no unifying metaphor or underlying principle. The experience is multifaceted, ambiguous, and emergent" (p. 139).

Eckstein (1995) describes a program of "foster family clusters," which is a synthetic extended family in which every family in the cluster has a role in every child's life, offering extensive support and a safety net. Though much of the work with these challenging children is focused within the cluster, efforts are made to keep the children's own families involved. The program, 1 of 10 sponsored by Lighthouse Youth Services, Inc., serves children from infancy to 18 years of age who have been abused or neglected or who are juvenile offenders.

Some suggest that specialized foster parents be considered para-professionals, and that they be carefully selected and trained. To create a therapeutic milieu for the children, they should also receive increased consultation, information about the child's needs and treatment plan, and financial and other support from supervising agencies (Kaplan & Fein, 1989; McFadden, 1996; Molin, 1994). These conditions, however, are not always met, because of caseworkers' high caseloads, lack of knowledge, and commitment (Wells & D'Angelo, 1994).

Transracial Foster Families

Transracial foster families need to address several unique issues, not the least of which is the racial identity of the children (McRoy, 1996). There has been considerable contention over transracial foster families, especially when white families foster Native American or African American children. Although the ICWA of 1978 placed limitations on the placement of Indian children with non-Indian families, it has been inadequately funded and unevenly implemented. In 1972, the NABSW condemned the placement of African American children with white families as "a growing threat to the preservation of the black family" (Kadushin & Martin, 1988, p. 637). Though this served to increase awareness of the importance of placing children in same-race families, African American children continue to be placed with white families. About one third of African American children are placed in white foster homes, and about two thirds of Hispanic children are placed in non-Hispanic foster homes. In contrast, 92% of white children are placed in white families (Barth, Courtney, Berrick, & Albert, 1994).

Relative Foster Families

Relative, or kinship, foster families are a form of extended family and have become more prevalent since the 1980s (Pecora, Le Prohn, & Nasuti, 1999; Scannapieco, Hegar, & McAlpine, 1997). The primary rationale for kinship care is permanency and continuation of family ties. Although there is a growing tendency to formalize kinship care as a form of foster care, there are still a great number of informal kin foster families, especially among people of color. Approximately 30% of children in foster families are living with relatives (Berrick & Barth, 1994; Berrick & Lawrence, 1995; Child Welfare League of America, 1994). In some urban areas, the number of kin foster families has reached or surpassed the number of nonrelative foster families (Voluntary Cooperative Information System, 1996).

Before the 1980s, there was considerable ambivalence toward kinship care among child welfare professionals. In New York, for example, grandparents were not permitted to act as foster parents until 1975 (Nisivoccia, 1996). This ambivalence continues despite the growing incidence of kin care. An analysis of states' policies on use of kinship care revealed a lack of clarity or consistency across states and a disagreement regarding policies guiding the placement of children with their relatives (Gleeson & Craig, 1994).

Compared with nonrelative foster parents, kin foster parents tend to be older (Berrick, Barth, & Needell, 1994) and significantly poorer, and were frequently dependent on public assistance to support the children in their care (Gebel, 1996; Le Prohn, 1994; McLean & Thomas, 1996). Compared with nonrelative foster parents, relative foster parents are more likely to be single (60% vs. 10% to 25%, respectively; Berrick et al., 1994; Le Prohn, 1994), and are less likely to work outside the home (Gebel, 1996). In most cases, kinship care is provided by grandmothers (Gebel, 1996; Nisivoccia, 1996; Scannapieco et al., 1997), and the majority of the children cared for by kin are African American (Le Prohn, 1994; Nisivoccia, 1996), reflecting norms of high involvement among African American grandparents (Longino & Earle, 1996; Pearson, Hunter, Ensminger, & Kellam, 1990).

Current practice suggests that kinship foster care has many advantages over foster family care. Because kin are biological family, they share with the child a common heritage, culture, and ethnic identity, which provide a sense of continuity and stability that helps cushion the trauma of foster care placement (Child Welfare League of America, 1994; Nisivoccia, 1996). Kin can provide the children with higher levels of attachment and continuity of family ties (Berrick & Barth, 1994; Child Welfare League of America, 1994; Courtney, 1994; Hegar, 1993; Nisivoccia, 1996; Scannapieco et al., 1997), provide more opportunities for continued contact between the foster children and their birth parents (Child Welfare League of America, 1994; Le Prohn, 1994), and provide a more stable placement than nonrelative foster parents (Berrick & Barth, 1994; Goerge, 1990). Staying with kin is associated with a greater likelihood of reuniting with the family and with a smoother transition into independent living once care is terminated (Child Welfare League of America, 1994; Courtney & Barth, 1996). Children in kin families are at less risk of maltreatment than are children in nonkin families (Zuravin, Benedict, & Somerfield, 1993). Finally, kin tend to be deeply invested and committed to the child in their care (Gebel, 1996).

Several studies examined the quality of care provided in kin foster care. Not surprisingly, in view of the impoverishment of many kin foster families, research shows that the quality of kin care as well as the outcomes for children of kin foster families are inferior to those of nonrelative foster families. This has been shown in terms of length of stay in care (Berrick et al., 1994; Courtney, 1994); quality of care for preschool children, including the provision of educationally stimulating toys and reading materials, affection, and attentiveness (Gaudin & Sutphen, 1993); and extensiveness of services provided (Scannapieco et al., 1997). Negative outcomes of kin care were also reported with regard to the children's health, behavior, and school-related problems (Dubowitz et al., 1994; Sawyer & Dubowitz, 1994). One study reports that at least some of the negative outcomes balance off in later years (Benedict, Zuravin, & Stallings, 1996). These findings should be interpreted with caution given the methodological limitations of outcome studies.

Kin foster families have dramatically less access to necessary resources than nonkin foster families (McLean & Thomas, 1996). Child welfare agencies fail to provide adequate services to relative caregivers, and caseworkers have less frequent contact with kinship caregivers than with nonkin foster parents (Berrick et al., 1994; Davidson, 1997; Gebel, 1996). Compared with Caucasian children, African American and Hispanic children who are fostered by kin are less likely to receive orders for mental health services, particularly psychotherapy and counseling (Garland & Besinger, 1997), and receive significantly fewer services both prior and subsequent to removal from their homes (Anderson, 1997; Courtney, 1994; Courtney et al., 1996; Garland & Besinger, 1997). Kin foster parents need both more adequate payment for their services and tangible items, such as beds, food, and clothing, in the initial stages of placement. In addition, they need respite time, day care, counseling for the child (Davidson, 1997), and help in advocating for health, mental health, and educational services (Berrick & Barth, 1994).

Several authors have attributed the deficient services to the difficulty relatives have with accepting agency supervision; they feel that being a biological family they have the sole responsibility and authority over the child. This ambivalence toward the intervention of caseworkers may reflect the relatives' failure to identify with the professional role (Le Prohn, 1994; Molin, 1994) and their need to reconcile family and agency expectations (Le Prohn, 1994; Molin, 1994; Nisivoccia, 1996). Relatives may wish to protect the privacy of their family life against the intrusion of state authorities, especially if they feel shame regarding the child's placement (Nisivoccia, 1996). From the family's standpoint, being a relative of the child and acting as his or her parents requires a new definition of roles. They must sort out when and under what circumstances to act as relatives and when to act as surrogate parents.

Adoptive-Foster Families

Adoptive-foster families plan on adopting the foster children in their care, but the children are not yet legally free for adoption because the parental rights have not yet been terminated. Although the child may be expected to be freed for adoption, these children might yet return to their birth parents at some time (Mica & Vosler, 1990). This type of family is relatively new. Until the 1980s, foster families were not allowed to adopt the children in their care. Infants, young children, and Caucasian children are much more likely to be adopted than older children or African American and Latino children (Barth, 1997).

The goal of such placements is to provide continuity of care. Nevertheless, the adoptive-foster family presents a sensitive dilemma. Until the child is legally free for adoption, any plans other than the return to the birth family may mislead the adoptive-foster parents and leave the social service agency open to be sued by both sets of parents (Mica & Vosler, 1990). From the adoptive-foster family's point of view, the situation may pose considerable uncertainty and anxiety, especially if they face a long wait for a legal decision to be made. If these families develop a strong bond, expecting to adopt the child, it will be very difficult for them to return the child if he or she is not freed for adoption (Hartman, 1985). It is unclear whether they may regard the child as "theirs," and to what extent they should integrate the child into their family, bond, and attach to him or her.

Even after the adoption is finalized, adoptive-foster families blur the distinctions between foster care and adoption (Mica & Vosler, 1990). As they have started their relationship with the child as foster parents and have acted as foster parents for an average of three to five years until adoption (McKenzie, 1993), it may not be clear when to drop the hyphen of adoptive-foster and become adoptive families.

Single-Parent, Gay, and Lesbian Foster Families

Placing children with single-parent foster families and with gay and lesbian families is becoming more common. Nevertheless, there are still negative attitudes about single-parent, lesbian, and gay families. For example, in August 1999, Utah banned gay couples and unmarried heterosexual couples living together from becoming foster families. There are more kin single-parent foster families than nonkin single-parent foster families. Among kin, 60% are not married (Fein et al., 1983; Le Prohn, 1994), whereas among nonkin foster families between 10% and 25% are not married (Berrick et al., 1994; Fein et al., 1983). For a detailed discussion of single-parent families and gay and lesbian families, see Chapters 4 and 6.

IMPLICATIONS FOR POLICY

Foster families are here to stay. Though there are presently about a half million children in foster care, this number is likely to increase for several reasons. First, there has been something of a backlash against family reunification. Underlying this shift has been frustration over the failure of the Adoption Assistance and Child Welfare Act of 1980 to meet its family preservation and reunification objectives. As a result, the Adoption and Safe Families Act was enacted in 1997 to expedite the termination of parental rights.

Second, many of the underlying conditions that contributed to the increases in out-of-home placements in the 1980s and 1990s continue unabated. These include the stresses on families caused by poverty; low wage rates; lack of affordable child care, health care, and housing; the lack of drug treatment programs; and increasing rates of incarceration. The United States is unique in maintaining a strict separation between public and private responsibility for caregiving. Most other industrialized countries provide universal child allowances, health care, and subsidized child care.

Third, though needs have increased, the social safety net continues to be pulled apart. The observation of Pecora and colleagues (1992) remains true today: "The nation's social service and public assistance programs have been battered by federal, state, and local budget cuts, while there have been increases in real need on the part of families and children" (p. 27). Instead of using the economic growth of the 1990s to rebuild the social infrastructure, the federal government and the states enacted tax cuts that benefit corporations and upper-income households, contributing to a further widening of the income gap. The move toward managed care has placed further restrictions on service provision. The failure to maintain services in an era of economic prosperity does not bode well for our meeting the needs of foster care when the inevitable downturn in the economy occurs.

Foster care and adoption in the United States have reached a state of near-catastrophe. State agencies fail to recruit enough families, and families are deterred by racially based criteria, long waiting periods, and cumbersome regulations. Programs languish because of inadequate funding and poor design. Child welfare appropriations have increased only modestly after two decades of steady erosion. Relatively little is allocated to services to families to prevent placement, whereas funding for foster care has increased dramatically to more than $3.9 billion in 1999 (Pecora et al., 2000). These funding disparities have created a system that favors the removal of children over the preservation of families. As Pelton (1989) has observed,

> In the absence of prevention-of-placement services, the foster care population varies with the amount of resources available for child removal, more than any other factor. . . . The pool of potential candidates for foster care is always quite large and consists mainly of children from families most deeply submerged in poverty. It is the "reasons" we find to remove such children that change and with them, the amount of resources that become available to do so. (pp. 108–109)

In addition to legislation, other conditions are needed to ensure the implementation of prevention-of-placement services. These include sufficient funding for family preservation, the incorporation of parental visits in the service plans, a case review system, well-staffed services and trained caseworkers, a flexible application of family reunification, and trained foster parents who are willing to collaborate with birth parents and caseworkers (Gambrill & Stein, 1985; Hess, 1988; Hess & Proch, 1993).

As Hess and Proch (1993) suggest, visiting "is an integral part of the family's service plan" (p. 119), yet "without unequivocal agency support policies and resources, visiting services will depend solely on the commitment of individual caseworkers or on court orders" (p. 132). Children should be placed in close geographic proximity to their birth families; in addition to facilitating visitation, this will permit the guidance and supervision of foster parents to enhance active contact between foster parents and birth parents (Hess, 1988; Hess & Proch, 1993).

Numerous studies advocate that the child placement goal should be to preserve sibling ties (Begun, 1995; Fein & Staff, 1992; Kosonen, 1996). If siblings are not placed together, frequent visits should occur from the beginning, with ample flexibility to allow opportunities for siblings to connect with one another (Begun, 1995).

Policy reforms are needed to strengthen relative foster homes. The current lack of standards for approving and monitoring relative foster homes creates great potential for harm to children. The Administration for Children and Families (ACF) should encourage states to extend existing foster home standards to relative foster homes or to develop reasonable and consistent alternative standards. It makes little sense for state agencies to remove children from parental home situations deemed unsafe only to place them in other situations that have not been thoroughly investigated and found to be safe. Children placed with relatives are the legal responsibility of the state agencies, and like all other children in foster care, they clearly deserve a basic level of protection.

The ACF should take an active role in encouraging states to establish clear and consistent policies and standards for using and supporting relative foster care placements. State agencies must then be held accountable for ensuring that all foster parents are aware of the benefits due them, and are offered such benefits as a matter of routine placement procedures. There is also a role for the ACF in the development of training packages that specifically address the needs of relative foster parents.

IMPLICATIONS FOR PRACTICE

Foster children need to be kept informed about major events affecting their lives to reduce the upheaval and trauma associated with the removal from their homes (Johnson et al., 1995). Kagan (1996) proposes several guiding principles and strategies for practitioners. These include engaging the parents of children in placement, mapping family resources, identifying split messages children hear from their family, and understanding the ensuing struggle children face following placement. Practitioners can help in mobilizing supportive networks and creating safety plans, fostering appropriate attachments with both birth and foster parents, and making visits and review conferences constructive times for change.

Foster parents' attitudes need to be addressed through training and supervision to help them cooperate and share authority with birth parents and caseworkers. Such training should emphasize the positive contribution of collaboration to the foster child's well-being, and it should stress the need for empathy toward birth parents. Because the expectation that foster parents collaborate with birth parents and caseworkers may arouse foster parents' resistance, training should explicitly address the skills necessary for a more collaborative role, while supporting their parenting and authority. However, only those foster parents who are able to collaborate with birth parents should be expected to do so, whereas others should be encouraged to opt for models that correspond better with their needs and abilities (Ryan et al., 1981; Seaberg, 1981).

IMPLICATIONS FOR RESEARCH

The research on foster care has not kept pace with the growing reliance on out-of-home placement of children. Much of the foster care literature is conceptual rather than empirical. Additional empirical research is needed to supplement the case studies and program evaluations. Given the potentially profound effects of legislative changes, it is especially important that research be funded to track the impact of legislation and to assess how it is being implemented. We need to know, for example, how the 12-month time limit for achieving reunification as required by the Adoption and Safe Families Act of 1997 affects foster care. We need assessments of the law's impact on the well-being of families and children. Ongoing research is needed to assess interventions and services to prevent out-of-home placement.

Continuing attention should be focused on the relationships between poverty and out-of-home placement. Many observers have suggested that one consequence of welfare reform may be an increase in out-of-home placements, because families lack the resources to care for their children. The relationships between the availability of welfare support and out-of-home placements merit close scrutiny, especially as welfare time limits begin to take effect.

The foster family itself has received little research attention. The family's structure, dynamics, and stages of development, as well as its boundaries and the roles and relationships among family members and with the birth family, all merit further study. Issues of loyalty, expectations, parenting, managing stigma and stereotypes, and family identity need also to be examined. More research is needed on placement to assess the effects of placement history and foster care, and on various types of foster families.

Further research is needed on recruitment of foster parents, on establishing guidelines for adequate reimbursement, and assessing foster parent training. We need to learn more about how caseworkers can be most effective in helping both the foster parents and foster children. Studies are also needed on the relative efficacy of the paraprofessional foster parent model and the resources it takes to sustain it.

If child welfare programs are to tie effectively into extended family care networks, more must be known about the participation of relatives in the child welfare system in general, and relative foster care placements in particular, including short- and long-term effects on children. With the growing reliance on kin foster families, we need to assess ways of supporting kin foster parents, including economic assistance, social and health services, and casework support.

Visitation policies and practices deserve continued research attention to assess the impact of visitation on children, parents, and foster parents, and to examine its role in facilitating reunification.

The transition of children out of foster care, especially for those who age out of the system, is a significant but understudied facet of the foster care system. We need to learn more about the kinds of interventions and services that can best facilitate a successful transition out of care.

DISCUSSION QUESTIONS

1. How do you account for the wide fluctuations in the number of children in foster care since the 1960s?
2. How would you define a foster family? Is it a substitute family? A replacement family? Should foster parents be considered as paraprofessionals, volunteers, or paid child care workers?
3. How does the acceptance of foster children affect the structure and dynamics of the foster family? What are the principal rewards and stressors for the foster family?
4. What is your assessment of the underlying class, gender, and racial dimensions of foster care in the United States?
5. What public policy initiatives could be taken to reduce the number of children in out-of-home placements?

6. Do you believe that laws and policies should move toward more rapid termination of parental rights when children are removed from the home? Should we instead permit more time for parents to reestablish their parental role? What are the principal arguments on either side of this issue? What additional considerations might you want to take into account?

7. Former Speaker of the House of Representatives Newt Gingrich advocated the total elimination of public welfare. He suggested that children whose parents could not support them could be removed from the home and placed in orphanages. What is your assessment of this proposal? What would you say to former Congressman Gingrich about it?

SUGGESTIONS FOR FURTHER READING

Barth, R. P., Courtney, M., Berrick, J. D., & Albert, V. (1994). *From child abuse to permanency planning: Child welfare services pathways and placements.* New York: Aldine.

Maluccio, A. N., Fein, E., & Olmstead, K. A. (1986). *Permanency planning for children.* New York: Tavistock.

McFadden, E. J. (1996). Family-centered practice with foster-parent families. *Families in Society, 77*(9), 545–557.

Molin, R. (1994). Foster families and larger systems: Image and identity. *Community Alternatives: International Journal of Family Care, 6*(1), 19–31.

Pecora, P. J., Whittaker, J. K., Maluccio, A. N., & Barth, R. P. (with Plotnick, R.). (2000). *The child welfare challenge: Policy, practice and research* (2nd ed.). Hawthorne, NY: Walter de Gruyter.

Chapter 3

ADOPTIVE FAMILIES

Adoption is a legal procedure whereby a person who is not a child's birth parent becomes the child's legal parent, acquiring the rights and assuming the responsibilities of a parent (Carrieri, 1991). Adoptions may be arranged independently (without agency supervision) or through either public or private agencies. The agencies investigate both the child's parentage and the suitability of the adoptive family. Placements are then reviewed by a court, which then issues a new birth certificate designating the adoptive parents as the parents. In addition to the legal arrangements, adoption is also a highly significant social event and a lifelong process.

About half of all adoptions today are by stepparents. These stepparent adoptions are considered here only in passing, because the issues relating to them are discussed in Chapter 5, "Stepfamilies." This chapter addresses all other adoptions, including infant adoptions, which comprise almost one third of all adoptions, and special needs adoptions, those occurring through public welfare departments and which account for about 20% of adoptions.

The adoption scene has changed dramatically in the past two decades. With fewer healthy infants available for adoption, there has been an increasing number of international adoptions, a steady movement toward more openness in adoption, and a growing diversity in the kinds of adoption placements (Daly & Sobol, 1997). Adoptive families today vary considerably depending on the characteristics of the adoptive parents and the adoptive child, and the auspices and type of adoption. The adoptive parents may be unrelated and unknown to the child, or may be previous foster parents, relatives, or stepparents. They may be middle-aged or younger, married couples or single persons, gay men and lesbians. The children may be infants or older children, may be healthy or have physical or emotional problems, and may be the same or of a different race and/or national origin as the adoptive parents. The adoption may be open or closed, conducted independently or through a public or private agency. These various circumstances all have implications for the structure and dynamics of the adoptive family.

In the past, most babies available for adoption were the children of unwed mothers. In recent years, however, the wider use of contraceptives and the greater availability of abortion have reduced the pool of adoptable children. Changing social attitudes toward unwed mothers has made it more possible for them to raise their children (Simon, Altstein, & Melli, 1994), a choice facilitated by the availability of welfare assistance and head of household tax benefits, and less necessary to make a plan for adoption. In 1992, only about 3% of children born to unmarried mothers were available for adoption (Sobol & Daly, 1992), dropping from 19% in 1965. However, the rate of relinquishment among unmarried black and Latina women has consistently been at or under 2% (Mosher & Bachrach, 1996). Many families now seek adoptive children outside the United States. Others make either legitimate private arrangements or illegal black-market transactions with the birth mother through a doctor or lawyer, often for a very high fee.

Along with the changes in the availability of babies for adoption has come a shift in attitudes about adoption. In the past, adoption was considered deviant, and was shrouded in secrecy; today, it is out in the open and regarded more positively. Yet the reality today lies somewhere in between the two ideological extremes that view adoption as inherently problematic or, conversely, as a wonderful solution that bestows the benefits of the nuclear family on childless couples and children lacking parental care. Although offering a solution of sorts, the adoptive family also carries unique risks and stresses related both to the inherent tensions within this family constellation and to the societal ambivalence about it.

HISTORICAL BACKGROUND AND THE SOCIAL-CULTURAL CONTEXT

Adoption was practiced by the ancient Romans, Greeks, Egyptians, and Babylonians, and is referred to in the Bible and other religious texts, with Moses being one of the most famous adopted children (Barth, 1992). Adoptions in preindustrial Europe were usually of orphans. The adoptive families were generally childless and were the child's relatives, godparents, or neighbors. Adoptions of nonorphans, an alternative to child abandonment, were usually by a family that was better off financially than the birth family (Phillips, 1997).

The first adoption statutes in the United States took effect in 1851. Before that time, children were transferred to substitute parents without legal recognition of the adoption. From the beginning of American colonization, formal procedures existed for recording births or name changes. This opened the door to informal adoptions. Often these informal placements were economically motivated. Child labor was in great demand, especially for farm owners, and adoption provided an alternative to paying adult laborers. In the latter half of the 19th century, industrialization brought massive immigration and growing urbanization. Families were often unable to support their children. Informal transfers of these children to other families, by either the indigent parents or the charitable institutions where parents sometimes left their children, promoted these types of placements. This situation also provided the impetus for the orphan trains between 1854 and 1929 that took children from the East Coast to western farm families. There was some hope or expectation that children available for informal adoptive settings would receive care, support, and perhaps education in their new home. Only if a formal will were executed, however, would the informally adopted child be permitted to share in the estate of the new parents. Children were often treated as chattel, with adoption being little more than a transfer of title. With the Industrial Revolution, which moved craft production out of the home and into factories, indenture became less relied on, and it was abolished with the passage of the Thirteenth Amendment in 1865 (Barth, 1992).

As the number of informal adoptions rose, the need for a formal adoption process became more apparent. In 1851, Massachusetts enacted the first adoption statute. It required judicial approval, consent of the child's parent or guardian, and a finding that the prospective adoptive family was capable of raising the child. In reality, the provisions of the Massachusetts statute and other state adoption laws were not implemented in the manner seen today. Though early adoption statutes required a finding of suitability of the prospective adoption home, this requirement was more form than substance. By 1929, all 50 states had adoption legislation and, by the 1930s, most statutes and courts required investigation of the adoptive home. These investigations had varying degrees of complexity.

Today, virtually every state requires some form of investigation into the suitability or fitness of those seeking to adopt. The investigation usually involves a report referred to as a *home study*.

The early adoption statutes defined a relationship between the adoptive parents and the child, yet the implications often remained unclear. For example, under some statutes adopted children retained the right to inherit from their birth parents. The treatment of adoption records was similarly confusing. Early adoption statutes made no provision for confidentiality or the maintenance of records. As a result, adoptive families and birth parents had no legal protection against intrusions on their lives following an adoption. In the early 20th century, statutes began to protect the confidentiality of adoption from the public at large, but not between the parties to an adoption. It was not until the 1930s that statutes were enacted to preserve the exclusivity of the adoptive home (Barth, 1992, 1995).

Between 1910 and 1920, the first private adoption agencies were established, and between the 1930s and 1950s, social workers began sealing birth and adoption records. This change in practice reflected the attitudes, mores, and myths of the time, as well as the increasing authority of psychoanalysis (Carp, 1998). Secrecy surrounding adoptions was believed to protect the birth parents, the adoptees, and the adoptive parents (Carp, 1998). The birth parents were protected from the stigma of pregnancy "out of wedlock." The adoptees were protected from the stigma of "illegitimacy," and from concerns about "bad blood" and "bad seed" connected to the "sins of the fathers." Children were also protected from considering themselves as different from other children, and from the confusion and potential conflicts in having two sets of parents. For the adoptive parents, often an infertile couple, the protection was from the stigma of raising an "illegitimate" child, acknowledging their infertility, and being adoptive rather than "normal" birth parents. Adoptive parents were expected to "forget" about the adoption, and "get on with their normal lives." To facilitate this secrecy and anonymity, there was considerable effort to match the physical and ethnic characteristics, as well as the religion, of the adoptive parents and the adopted child (Anderson, Piantanida, & Anderson, 1993; Barth, 1995; Kadushin & Martin, 1988).

Until World War II, most adoptions were made by white, middle-class parents who adopted local white infants (Barth, 1995). Healthy Anglo babies were plentiful at a time when an unmarried woman had little or no choice whether to place her baby for adoption. Social workers had complete control over adoptive placement decisions, and services were geared toward providing the most perfect baby for adoptive applicants (Kadushin & Martin, 1988).

The circumstances of adoption changed dramatically after World War II. The involvement of Americans in wars outside the United States, in Europe, Japan, Korea, and later in Vietnam, coupled with a decline in infants available for adoption in the United States, gave rise to the practice of international adoption (Hollingsworth, 1998). As the children were usually very different in appearance from their adoptive parents, secrecy about the adoption became irrelevant. These early transracial adoptions challenged the prevailing stigma attached to the adoptive triad—namely, the adoptive parents, the adoptive child, and the birth family.

The growing acceptance of adoptive families who were "out of the closet" as nonblood families, paved the way for white parents adopting African American children (Bartholet, 1993; Rosettenstein, 1995; Rushton & Minnis, 1997). This practice was facilitated by liberal child welfare organizations that promoted transracial placements to help disadvantaged black children (Rosettenstein, 1995) and by what at the time were thought to be progressive attitudes promoting integration.

Propelled by the example of the civil rights movement of the 1960s, adoption-related liberation movements emerged, including the Adoptee's Liberty Movement (ALMA) and birth fathers' rights. Birth parents and adult adoptees began to speak out about their experiences, their rights, and their needs, and adoptive parents demanded more information on the children whose futures were entrusted to them.

PREVALENCE AND DEMOGRAPHIC CHARACTERISTICS OF ADOPTEES AND ADOPTIVE FAMILIES

The U.S. government does not maintain records on adoption, and state data are incomplete. Most adoptions occur outside the public child welfare system, and data on private adoptions are scarce. Therefore, the exact number of adopted children is not known, and estimates vary from 1 million to 5 million (Hollinger, 1998). Between 2% and 4% of American families have adopted a child (Moorman & Hernandez, 1989; Mosher & Bachrach, 1996).

Characteristics of the Adoptive
Parents and the Adoptive Act

According to the NCHS (1997), about a half million people are, at any one time, seeking to adopt a child, though only about 100,000 have applied to an agency. There are approximately 5 or 6 adoption seekers for every actual adoption (Hollinger, 1998; NCHS, 1997). The waiting time to adopt a healthy American infant is between 1 and 7 years; the waiting time for an international infant is between 6 and 18 months (Simon et al., 1994).

Those most likely to consider adopting a baby are childless women; women with fecundity impairments, pregnancy loss, and previous child deaths; and women with higher levels of income and education (Bachrach, London, & Maza, 1991; Mosher & Bachrach, 1996). Between 11% and 24% of couples with infertility problems take a step toward adopting a child (Mosher & Bachrach, 1996). Furthermore, single parents are adopting in greater numbers—currently representing from 12% to 25% of adoption seekers (Meezan, 1980; Shireman, 1995).

Adoption and seeking to adopt are influenced by the cost, the limited supply of babies available for adoption, the experience of infertility, and the individual's identity as a parent (Bachrach et al., 1991; Bartholet, 1994; Brodzinsky, 1997). The meanings of reproduction, infertility, and parenthood are socially constructed. The popularity of new reproductive technologies builds on deeply rooted social biases that favor birth children and families founded on biological ties (Bartholet, 1994; Miall, 1995). This value bias constructs infertility as a problem requiring high technology medical treatments to produce biologically related children. Adoption is considered by many as inferior to biologically reproducing a child, a choice of last resort. This bias conditions infertile couples to focus on treatment options rather than to consider adoption, while birth mothers are made to feel that it would be unnatural to surrender their children for others to raise.

Most adoptions are relatively costly. Estimates for agency adoptions range from about $10,000 to $20,000. Public agency adoptions are free or entail a minimal fee, although attorney fees are required in finalizing the adoption. The cost for international adoptions ranges from $5,000 to $20,000 (Simon et al., 1994).

LEGAL AND POLICY ISSUES

Though adoption is regulated by state statute, several federal laws have had significant implications for adoption practices. These include the 1978 Indian Child Welfare Act (ICWA, Public Law 95-608), the Adoption Assistance and Child Welfare Act of 1980 (Public Law 96-272), the Adoption and Safe Families Act of 1997 (Public Law 105-89), and the Multiethnic Placement Act of 1994 (MEPA, Public Law 103-382). These laws apply to foster care as well as to adoption, and the reader is advised to refer to the discussion of these laws in Chapter 2 to get an understanding of the federal policy context for adoption. Here, I consider the following state legal and policy issues: (a) parental consent to an adoption, (b) open records and reunion with birth parents, (c) auspices of adoption, and (d) pre- and postplacement services.

Parental Consent to an Adoption

Parental consent to an adoption is a requirement of most adoption statutes. Consent is the most common method to achieve a voluntary termination of parental rights. Who is defined as a "parent," however, varies from state to state. Birth but unwed fathers had no recognized role until the 1970s. In many states, unwed birth fathers still do not have a presumptive right to give consent or to veto an adoption, but merely a constitutional right to notice and an opportunity to be heard. In some cases, the unwed father may "earn" the right to consent or veto by establishing paternity following the child's birth.

Statutes detailing the grounds on which parental rights may be involuntarily terminated commenced in the 1970s. In *Santoski v. Kramer,* 455 U.S. 745 (1982), the U. S. Supreme Court held that parents have a fundamental interest in the care, custody, and control of their children, but not an absolute right. The due process clause of the U. S. Constitution requires that severance of a parent's rights be supported by clear and convincing evidence.

State statutes generally view involuntary termination of parental rights as an action of last resort. Statutes usually require that reasonable efforts be made to preserve the family relationship. What efforts must be taken and to what length those efforts must be made prior to termination varies from state to state.

Open Records and Reunion With Birth Parents

Most U.S. states require the sealing of agency records, though under pressure from adoptees wishing to know their "true" identity, states increasingly have granted adult adoptees access to their original birth certificates. In only four states (Alaska, Kansas, Oregon, and Tennessee) may all adopted adults obtain copies of their original birth certificates, though as of February 1998, 24 states had mutual consent registries and "search and consent" statutes (Hollinger, 1998). In three states (Alaska, Kansas, and Tennessee), state legislatures opened the records; in Oregon, however, voters, not legislators, opted to open birth certificates.

This new trend to open sealed adoption records signifies a reversal of public attitudes. Until the 1940s and 1950s, most states had an open adoption policy. For example, in Washington State, adoption records were open until 1943, and in Oregon until 1957. From the end of the 1950s, the records were closed to protect the adoptee from the stigma of being illegitimate.

Mutual consent registries permit parties to an adoption to register their willingness to meet at some point in the future, but they allow the release of identifying information only when a birth parent and an adult adoptee both file formal consents to the disclosure of their identities (Hollinger, 1998). Search-and-consent statutes provide that when a birth parent, on being contacted by an individual or agency acting as a "confidential intermediary," consents to the disclosure of his or her identity to the adoptee, the disclosure may then be authorized by a court (Hollinger, 1998). Several states (New Jersey, Nevada, Iowa, and North Carolina, in addition to the District of Columbia) allow access to adoption information for "good cause" shown to a court (Hollinger, 1998).

Until the 1960s, both birth and adoptive parents were explicitly or implicitly promised anonymity. Little, if any, information was shared between them. The parties involved were encouraged to "get on with their lives" and "put this event behind them." They had no preparation to deal with future issues that were bound to arise. With the sealing of records there was also little or no legal recourse for the adoptee to access information. Adoptees who held questions of identity, ancestry, and genetics had nowhere to turn for answers. Adoptive parents had been assured that if they were good parents, no curiosity would exist. Therefore, when faced with questions, they often felt insecure and inadequate, believing that they had somehow failed (Alty & Cameron, 1995; Anderson et al., 1993).

The main arguments for the closure of the adoption records were to safeguard the adoptive family's privacy and stability. Closure was held to be necessary to uphold guarantees of confidentiality made to birth parents and adoptive parents, and to protect the adoptees from potentially disturbing information about the circumstances of their conception, such as incest or rape. Those favoring sealed records point out that few adoptees actually search for their birth parents, and that birth parents generally do not want to be found. Some maintain that open records will discourage parents from placing their children for adoption and will cause mothers to opt for abortion instead (Burke, 1996).

Proponents of open records argue that open adoption records permit adoptees to establish their identity and that to deny adoptees access to birth certificates and court records violates their civil rights. In addition, a contract with birth parents to ensure privacy denies the rights of children who did not give their consent to the contract. Furthermore, though only 2% of adoptees search for their birth parents each year, the cumulative number over 10 years is about 2.5 million (Burke, 1996). Finally, they argue that percentages and numbers do not matter, in that all adopted children search. It may not be a literal search, but it is meaningful nonetheless. It begins when the child first asks herself or others, Why was I adopted? Who are my birth parents? Where are they now?

Auspices of Adoption

Adoption can be done independently or through agencies. Each alternative offers different benefits, preparatory services, and postadoption support (Barth, 1992; Berry, Barth, & Needell, 1996). Independent adoptions are made by parents who place their children in an adoptive family without the intervention of an agency (Carrieri, 1991). Barth (1995) estimates that about 25,000 children are adopted independently each year.

Agency adoptions are conducted through public or private (attorney facilitated) agencies, and follow voluntary or involuntary relinquishment of the birth parents' rights to the child. Since the 1980s, with the adoption of permanency planning legislation, public agency adoptions have increased dramatically (Barth, 1995). Usually, children adopted through public agencies have been in the foster care system for months or years, and are identified as having special needs. The adoptive parents these agencies serve tend to have lower incomes and less education, to be older, and to have more children than parents adopting through private agencies (Barth, 1995). Independent adoption is an alternative for those who do not meet agency criteria and/or those wishing to take a more aggressive role in finding a child. For the birth parent, an independent adoption may be viewed as a way to be more in control of selecting the adoptive home, though private adoption agencies are generally flexible in permitting the birth parents and the adoptive parents to plan as to how the adoption will proceed.

Public agencies have been found to provide more preparatory services and postadoptive services (e.g., visiting, counseling, and providing information about the child and birth mother) than either private or independent services. However, both private and independent services offer more opportunities to meet with the child's birth family (Berry et al., 1996).

Pre- and Postplacement Services

Preplacement services include screening potential adoptive families and providing the adoptive parents with information about the child. The major function of the screening process, done through home study, is to protect the child from harm by checking the fitness of the adoptive family. Home studies, a practice initiated nearly 150 years ago, also clarify the intentions and flexibility of the adoptive parents regarding the characteristics of the child they wish to adopt. Some scholars argue that all who wish to become adoptive parents should be presumed fit and should not be screened, exactly as birth parents are not screened (Bartholet, 1993).

Studies confirm that thorough background information is vital for the successful adoption of special-needs children (Rosenthal, 1993; Rosenthal & Groze, 1994; Rosenthal, Groze, & Morgan, 1996). Nondisclosure of medical and other health-related information about the child may be grounds for civil suit as "wrongful adoption" (Kopels, 1995).

Agencies usually maintain contact with the adoptive family during the first three to six months following the adoption. In special-needs adoptions, these contacts are meant to reassure the child of continuity with his or her past and to provide the family with needed support (Barth, 1995). Postplacement contact is also important as a means to detect problems before they escalate. There is also a case to be made for ongoing postplacement services, especially for special-needs and international adoptions (Barth, 1995; Barth & Berry, 1988; Serbin, 1997; Shireman, 1995).

Some programs offer a hotline for adoptive families in which experienced adoptive families offer support and advice (Pecora, Whittaker, & Maluccio, 1992), and many agencies conduct support groups for adoptive families (Barth, 1995).

OPEN AND CLOSED ADOPTION

Closely related to the issue of disclosure in adoption records is the growing trend over the past 20 years for open adoption. The majority of infant adoptions in the United States are now open to some degree; birth parents are insisting more and more on a degree of openness in making a plan for placing their children (Burke, 1996). Open adoption confers permanent responsibility for the care, custody, and control of the child to the adoptive parents, while maintaining communication and/or contact with the child's birth parents before and/or after the adoption (Alty & Cameron, 1995; Carrieri, 1991; Silverstein & Demick, 1994). The contact can be minimal, limited to exchanging names, or it can be highly interactive, with continuous visitation of the birth parents and/or the birth family, including grandparents and siblings (Alty & Cameron, 1995).

There are two opposing policy considerations affecting openness in adoptions. One is the children's consent to decisions affecting their lives, stressing the child's rights. The other is the doctrine that stresses the best interest of the child, which gives the state the authority to act on behalf of the child if the child is either too young or not able to decide for him- or herself. Usually, when older children are involved, their consent is sought by judges (Daly & Sobol, 1997).

During the past 70 years, secrecy and denial have characterized adoption practice. This closed system of adoption has its roots in the assumption that adoption is a one-time legal event and that the adoptive family replaces the birth family "as if" the child were born to them (Kirk, 1964). Despite the movement toward more openness, this doctrine remains a central tenet of the law governing adoption in the United States, with contemporary adoption statutes continuing to emphasize confidentiality and requiring the relinquishment of the birth parents' rights (Cook, 1992; Daly & Sobol, 1997). More recently, professionals have begun recognizing that adoption is a lifelong process with profound effects for the adoption triad members throughout their lives (Rosenberg & Groze, 1997).

Open adoption represents a dramatic shift from the notion that adoptive families are equivalent to birth families, and it renders adoptive families more similar to foster families and joint-custody divorced families. To date, most open adoptions are voluntary, although there is a growing tendency to require adoptive parents to agree that the birth parents can visit their child postadoption as part of the adoption agreement. Open adoption is most prevalent in the adoption of older children and in stepparent adoption. In contrast, when the adoption occurs because of the abuse of the child by the birth parents, open adoption is usually not permitted, and the court order may override the wishes of the birth parents to have an open adoption (Alty & Cameron, 1995). Between 1988 and 1989, 55% of the adoptive families in California had contact with the birth family within the two years following the adoption (Berry, as cited in Barth 1992).

The arguments for both closed and open adoptions reflect differences in ideology rather than the research evidence (Alty & Cameron, 1995; Baran & Panor, 1990). Goldstein, Freud, and Solnit (1973), citing the importance of bonding and permanence, held that contact with birth parents threatened the attachment with the psychological (i.e., adoptive) parents and generated conflicting loyalties for the child. Their books, *Beyond the Best Interests of the Child* (1973) and *Before the Best Interests of the Child* (1979), were highly influential. Others believed that closed adoption facilitates family stability (Alty & Cameron, 1995; Austinson, 1995) and that open adoption may dissuade potential adoptive parents from adopting (Alty & Cameron, 1995). Kraft, Palombo, Woods, Mitchell, & Schmidt (1985) concluded that though there are benefits to open adoption, these are primarily related to the mother and the child and are at the expense of the adoptive parents.

The value of open adoption, and especially its effect on the child, has not yet been adequately assessed (Austinson, 1995; Barth, 1992), although findings from small, nonrepresentative studies do suggest that openness has more positive than negative consequences (Alty & Cameron, 1995; Gross, 1993). Adoptive mothers who experienced open adoption have significantly more favorable attitudes toward both the birth mother and the adopted child, and demonstrate significantly more favorable parenting attitudes two years after the adoption (Lee & Twaite, 1997). Contrary to clinical assumptions, adoptive parents who experience open adoption are less concerned about attachment to their adoptive child (Silverstein & Demick, 1994). Contact with the birth parents may also help adoptive parents to come to terms with their infertility rather than suppressing and disguising their feelings about it through the pretense that they are the birth parents (Churchman, 1986; Silverstein & Demick, 1994).

Proponents argue that the secrecy and denial of conventional, or closed, adoption violates the rights of the adopted child and negatively affects the adoptive triad (Rosenberg & Groze, 1997). In contrast, they consider open adoption to be in the best interests of the child (Alty & Cameron, 1995; Barth, 1992) and beneficial for the two sets of parents (Rosenberg & Groze, 1997).

Birth parents clearly favor open adoptions (Cushman, Kalmuss, & Namerow, 1997; Gross, 1993). Visiting and telephoning the adoptive family, as well as indirect contact through pictures or letters, were associated with birth mothers experiencing lower levels of grief, worry about the baby, and regret over the adoption decision (Alty & Cameron, 1995; Cushman et al., 1997; Rosenberg & Groze, 1997). Birth mothers who experienced open adoption showed attachment to their pregnancies, sought support and prenatal care, and were able to come to terms with the loss of their babies. In closed adoptions, an essential part of the child's history and self is cut off (Rosenberg & Groze, 1997; Silverstein & Demick, 1994); open adoption helps the child cope with feelings of rejection by the birth parents and helps the child establish his or her identity (Alty & Cameron, 1995).

TRANSRACIAL ADOPTION

Transracial adoptions, also referred to as interracial, interethnic, or transethnic adoptions, involve the adoption of a child by parents of a different race or ethnicity. In practice, transracial adoption refers mostly to the adoption of children of color by white families (Hollingsworth, 1998; McRoy & Hall, 1996).

Although international adoptions, discussed in the next section, frequently involve children who have a different racial and cultural background and, in that sense, should be considered interracial adoptions, domestic interracial adoptions of African American children by white parents is a uniquely contentious issue.

In reaction to the increase in transracial adoption in the 1960s, the NABSW in 1972 demanded the cessation of whites adopting African American children. Their concern was that transracial adoptions would result in cultural genocide. For a while, their position influenced family court judges and child advocates to pursue same-race adoption for African American children (Curtis, 1996). Nevertheless, there has been growing abandonment of race-matching adoption policies and increased reliance on transracial adoption (McRoy & Hall, 1996). This has been propelled by the declining availability of white babies for adoption, the increasing numbers of white families seeking to adopt, the rapidly growing numbers of African American children in foster care, and difficulties in finding African American placement families. The MEPA forbade federally funded agencies from solely considering race, culture, and ethnicity in making foster care and adoption placement decisions. This shift in policy and the Interethnic Adoption Provisions Act of 1996 (IEAP, Public Law 104-188), which prohibited states altogether from considering race or ethnicity in determining the best interest of the child, enraged many African American social workers (Curtis, 1996). The arguments for and against transracial adoptions cannot be separated from the bitter history of the race relations in the United States. It is not surprising that the most heated arguments about adoption concern African American children.

In the absence of national data, the number and characteristics of transracial adoptions are unknown. Based on NCHS data, Simon and colleagues (1994) report that in 1987 no more than 1% of all U.S. adoptions were transracial. McRoy and Hall (1996) estimate that each year about 1,200 black children are transracially placed. Although some argue that transracial adoption is practiced mostly with older children when there is concern that the child will not be adopted at all (Barth, 1992), others maintain that most transracial adoptions are of healthy infants, not older children with special needs (McRoy & Hall, 1996; Willis, 1996).

Practitioners and policy makers agree that children benefit from same-race adoptions, because such an adoption is important for the child's racial/ethnic identity. However, some practitioners, as well as the Child Welfare League of America, stress that when same-race adoptions are not possible, the child should not be denied adoption (Barth, 1992; Simon et al., 1994). As transracial adoptions are politically controversial, many agencies choose not to place children in transracial homes, even if that means the child is denied adoption (Barth, 1992).

Supporters of transracial adoption cite studies showing that children placed in transracial families do as well as other adopted children (Bagley, 1993; Simon & Altstein, 1987, 1996). These findings, however, have been challenged as reflecting a Eurocentric bias (Lovett-Tisdale &

Purnell, 1996). The research indicates that compared with same-race adoptions, children raised in transracial families had a well-adjusted sense of identity (Bagley, 1993), identified themselves as black or of mixed race in similar proportions, were usually well adjusted, and had good or very good self-esteem (Vroegh, 1997). Adoptive parents described their transracially adopted children as well bonded and as having quite positive self-esteem (Hoopes, Alexander, Silver, Ober, & Kirby, 1997). Based on a review of research regarding the transracial adoption of African American children, Alexander and Curtis (1996) conclude that the children have not been psychologically harmed by the placements.

A survey of 368 African American state university students found that the majority did not oppose transracial adoption by white families as long as the child is allowed to interact with other African American children and white adoptive parents obtain knowledge of black history. Nevertheless, 59% preferred that black parents decide whether their children should be adopted by black or white parents, and almost half believed that white adoptive parents are not sensitive to the racism faced by African American youth (Chima, 1996).

Assessing the studies on transracial adoptions, Simon and Altstein (1996) conclude that "nowhere in the arguments against transracial adoptions are data presented which show that the practice does not serve the children's best interest. The arguments against transracial adoption have no empirical base. They are ideologically and politically driven" (p. 8). Proponents of transracial adoptions further argue that the call for banning these adoptions is based on a binary opposition of black and white that denies differences within these categories and similarities across them, and that it reflects racist stereotyping (Macey, 1995).

On the other side, opponents of transracial adoption maintain that instead of adopting these children, the reasons for their being available for adoption should be corrected (Hollingsworth, 1998). They consider the practice to be racist in presuming that whites are more capable of raising black children than blacks (Abdullah, 1996; Goddard, 1996). Fueling the debate is the large number of African American children who are removed from their birth families. African American children are at especially high risk of being placed for foster care or adoption due to poverty, a situation that in part reflects discrimination and racism (Goddard, 1996). Over 46% of African American children lived in poverty in 1993, as did 41% of all Latino children, compared with 14% of white children (Hollingsworth, 1998). Many African American families lack basic resources, including employment and educational opportunities, sufficient wages, housing, and health insurance. With so many African American men in prisons, a substantial number of African American families are deprived of the income and support of males. As Penn and Coverdale (1996) state,

> Despite America's great wealth, millions of African American children share the plight of children from some of the poorest countries in the world. . . . [J]ust as we know that the problems faced by Bosnian, Ethiopian, Colombian, Liberian, Biafran, Rwandan, Asian, and Latin American children cannot be solved by benevolent foreigners who lovingly adopt, so we also know that transracial adoption is no real solution to the problems that plague African American children. (p. 243)

Opponents of transracial adoption also question the positive research findings as biased in measuring irrelevant variables, such as IQ, self-esteem, or adjustment, rather than racial identity, and in applying white, European American standards as the yardstick (Penn & Coverdale, 1996). Furthermore, they argue, the racial identity measures that have been used are inappropriate, invalid, or unreliable (Abdullah, 1996; Willis, 1996).

Most of the studies on transracial adoption of African American children were done during the children's early and middle childhood years, missing the stage when racial identity is most meaningful (Willis, 1996). The studies have failed to address crucial questions regarding the development of adopted children, the contexts of families engaging in transracial adoption, and the age of the adoptees at the time of the adoption (Harrison, 1996). The researchers generally solicit the opinions of the adoptive parents rather than those of the adopted children, and the white parents' point of view may be biased (Penn & Coverdale, 1996).

To comprehend fully the meaning of transracial adoption from an African American perspective, transracial adoptions must be considered within an African-centered frame of reference (Abdullah, 1996; Goddard, 1996). Racial and ethnic identity refers to one's sense of belonging to a particular racial or ethnic group, the acquisition of behaviors specific to that group, and how one differentiates oneself from members of other racial or ethnic groups (Goddard, 1996; McRoy & Hall, 1996). The socialization of black children is not done solely by the parents, as "it takes a whole village to raise a child" (Taylor & Thornton, 1996; Willis, 1996). Racial identity is crucial for black children. It asserts both positive aspects like black pride and black culture affirmations as well as negative aspects such as acceptance of negative stereotypes (Taylor & Thornton, 1996). It involves absorbing the black experience, including slavery and the collective history of whites' cruelty and racism against blacks (Griffith, 1995). It helps prepare the children for coping in a racist society (Bausch & Serpe, 1997; Willis, 1996).

The need for other races to adopt African American children is also indicative of deficiencies in an adoption system that places barriers against potential African American adoptive families. Many well-suited African American families who could provide adoptees with a warm, nurturing environment are rejected because they lack the economic and material resources (Hollingsworth, 1998; McRoy & Hall, 1996) and because of "structurally discriminatory eligibility criteria [that] screen out potential Black families" (Hill, 1998, p. 21) on the basis of marital status, age, economic status, and having birth children (Hill, 1998). High adoption fees, the perception among African Americans that formal adoption is equivalent to the purchase of children, the failure to recruit African American adoption workers, and the lack of culturally competent placement workers and specialized minority programs also stand in the way (Hollingsworth, 1998; Lovett-Tisdale & Purnell, 1996; McRoy & Hall, 1996; McRoy, Oglesby, & Grape, 1997).

Willis (1996) challenges the notion that, unless adopted by white parents, black children will remain unadopted as a deliberate manipulation of the facts. According to Willis, healthy African American babies are not waiting to be adopted. Prospective white and African American parents compete to adopt them. It is, rather, the older black and white children with special needs who are waiting to be adopted, and prospective parents are not lining up to adopt them.

INTERNATIONAL ADOPTIONS

International or intercountry adoptions were almost unheard of until after World War II. Since then, the number of intercountry adoptions has grown steadily, reaching 13,620 in 1997 according to the U.S. Immigration and Naturalization Service (INS), or about 10% of adoptions in the United States (Barth, 1995). The primary sending countries in 1997 were China (3,616 children), Taiwan (3,333 children), the Russian Federation (3,816 children), Korea (1,654 children), and Romania (554 children).

As with transracial adoption, international adoption raises difficult policy and moral issues. International adoptions are expensive and often require a lengthy trip to the child's country of origin. The adoptive parents are a privileged group from an affluent society (Riley, 1997). The "sending" nations are usually less developed countries experiencing the aftermath of war and poverty, lacking either the resources to provide for abandoned or orphaned children or the ability to stop the flow of adoptions out of their countries. Hence international adoptions have been criticized as a form of imperialism in which wealthy industrialized nations exploit impoverished and distressed nations by taking away their children (Serbin, 1997). As Riley (1997) describes it, international adoption is

> an irony, a contradiction, a usually well-intentioned action which is possible because of the differences in access, privilege, and norms of two different societies, and the differences in expectations, privileges, and opportunities given to women and men within both societies. (p. 100)

Seen in that light, foreign children are commodities for the consumption of richer Western nations, not differing much from the shipment of other "exotic" commodities imported from the East under colonial regimes (Riley, 1997). Furthermore, international adoptions are tainted by racism. People living in Western countries adopt few children from Africa. The most desired children are either white (from the former U.S.S.R. or Romania), light skinned (Latin American), or "cute" and "exotic" (Chinese girls; Riley, 1997). Nevertheless, on an individual level, the adoption of these children frequently means saving them from early mortality, hunger, and conditions that would severely impair their ability to develop into healthy adults (Riley, 1997).

International adoptions are governed by three sets of laws: those of the country of origin (the child's birth country), those of the host country, and those of the state where the adoptive parents live. Most countries require that the child be adopted in the country of origin, and require the adoptive parents to remain in the country as long as it takes to complete the adoption process. These requirements, along with the long and often frustrating wait, the expense, and the fact that only a few countries allow the adopted child to be relocated to the United States, constitute major barriers to international adoptions (Simon et al., 1994). After the requirements of the country of origin are fulfilled, the child needs a passport in order to travel to the host country. The INS requires that the adoptive parents be approved, based on a home study, and that the adoptive child meet the INS definition of an "orphan." State laws may require that the child be legally adopted in the United States, even if he or she was already legally adopted in the host country. Before finalizing the adoption, some states require a period of residency with the adoptive family. The growing prevalence of international adoptions, and the problems it presents, has been recognized in three international treaties since 1984: The UN Human Rights Treaty, the Hague Convention on Inter-Country Adoption, and the Inter-American Convention (Simon et al., 1994).

Once an international adoption has taken place, it poses several unique challenges. These may include the differing racial, ethnic, and/or cultural backgrounds of the child and adoptive family, as well as the residues of institutionalization, because many intercountry children have lived in orphanages before being adopted.

Families who adopt children internationally are frequently faced with not only the visibility of the adoption, but also the recognition of the child's original culture (Trolley, Wallin, & Hansen, 1995; Westhues & Cohen, 1998). If the child is older at the time of the adoption, these differences may also require that the child undergo acculturation. Nevertheless, international adoptions are the most prevalent form of adoption in many countries. For example, in Canada, international adoptions constitute 60% of the total adoptions (Marcovitch, Cesaroni, Roberts, & Swanson, 1995), and in Holland 90% (VanDulmen, 1998).

Most of the research on international adoptions has been on Romanian children and on the impact of institutionalization prior to adoption. This is due, to a large extent, to the media's coverage of the terrible conditions in Romanian orphanages following Ceaucescu's death. The first television exposés were in 1990, showing that the children who survived the orphanages suffered from near starvation; lack of medical attention, clothing, and heating; and spending most of the day in their cribs, suffering from extreme deficiency of human contact, caring, and stimulation. These images drew a large number of would-be adoptive parents from around the world.

Adopted children who have been institutionalized tend to exhibit a number of problems following adoption, including medical difficulties, such as increased risk for tuberculosis and hepatitis or below-normal weight and height; developmental delays, such as a delay in fine and gross motor skills, or in social and language skills; attachment risks, such as a lack of trust, avoidance of intimate relations, clinging, and anxiety; and behavioral risks, such as temper tantrums and fearfulness

(Groza, 1997). Despite the risks posed by institutionalization, several studies (e.g., Groze & Ileana, 1996) and reviews of adoption studies (e.g., Groza, 1997) suggest that not all the children who have been institutionalized exhibit these problems, and that a significant number of children improve considerably in their adoptive homes.

Many of the developmental delays of the Romanian adoptees were made up postadoption (Morison, Ames, & Chisholm, 1995). Most children, with time, exhibited appropriate development and good parent-child relationships (Groze & Ileana, 1996), were well adjusted, and functioned in the normal range (Marcovitch et al., 1997). Similarly, a study in the Netherlands, on 80 internationally and interracially adopted children who had been placed before the age of 6 months, found that most—74%—had secure infant-mother attachments (Juffer & Rosenboom, 1997).

Finally, some studies found no relationship between preadoption history of Romanian children adopted by U.S. families and adoptees' development (Groze & Ileana, 1996) or attachment outcomes (Marcovitch et al., 1997).

FAMILY STRUCTURE

Although they look like nuclear birth families and have many of the same experiences, adoptive families differ in both structure and dynamics from the "traditional" families in which two heterosexual parents raise their shared birth children (Brodzinsky, Lang, & Smith, 1995; Watson, 1996). As Anderson and colleagues (1993) describe it,

> The differences and complexities inherent in both the process of the adoption and the families created in this way . . . impact and alter the way in which [adoptive] family members attribute meaning to normative events, create their family structure, and respond to life-cycle transitions. (p. 255)

This view of the adoptive family as different from the nuclear birth family is relatively new, and it marks a significant change from the earlier view that adoptive families are essentially the same as traditional nuclear families. To create an illusion of a traditional family, social workers used to rely on a number of carefully designed strategies to conceal the adoption. The common practice of adopting infants and carefully matching the ethnicity and race of the birth child and the adoptive parents helped maintain secrecy. The adoptive parents did not reveal to others, and often not to the adopted child, that the child had been adopted. The absolute lack of contact with the birth parents following the adoption and the sealed birth records prevented adoptees from learning about their birth parents and their past. The rationale of all these measures was supported by attachment theory (Bowlby, 1982), which views the development of secure attachment to the mother in the first months of life as having crucial long-term consequences, especially for the development of basic trust. Based on this theory, it was assumed that the bond between the adoptive mother and the baby needs to be free of disruptions, and the earlier the adoption, the better the ability of the child to develop a secure attachment. The effort to conceal the adoption and create an illusion that the child is a birth child was also supported by the belief that the traditional nuclear family was the ideal family form. If for some reason it was impossible to attain this ideal, the "second best" was to create the illusion of a traditional family.

Although the belief remains that the traditional family is the ideal, today's adoptive families are much less able or willing to be "closeted." This reflects the increasing adoption of children who are visibly different from their adoptive parents (i.e., international, intercultural, interracial, or older children). The growing awareness and acceptance of adoptive families allows the adoptive parents, the adoptees, and the birth parents to come out of the closet, a trend reflected in the availability of books for children and adults describing the lives of adoptive families. The greater openness has also been reinforced by the increasing prevalence and acceptance of other nontraditional families.

Nevertheless, despite the greater openness, these families, like other once-stigmatized nontraditional families, are still fighting for social approval and acceptance. They may often try to act like, and if possible to pretend that, they are traditional families. Parents' expectations may be shaped by powerful adoption myths based on the idealization of the traditional nuclear birth family. The mythical happy family, in which all members love, support, and respect each other and live a life filled with caring and rewarding experience, does not match the daily lives of adoptive families. Power and Krause-Eheart (1995) suggest that a new collective story is needed that will offer a more realistic guide to the adoption of older children with special needs and, I would add, to adoption in general. There is evidence that the more the adoptive parents view their families as different from traditional families, the more secure they feel about their competence as parents, about the child's birth parents, and about their child's separateness from themselves (Silverman, Campbell, & Patti, 1994).

The recognition that adoptive families differ from nuclear families calls for a shift in addressing these families. Rather than focusing on the adopted child, we need to consider the entire adoptive family. Historically, the focus has been on the adopted child as the "identified patient." Both popular belief and research stressed the psychopathology of adopted children. A disproportionately large number of adopted children and adolescents were in the past referred to mental health professionals (Kirschner, 1996; McRoy, Grotevant, & Zurcher, 1988; Wegar, 1998).

Several unique structural features of the adoptive family set it apart from the traditional family. These include (a) their being created following losses, (b) the presence of residential and nonresidential family members, and (c) the ambiguity of family roles.

Families Created Following Losses

Adoptive families are created on the basis of several losses. For the adopted child, the loss is of the birth family, roots, and history. For the birth parents, it is the loss of the child, the separation from the child, and the loss of future parenting. For the adoptive parents, adoption represents the loss of fertility and of the birth child they will never have (Anderson et al., 1993; Brodzinsky et al., 1995).

From the adopted child's perspective, being adopted requires dealing with the transition from one family or institution to another family, and then developing attachment to the new family. The younger and healthier the child and the more the child resembles the adoptive parents, the smoother this transition (Hajal, 1996). Yet even for an infant or a baby the transition means the loss of the parents who gave them life and the loss of a primary bonding, belonging, and security (Anderson et al., 1993; Brodzinsky et al., 1995). It is also a loss of familiar faces, sounds, smells, and foods, coupled with an exposure to new ones. For an older child, the transition and the losses are even more complex, because the child remembers his parents and past. Regardless of the age of the adopted child, the adoption implies a disruption of the child's past, origins, history, birth parents, and family. This disruption and loss of history may have an acute impact on the adoptive child as he or she defines and forms his or her sense of self-identity (Hajal, 1996; Kaiser, 1996).

Parallel to the loss experienced by the adoptive child and his or her birth parents, adoptive parents, too, are subject to loss insofar as adoption is the result of inability to conceive a birth child. Whether or not this inability is due to infertility, adoption follows the loss and mourning of the fantasized birth child that will not be born (Hajal, 1996). The extended family may also experience a sense of loss, as they may find it difficult to accept the adoptive child, especially if the child is of a different race, ethnicity, or country (Hajal, 1996). Adoptive parents often need to realign their relationship with their extended family and with the community to accept the child (Hajal, 1996; Kaiser, 1996).

If the adoption is a result of infertility, this issue remains unresolved. It may symbolize a deficit in the parents' perceived sexuality and identity, and may contribute to marital tensions (Hajal, 1996). Stigma about infertility and adoption may lead to secrecy and an attempt to create the appearance of a "normal" family (Kaiser, 1996).

The abruptness of the actual adoption and the lack of preparation to parenthood also set the adoptive family apart from birth families who have the time of pregnancy to prepare (Hajal, 1996; Kaiser, 1996). This may be especially difficult for first-time parents and with older children. This instant parenting is made even more complicated in that the adopted child is experiencing a sudden and dramatic transition as well.

Residential and Nonresidential Family Members

The birth parents of the adopted child are linked for life: forever a part of the history, present, and future of the adoptive family, even if there is no contact between the families (Kaiser, 1996). Regardless of whether the adopted child will ever connect with the birth parents or search for them, once a child knows that he or she is adopted, he or she will forever feel related to the birth family, exactly as the birth parents will always feel related to their child. Adoptive families comprise a metafamily that includes multiple parental figures and family members: the adopted child's birth family (Hajal, 1996). If the adoption is an open adoption, the metafamily joining the adoptive family is not a "shadow" family, but a very real family that visits with the child and is related to the adoptive family in a powerful way. As this suggests, the adoptive family needs to accept the child's birth family and his or her history (Hajal, 1996).

In traditional closed adoptions, adoptive parents may have thoughts about the birth parents that might, in their imagination, stand between

themselves and the child. For the adoptive parents, the birth parents—
and especially the mother—are a constant presence, the "ghost in the
nursery" (Silin, 1996, p. 259). Adoptive parents may find themselves
wondering what the birth parent would think of their parenting, and may
have fantasies that the birth parents will want the child back or that the
child would prefer the birth parents. The adoptive parents may also fear
that the birth parents perceive them as competitors. This fear is increased
by the lack of information about the birth parents, the nature and conditions of the pregnancy and birth, and the development of the child prior to
the adoption. In traditional closed adoptions, the adoptive parents usually receive some information about the birth parents, their physical
characteristics, education, perhaps something about the birth, and other
facts. But this information will never compare to the intimate knowledge
of blood relatives, and the adoptive family will always sense that an
essential part of family history is missing (Kaiser, 1996). The lack of
information and the genealogical discontinuity may be used as arguments against the adopted child when difficulties arise, attributing negative qualities to the child's heredity (Kaiser, 1996).

The meaning of multiple parental figures is most dramatic when the
adoption is made without the consent of the parents. When the parents
oppose the adoption, the court process may generate antipathy toward
the birth parents that the "winning" adoptive parents may later convey to
the children and that, in turn, may be internalized by them (Ryburn,
1997).

From the adoptive children's perspective, being raised by non–birth
parents may create several difficulties. If the children know that they are
adopted, but have no contact with the birth parents or information about
them, they may either idealize or demonize the birth parents. In either
case, adopted children often experience a sense of loss and grief over the
parents that relinquished them, and that sense of loss may be especially
intense if the child is older (Hajal, 1996). Adopted children may also
have difficulties in establishing a sense of identity, belonging, and personal roots. Young children do not fully comprehend the meaning of
adoption and the reasons for their being adopted, and older adopted children may feel powerless because they did not actively participate in the
decisions about their removal and placement. Adopted children may
view loyalty to the adoptive parents as disloyalty to the birth parents, and
their fantasies about birth parents may result in an ambivalence toward
both birth and adoptive parents (Kaiser, 1996).

Interracial and international adoptions raise other issues. With the awareness of the importance of maintaining the child's cultural and/or ethnic heritage, interracial and international adoptive families frequently try to incorporate the child's background into the family. They do so by drawing on elements of the child's original culture, including foods and holidays; by learning the child's original language, or at least ensuring that the child learns it; by seeking out a social network from the child's original culture; and by traveling to the child's home country.

Role Ambiguity

Adoption, by definition, changes the usual patterns of family connections (Watson, 1997). Even if the adoptive parents and the child never meet the birth parents, adoptive families are always aware that the birth parents exist, and this casts a shadow on their exclusiveness. Adoptive parents cannot avoid wondering who the birth parents are, why they gave the child up for adoption, and whether they will show up to claim the child. For adopted children who know that they are adopted, similar questions are unavoidable. Regardless of whether they actually search for their birth parents in the literal sense, adoptive children are in search of their birth parents all their lives (Brodzinsky et al., 1995). The illusory notion that the adoptive family is a nuclear family may force adoptive families to deny their difference, thus creating tensions between their actual experiences and the social expectations that they have internalized. These tensions may contribute to a sense of living "in secret," of being deviant, and in many ways of being closeted.

For the open adoption family who maintains at least some contact with the birth family, the situation is both simpler and more complex. It is simpler because the family is not living in secret, and their daily experiences are acknowledged and legitimized. The simplicity results from the fact that these families do not hide; they do not need to keep a secret from themselves, their extended family, and their community. They are "permitted" to feel what they feel, express their fears, fantasies, and concerns. It is also easier for the adoptive families because they have access to the information that may haunt the closed adoption families. The birth parents are not viewed as ghosts, but as real human beings, and their history, as well as the child's history, can be shared. Nevertheless, open adoptive families need to define for themselves how to conduct their family situation. Being a metafamily with multiple parents, having both residential and nonresidential family members, requires a new definition of a family. Because open adoptions are relatively new, there are no guidelines. Therefore, these adoptive families may experience role ambiguity in their relationships with the adoptive child, the child's birth family, their own extended family, and the systems outside their family, including school and the community. When the adoption is open and visible, strangers may inquire about the adoptive child's background, invading the adoptive family's privacy in a way that would not be done with other families. Teachers and other professionals may attribute any problems to the child's origins. Such attitudes undermine the adoptive parents' identity, delegitimizing and disempowering them.

The presence of residential and nonresidential family members extends the membership of adoptive families beyond the family's household; however, the physical boundaries of these families are incongruent with their psychological boundaries (Pasley & Ihinger-Tallman, 1989). Family theorists have called this situation a family boundary ambiguity (Boss & Greenberg, 1984; Pasley & Ihinger-Tallman, 1989). As too-open family boundaries may result in the loss of the family's sense of identity, maintaining open family boundaries requires finding the right balance of family cohesion and integrity (Pasley & Ihinger-Tallman, 1989).

A related issue for adoptive parents is that of entitlement, in which the adoptive parents feel that they have the legal and emotional right to parent their child (Reitz & Watson, 1992). The need to prove to themselves and to others that they are legitimate and good parents starts even before the actual adoption, as the adoption agencies assess the parental competencies of potential adoptive parents (Hajal, 1996; Kaiser, 1996). Post-adoption, and especially in the early stages of adjusting to parenthood and bonding with the child, adoptive parents may question their entitlement (Anderson et al., 1993; Grotevant, 1997; Reitz & Watson, 1992). This wondering may resurface when the child is old enough to pose questions about his or her birth parents, origin, and the adoption; when the child reaches adolescence; or when the community raises the adoption as a possible source of the child's problems. In all these instances, the child may challenge the parents' rights to act as parents, to discipline, or to set limits (Cohen, Coyne, & Duvall, 1996). If the parents perceive themselves as lacking entitlement, they may, in turn, feel unworthy of providing structure or disciplining their child (Reitz & Watson, 1992; Watson, 1996).

THE DYNAMICS OF THE ADOPTIVE FAMILY

Several key issues are commonly confronted by the adoptive family: (a) bonding and attachment, (b) telling the child about the adoption, (c) searching and reuniting with the birth family, (d) relations between the birth parents and the adoptive parents, and (e) stigma of the adoptive triad.

Bonding and Attachment

The widely influential theory of John Bowlby (1982) holds that attachment is a persisting affective tie that binds one person to another. It develops in a child initially through interactions with primary caretakers, and continues to develop and stabilize as the child ages (Johnson & Fein, 1991). Through the attachment relationship, the child develops a sense of security, expectations about others, and conceptions of self.

Watson (1997) defines bonding as a sense of "being connected to someone without conscious effort, intent, or awareness of how it happened" (p. 165), and suggests that the number of bondings is limited. He defines attachment as "the learned ability to make psychologically rooted ties between people that gives them significant meaning to each other" (p. 165). The capacity to make attachment and to disengage from attachments that are developmentally inappropriate is learned in early childhood.

It is widely believed that older adopted children, and adopted children who experienced some trauma prior to their adoption, will have some difficulties in bonding and developing an attachment to their adoptive parents (Hajal, 1996; Silin, 1996). This is supported by studies of children adopted from Romanian orphanages (e.g., Mainemer, Gilman, & Ames, 1998; Marcovitch et al., 1995; Marcovitch et al., 1997), as well as of children who had multiple placements prior to their adoption and/or histories of abuse (Groze & Rosenthal, 1993).

Telling the Child of the Adoption

With respect to conventional or "closed" adoption, there is a long history of debate over whether or not to tell the child about the adoption, and, if so, when and how. Professionals favor telling the child as soon as possible. Although adoption can be a difficult concept to understand correctly before the child is about 10 years old (Barth, 1992), the child should be told in a sentence or two about the adoption early. This prepares the child to handle the questions of teachers and friends. Barth (1992) suggests that the exact wording does not matter, although it is important that the adoptive family acknowledges the differences between themselves and birth families, especially when there are racial, ethnic, or cultural differences.

On the basis of clinical experience, Nickman (1996) suggests that parents should talk with the adopted children about their relationship with birth parents, even if they have never known them. This allows the children to experience and share the birth parents' sense of loss and bereavement, and to construct an inner representation of their birth parents. It can also help integrate the adoption into the child's growing self-esteem, and hence become less important over time. Research suggests that adoptive parents who are comfortable with their own feelings about their child's history and birth parents are best able to make the child feel valued when discussing that history (Silin, 1996). Nevertheless, it is quite common that when the child is able to comprehend the meaning of his or her adoption, usually between the ages of 8 and 11, the child may grieve for the birth parents and experience anger, rejection, and pain. This may be manifested in various ways, including irritability, withdrawal, and negative attitudes toward the adoptive family, peers, and school.

Searching and Reuniting With the Birth Family

An internal search on the part of adoptive children for their birth parents is a quest to achieve a sense of wellness and congruence (Brodzinsky et al., 1995), as well as to establish a continuous sense of identity and belonging (Krueger & Hanna, 1997). From an existential perspective, the quest for one's birth parents and origins is part of the quest for authenticity, meaningfulness, being, and freedom (Krueger & Hanna, 1997).

Most searching adoptees are women, and they generally seek their mothers (Moran, 1994); adoptive men, in contrast, tend to seek their birth fathers (Pacheco & Eme, 1993). Some studies have found that adult adoptees who search for their birth parents differ in some significant respects from adoptees who decide not to search. Aumend and Barrett (1984) found that compared with searching adoptees, nonsearching adoptees had significantly more positive self-concepts and self-esteem, and more positive attitudes toward their adoptive parents.

In addition to the decision to search for their birth parents, adoptees also need to decide whether to tell their adoptive parents about their search. Research suggests that adoptive parents who view the adoptive family as identical to a birth family are more likely to feel their competence as parents threatened by a search, whereas families who view the adoptive family as different do not feel threatened as parents (Silverman et al., 1994).

Adoptees may go through several stages in seeking the birth parents and reuniting with them. Moran (1994) described them as paralysis, eruption, loss and grief, and empowerment. Adoptees and birth parents who wish to establish a relationship do so in a context of social disapproval (Modell, 1997). Nevertheless, studies show for most adoptees who reunite with their birth parents positive results in terms of improved self-concept, self-esteem, and ability to relate to others (Pacheco & Eme, 1993; Ryburn, 1996).

Relationships Between
Adoptive Parents and Birth Parents

In view of Western norms about the primacy of blood relations, there is a tendency to view the birth parents, and especially the birth mother, as endangering the bond between the child and the adoptive parents. In the past, when only closed adoptions were possible, the relationship between adoptive parents and birth parents was assumed to be inherently conflictual. The adoptive and birth mothers were viewed as potential competitors for the child's love and loyalty: It was seen as a competition between the good, caring woman, often from a middle or upper social class (the adoptive mother), and the bad promiscuous woman, often from a disadvantaged social class, who abandoned her child (the birth mother; Mass, 1994). Yet, if the two mothers manage to move beyond the stereotypes, they may learn to view each other as collaborators who share a child whose best interests are dear to both of them.

The contact patterns between birth and adoptive families can vary considerably, and are distinguishable by intensity and frequency as well as by the emotional significance of the developing relationship to the adoptive parents. Actual contact between the adoptive and the birth parents is almost always with the birth mother rather than with the father (Avery, 1998). With time, contact between adoptive and birth parents tends to decrease or cease altogether, primarily among adoptive families who chose openness at the recommendation or insistence of the adoption agency or agent (Berry, Dylla, Barth, & Needell, 1998). Gross (1997) found three contact patterns between birth and adoptive families, which he labeled as *acceptors, embracers,* and *rejecters* based on the adoptive parents' attitudes. Acceptors, predicted to be the most prevalent type, value having information about each other before the adoption, and, after the adoption, wish to have limited contact consisting of letters, phone calls, or meetings at special events like birthdays and holidays. Embracers are parents who will want ongoing meetings and contacts between the family members, developing emotional bonds and viewing each other as part of the one family. Rejecters, the least prevalent, are those families initially committed to open adoption, but who, following the adoption, do not want to have contact with the child's birth family.

Adoptive parents tend to favor greater openness in adoption and to feel comfortable with postplacement contact with birth parents (Avery, 1998; Berry, 1993; Berry et al., 1998; Etter, 1993; Gross, 1993). Several studies argue that contact between adoptive and birth parents, facilitated by open adoption, helps the adoptive parents view the birth parents as real people rather than as monsters or phantoms that threaten their relationship with the adopted child. This, in turn, may help adoptive parents view the birth parents with greater tolerance, acceptance, and empathy, which ultimately may benefit the child (Baran & Panor, 1990; Silverstein & Demick, 1994).

Stigma and the Adoptive Triad

Adoptive families have been subject to stereotypes stigmatizing all parties in the adoptive triad, which comprises the adoptive parents (and especially the adoptive mother), the adopted child, and the birth parents. This is especially true in visible adoptions, where there are racial or ethnic differences.

There are numerous myths reflecting the stigma of adoption. The most salient are (a) that because blood ties are important for bonding and love, in adoption bonding and love are second best (Bartholet, 1993; Miall, 1987; Wegar, 1998); (b) that adopted children are second rate because of their unknown genetic past (Miall, 1987; Wegar, 1998); and (c) that adoptive parents are not "real" parents (Bartholet, 1993; Miall, 1987).

Stigma and the Birth Parent. Birth parents in general, and the mothers in particular, are often stigmatized as "fallen" women and cruel parents who abandoned their children (Wegar, 1998). This negative stereotype may generate a sense of guilt about relinquishing the child and pressure to keep both the birth and the adoption secret (Kaiser, 1996). Contrary to popular belief, however, most birth mothers have had a long-term and steady relationship with the fathers. Kaiser (1996) reports that in less than a quarter of the cases the father is unknown or involved in only a brief encounter with the mother.

Several studies document the grief, depression, isolation, guilt, and shame experienced by birth mothers (and fathers) who relinquished a child for adoption (Cushman et al., 1997; De-Simone, 1996; Logan, 1996; Menard, 1997; Weinreb & Konstam, 1995). Such emotional reactions were associated with the birth mother's perception of being coerced into relinquishment by others (De-Simone, 1996), as well as with closed adoption.

Stigma and the Adoptive Family. Involuntarily childless women tend to perceive childlessness as a negative, stigmatized attribute (Cook, Golombok, Bish, & Murray, 1995; Miall, 1987). This reflects social attitudes that equate womanhood with biological motherhood, and that construct infertility as a problem to be solved by high-technology medical intervention (Wegar, 1998). The social preference for reproductive technologies implies that adoption is "second best," thus keeping infertile couples away from adoption (Bartholet, 1993; Miall, 1995). With the stigma of adoption and preference for biological parenthood, the relationship between a child and adoptive parents is often assumed to be inherently problematic. Adoptive parents, and especially the adoptive mother, have been described as overprotective and overindulgent, insecure, and lax disciplinarians (Miall, 1995). Such stereotypes are sometimes reflected in the screening process that adoptive parents undergo to examine their suitability to parent (Bartholet, 1993). Adoptive families also need to deal with the stigmatic community attitudes toward adoption in general, and toward interracial, ethnic, and intercountry adoptions in particular (Hajal, 1996).

One study of adoptive families suggests that lacking the social legitimacy conferred by consanguinity, adoptive parents and their children tend to experience their relationship as contrived and deviant. This sense of deviance stigmatizes the motivational context of adoption, imparts a sense of secrecy and fantasy about the deviant origins of the adopted child, creates a sense of disvalued identity, and may generate dysfunctional behavior in adoptees (Kressierer & Bryant, 1996).

Stigma and the Adoptees. The adoptive children are often stereotyped as deficient, damaged, and emotionally disturbed, especially if they are different from their adoptive family in terms of ethnicity or race (Bartholet, 1993; Miall, 1995). One manifestation of this stereotype is the assumption that, because they were adopted, adoptees are susceptible to a host of emotional problems (Bartholet, 1993; McRoy et al., 1988; Wegar, 1998). The stigmatization also reflects negative feelings toward the children's mother that are extended to the children, who are viewed as "children of sin," having inherited the mental and moral weaknesses of their birth mothers (Wegar, 1998). Even as adults, regardless of how well they are doing, former adoptive children tend to experience this sense of stigma. March (1995) found that the major motivations for reunification with the birth parents was the adoptees' sense of being discriminated against by others who questioned their unknown birth kinship ties and their own view of their adoptive status as socially stigmatized. Kressierer and Bryant (1996), however, consider searching for the birth parents "a deviant inquiry" that renders the adoptive parents to be inauthentic, negates the years of nurturing by the adoptive parents, and symbolically rejects them.

In the view of Kressierer and Bryant (1996), the adoption and the relationship between the adoptive parents and the child are by definition deviant due to the stigmatized context of adoption, as well as the secrecy and deception surrounding it. These negative stereotypes of the adoptive triad should be considered in the context of adoption attitudes and policies that reinforce gender, social class, and race inequalities (Wegar, 1997, 1998). Bartholet (1994) argues that to a significant degree, adoption typically involves

> the transfer of children from those who suffer various forms of deprivation to those who are relatively privileged. Poor birth mothers give up their children to well-off adoptive couples; Third World nations give up their children to the industrialized Western nations; black and brown people give up their children to whites. (p. 178)

And, as Wegar (1998) states,

> By failing to take into account the impact of cultural norms and assumptions regarding infertility, childlessness, femininity, and the significance of the blood relationship, researchers have inadvertently defined the adoptive bonds as inferior to biological kinship . . . [and] contributed to the pathologizing of adoption. (p. 45)

IMPLICATIONS FOR CHILDREN

The extent to which being adopted increases a child's risk for the development of adjustment problems has been debated for decades. For many years, both research and popular beliefs focused on the alleged psychopathology of adopted children as reflected in the term *adopted child syndrome,* an extreme form of adoption-related psychopathology characterized by provocative, antisocial behavior and associated personality disturbances (Bartholet, 1993; Kirschner, 1996; McRoy et al., 1988; Wegar, 1998). The assumption that adoptees are at risk of psychological problems has found support in the disproportionate number of adopted children referred to mental health professionals (Feigelman, 1997; Haugaard, 1998). This, however, may reflect biases in referral and be a self-fulfilling prophecy that adoption inevitably brings adjustment problems (Haugaard, 1998). In recent years, this focus on psychopathology has been challenged (Haugaard, 1998; Kirschner, 1996).

Several studies have found that adopted children exhibit emotional and behavioral problems, as well as feelings of insecurity and tension. The problems tend to be manifested especially during adolescence (Hoksbergen, 1997; Rosenthal & Groze, 1994), and seem to diminish when the adoptees reach adulthood (Feigelman, 1997; Sharma, McGue, & Benson, 1996b). The highest rate of adolescent problem behaviors was among children who either were adopted at an older age or had experienced adverse care prior to adoption (Groze & Ileana, 1996; Howe, 1997; Sharma et al., 1996b). Adopted women tend to exhibit more positive outcomes than men (Collishaw, Maughan, & Pickles, 1998; Sharma, McGue, & Benson, 1996a). Other studies, especially those examining adoptees who are not undergoing psychological treatment, show a less decisive picture regarding the prevalence of behavioral and emotional problems among adopted adults. Collishaw and colleauges (1998) found that, compared with a general population of nonadopted adults, those who were adopted as children showed very positive adjustment in employment, social support, receipt of state benefits, housing, family life, relationship and parenting histories, and psychological well-being. Similarly, Feigelman (1997) found that during adulthood adoptees did not differ significantly from nonadopted adults in their educational attainment, employment success, asset accumulation, home ownership, marital stability, and drug use.

Adoptees raised in closed adoptive families often live in an atmosphere of secrecy and denial. This, in addition to the fact that a coherent sense of identity requires the integration of one's past, present, and future, may affect the adoptees' identity development. Because an essential part of the adoptees' roots, genealogical continuity, and history is discontinued and is partially in the dark, adoptees frequently experience identity conflicts (Grotevant, 1997; Rosenberg & Groze, 1997). They also often experience an identity crisis, especially during adolescence (Anderson et al., 1993; Hajal, 1996), and tend to have a low level of self-esteem and a sense of inferiority (Kaiser, 1996). Based on her own experiences as an adopted child and on letters from adopted men and women, Lifton (1996) suggests that adoptees often feel as if they have no self. They feel alienated, unreal, and invisible to themselves and others. Identity crisis is especially acute with transracial and international adoptions, and when the children's ethnicity or race is different from their peers and community (Anderson et al., 1993). A few studies, however, did not find any support for the belief that adoptees have low self-concepts or identity conflicts (e.g., Aumend & Barrett, 1984; Groze, 1996b).

At this point, there is enough empirical evidence to indicate that adoption is not necessarily linked with psychopathology, and that children adopted in infancy who did not experience trauma prior to their adoption do well in their adult years (Barth, 1994; Bartholet, 1993; Rosenthal, 1993; Wegar, 1998). Based on a review of existing research, Haugaard (1998) concludes that the risk associated with adoption is modest or nonexistent.

VARIATIONS WITHIN THE ADOPTIVE FAMILY

Adoptive families vary considerably on such dimensions as the origin, ages, and number of children adopted, and the characteristics of the adoptive parent or parents. Previously, restrictions placed on prospective parents limited the placement options for "hard-to-place" children, namely older children, siblings, minority children, and children with special needs. Since the 1980s, the policy has been to encourage the adoption of these children, resulting in a corresponding flexibility in the requirements for "suitable" adoptive families (Barth, 1992).

This section considers several variations among adoptive families: stepparent adoptions; relative adoptive families; adoptions of children with special needs; single-parent adoptive families; and surrogate adoptive families. Other adoptive families, not addressed here, include foster-adoptive families and gay or lesbian adoptive families. As many of the same family variations apply as well to foster families, the reader is advised to refer to the discussion of these families in Chapter 2.

Stepparent Adoption

Stepparent adoption refers to the formal adoption of the children of one spouse, who have usually resided with the stepparent prior to the adoption (Barth, 1995). Stepparent adoptions, which are about twice as common as non-stepparent adoptions, differ from other adoptions in that one parent is a birth parent. Furthermore, in contrast with other adoptive families, the child in adoptive stepfamilies is already legally living with the adoptive stepparent.

Frequently, stepparent adoption follows the death of a child's parent and the stepparent is legally replacing that birth parent. If the nonresidential birth parent is alive, he or she needs to give consent to the adoption. Because stepparent adoptions have an impact on the distribution of the family's property, the adoption is usually formalized in superior or probate court (Barth, 1995).

Relative Adoptive Families

Relatives who adopt a child were usually his or her foster parents before the adoption. Adoption by kin has increased significantly in recent years, and in 1992 it represented 14% of all adoptions of foster children (Barth, 1995). Kinship adoptions are more likely to be by single parents and by older, less-educated, poorer persons than are other adoptions (Barth, 1994).

Adoptive Families With Special-Needs Children

Children with special needs are defined by federal law as having a specific condition that makes them hard to place in a permanent home. In most instances, raising them poses special challenges to the adoptive family. Although state regulations vary in the interpretation of these conditions, they usually involve older age (usually 3 years or older); having a physical, mental, or emotional disability; being part of a sibling group (usually of three or more siblings); or being a member of an ethnic minority group (Barth, 1995). Although the state must make a reasonable effort to find a family that will adopt the special-needs children without assistance, if these efforts fail, the adoptive family should be provided with medical and/or financial assistance. Several studies by Rosenthal and his colleagues (Rosenthal, 1993; Rosenthal & Groze, 1994; Rosenthal et al., 1996) indicate that financial adoption subsidies may be the single most important postadoptive service for special-needs families. Furthermore, special-needs children generally cannot or should not be returned to their birth families (Barth, 1995). The vast majority have been placed with foster families before the adoption (Barth, 1994). Special-needs adoption of foster children accounts for about 10% of all exits from foster care (Barth & Berry, 1988). It is estimated that about 35,000 such children need to be placed each year (Groze, 1996b).

Since the 1970s, there has been a growing emphasis on the right of every child to a permanent home, accompanied by practice approaches to recruit adoptive families for children formerly considered hard to place, or even unadoptable. There is now ample evidence that special-needs adoption is a viable option, particularly for disabled children (Lightburn & Pine, 1996). Although most studies address special-needs children as a single category, this category comprises distinctive subgroups of children with very different characteristics—older children, siblings, and children with physical, emotional, or mental disabilities. Some have a history of trauma, including physical and sexual abuse, abandonment, AIDS, and multiple foster placements prior to adoption, because special-needs children frequently wait long periods of time before being adopted.

The adoption of older children requires considerable readjustment. Although the adoptee may experience resistance and ambivalence, the adoptive family explores the new arrangements at individual, dyadic, and family levels. The adoptive parents often come to realize that special-needs children require excessive emotional work. Coping with difficult behaviors and emotional problems, including the inability of the children to receive or give warmth and affection, can pose a difficult challenge. Adoptive parents may find that they do not feel unconditional love toward their adopted children; against their best intentions, they may feel intense anger toward them (Power & Krause-Eheart, 1995). These difficulties are intensified by prevailing adoption myths and by a tendency both to underestimate the influence of the child's past and to overestimate the adoptive parents' ability to undo the past and produce happy, successful children (Power & Krause-Eheart, 1995). Raising special-needs children also requires special support and services for the adoptive families. These include financial and medical subsidies, respite care, counseling, and educational services (Groze, 1996b; Rosenthal et al., 1996).

Regardless of the difficulties, a majority of parents were found to be positive about the adoption of children with special needs (Groze, 1996a, 1996b) Furthermore, despite the significant behavioral problems (Groze, 1996a, 1996b), research shows that these problems do not impair the ability and willingness of the adoptive families to provide a family and a home, to appreciate the children's progress, and to view life with the children as meaningful (Groze, 1996b; Rosenthal et al., 1996). The disruption rate for older children and children with special needs is between 10% and 15% (Barth & Berry, 1988); it is lower for children with developmental disabilities, and higher for children with severe emotional difficulties (Rosenthal et al., 1996).

Interestingly, one study found that adoption outcomes for special-needs adoptive families ($N = 133$) were most positive for single-parent, foster, less-educated, poorer, and minority families (Groze, 1996a; for additional information on special-needs adoptive families, see Groze, 1996b, which is based on a study that followed special-needs adoptive families over four years).

Single-Parent Adoptive Families

Adoption by single parents began in the mid-1970s, and has steadily increased (Anderson et al., 1993) because of the need to widen the pool of adoptive parents for special-needs children. This need also coincided with the growing acceptance of single parenthood. Single-parent adoptions are still in the minority, and they tend to be by the child's relative (usually the grandmother), and/or to involve special-needs children (Barth & Berry, 1988).

Several studies found that single adoptive parents have high emotional maturity, tolerance of frustration, and independence, and provide a network of supportive relatives (Barth, 1992; Barth & Berry, 1988). Based on a review of the literature and a longitudinal study of 118 black or mixed-raced children placed in adoptive homes, Shireman (1995) found that single persons who adopt are well able to carry out the responsibilities of parenting, and that single-parent homes have unique strengths and may be the placement of choice for some children. Special-needs children adopted by single parents were found to be doing as well as, or perhaps even better than, children adopted into two-parent homes (Groze, 1996a; Groze & Rosenthal, 1991; Owen, 1994; Shireman, 1995).

Surrogate Adoptive Families

Surrogate mothers agree to become pregnant and give birth to a child on behalf of another person or couple, usually through donor insemination or implantation of an embryo. Surrogate adoptive families sign a contract with the birth mother stating that she will relinquish her parental rights when the baby is born. Nevertheless, once the child is born to the surrogate mother, he or she must still be adopted. Current adoption laws give the surrogate birth mother the opportunity to change her mind and keep the child despite the contract to relinquish the baby. Some states have outlawed surrogate parenting altogether.

Another form of adoption involves embryo transfer, in which the egg of a donor is impregnated and then transplanted into the body of the birth-mother-to-be. Although the mother bears the child as with a surrogate birth, the child is not genetically related to her. The policies and practice concerns regarding this type of parenting will flourish as reproductive technology advances (Pecora et al., 1992).

IMPLICATIONS FOR PRACTICE

Therapists rarely consider adoption issues when treating adoptive families, and rarely mention adoption as an issue in their treatment plan (McDaniel & Jennings, 1997). Similarly, the special needs of international adoptive families have seldom been addressed in family therapy literature (Deacon, 1997). As the research summarized in this chapter indicates, these are serious omissions.

Before adoption, adoptive families—especially families adopting older children, children with special needs, and international children—need to obtain comprehensive background information about the present and future needs of the children. Families also need to be prepared for the challenges these children may present and the potential services they might need at different developmental stages (Rosenthal et al., 1996).

Following the adoption, adoptive parents need to have a "pregnancy period" to work through the psychological tasks of integrating a child into the family (Trout, 1996). They also need continuing support from the adoption agency and from the community (Shireman, 1995), as well as education and counseling on adoption issues, child development, and planning for the child's future (Rosenthal et al., 1996). Adoptive families, especially with older children and children with special needs, may also need financial assistance. Furthermore, they may benefit from the availability of respite services (Groze, 1996b; Rosenthal, 1993; Rosenthal & Groze, 1994; Rosenthal et al., 1996).

Several approaches have been described that may benefit adoptees and their families. These include videotaping visits from birth parents (Clegg & Toll, 1996), and participating in groups where adopted children, especially those with special needs, can share their experiences in a supportive environment (Moroz, 1996).

Adoption agencies can improve the adoption rate of black children by African American families by hiring more black social workers and support staff (Lovett-Tisdale & Purnell, 1996; Taylor & Thornton, 1996). Several minority adoption programs have shown success in finding African American adoptive families for African American children. Examples include the Institute for Black Parenting, Project Hustle, and One Church, One Child (McRoy et al., 1997), and a self-help program in Georgia described by Jackson-White, Dozier, Davenport, and Gardner (1997).

IMPLICATIONS FOR RESEARCH

The adoptive family merits greater attention from researchers as a unique family structure. As is true of the family in general, adoption policies and practices are constantly evolving, and the research needs to keep pace to address a host of contentious issues. Much of the research on adoption is inconclusive because of the small, nonrepresentative samples used and the methodological limitations, including cross-sectional designs. We increasingly recognize adoption as a lifelong process, and the social context of adoption is in constant flux. Therefore, we need more longitudinal studies based on samples that are more representative in terms of race, ethnicity, income, family configuration, and adoptive circumstances. Such studies are needed to chart the experience of adoptive families, adoptees, and birth parents over time and at key stages of the family life cycle.

Although open adoption is becoming more normative, the debate about the relative merits and consequences of open and closed adoptions has not been sufficiently informed by empirical evidence. Research is needed on the effects of open adoption on children, adoptive families, and birth parents. Furthermore, current changes in the legislative arena provide rich opportunities to assess the implications of contrasting state laws: those that safeguard birth parent identity, those that provide for mutual search-and-consent registries for adoptees and birth parents; and those that have opened birth and adoption records to adoptees. The relative merits of these contrasting policies are likely to be debated for years to come, and empirical research is sorely needed to inform these policy debates. On an individual level, we need to learn more about the characteristics of those who opt to search for parents or children, and those who choose not to, and we need more information about the implications of reuniting for the adoptee, the parents, and the adoptive family.

As the United States becomes more racially diverse, transracial adoption will undoubtedly continue to be subject to debate. All research studies on adoption need to take race, ethnicity, and social class differences into account. More studies, and especially culturally sensitive studies, are needed on the effects of transracial adoptions. We need to examine carefully the circumstances that give rise to women relinquishing their children for adoption, especially economic conditions that can be addressed by public policy. The barriers to adoption faced by families of color need further investigation with a view toward finding ways to make it easier for them to adopt.

International adoption is yet another area that can benefit from ongoing study. As the practice grows and children are adopted from more countries, more diverse samples will become available for studying the adjustment of international adoptees and for assessing pre- and postadoption services. With the growing attention to globalization, we should encourage research that examines the economic and political context of international adoption.

Preplacement home study practices have evolved over time and are circumscribed by agency resources and legal requirements. More research is needed on the predictive efficacy of home study practices. With the increases in special needs adoptions, we also need to learn more about the kinds of pre- and postadoption services and financial assistance that are necessary to ensure a successful adjustment.

DISCUSSION QUESTIONS

1. Interracial and international adoptions pose especially vexing policy and moral dilemmas when considered from the contrasting perspectives of the adoptive parents, the children, the birth parents, and society. Can you think

of ways these dilemmas might be reconciled? What, if any, policy changes would you favor? Why?

2. In 1998, the state of Oregon enacted legislation opening adoption records to adoptees. It was challenged by birth parents as unfairly violating the secrecy they had been assured. What is your view? Should adoption records be opened? Should any conditions be attached?

3. Some scholars characterize adoption as a kind of commodity exchange between more- and less-privileged members of society. Others point out that it is an exchange that benefits all parties. What do you think? What are the arguments on each side of the issue? What are the implications for public policy?

SUGGESTIONS FOR FURTHER READING

Barth, R. P., & Berry, M. (1988). *Adoption and disruption: Rates, risks, and responses.* New York: Aldine.

Groza, V. (1997). Adoption: International. In *Encyclopedia of social work, 1997 Supplement* (19th ed., pp. 1–14). Washington, DC: National Association of Social Workers.

Hajal, F., & Rosenberg, E. B. (1991). The family life cycle in adoptive families. *American Journal of Orthopsychiatry, 61*(1), 78–86.

Reitz, M., & Watson, K. W. (1992). *Adoption and the family system: Strategies for treatment.* New York: Guilford.

Willis, M. G. (1996). The real issues in transracial adoption: A response. *Journal of Black Psychology, 22*(2), 246–253.

Chapter 4

SINGLE-PARENT FAMILIES

Single-parent families, perhaps more than any other family type, are considered by many to be problematic (Kamerman & Kahn, 1988). Viewed against the backdrop of an idealized nuclear family, the increase since the 1970s in divorce, unmarried childbearing, and single-parent families has been looked on with alarm.

Single-parent families face numerous stresses, foremost among which is economic hardship. The stresses of single parenthood are exacerbated by discrimination and punitive attitudes toward female heads of families, and especially toward African American women. The stigma against single-parent families is reflected in social policy, political discourse, social science research, and the attitudes of many helping professionals.

With the demise of what was once a family wage, it now takes two wage earners to maintain even a modest standard of living. Women's caretaking responsibilities are not recognized as real work, and are consequently uncompensated. Nearly half of single-parent families live in poverty, and their impoverishment has profound social implications. Although the financial and resource constraints that entrap so many single-parent families could be eased by social policies that are common in other advanced industrial nations, the United States is hampered by prejudice against single-parent families fueled by racial stereotypes and sexism. Many of the stresses experienced by single-parent families are also experienced by women in two-parent families. However, for single-parent families, the problems are magnified.

This chapter examines single-parent families, their demographic characteristics, the historical context, and policy issues. It considers the experience of divorce from the custodial mother's perspective, and examines the implications for the children. Though the primary focus is on the most prevalent type of single-parent family headed by the mother following divorce, father-headed families and other kinds of single-parent families are also discussed.

PREVALENCE AND DEMOGRAPHIC CHARACTERISTICS OF SINGLE-PARENT FAMILIES

Single parenthood may result from divorce, separation, the death of a spouse, births to unmarried women, adoption, or foster care (Lino, 1995). In the latter half of the 20th century, divorce and unmarried childbearing have supplanted widowhood as the leading causes of single parenthood. The proportion of children living with single parents in 1900 was not that different from that in 1960: 8.5% then, as compared with 9.1% in 1960. Most single-parent families in the 19th century resulted from the death of a spouse. In 1900, approximately 75% of African American and white single parents were widows (Bohannan, 1997; Gordon & McLanahan, 1991). In contrast, in 1991, 60% of single-parent families resulted from divorce or separation, 34% from births to unmarried women, and only 6% from the death of a spouse (Norton & Miller, 1992). The percentage of children living in single-parent families increased sharply during the 1970s and 1980s. By 1992, 24.7% of children under 18 lived in single-parent families.

The United States has the highest divorce rate in the world, having risen steadily from 1966 to 1979. By 1988, the rate had declined, and has since remained fairly stable (NCHS, 1989–1990). Between 56% and 62% of marriages in the United States end in divorce (Bumpass, Castro, & Sweet, 1991). Since 1980, divorce rates in other countries have also risen and the gap between them and the United States has narrowed slightly (Stacey, 2000). Whereas the increase in divorce fueled the growth in single-parent families in the 1960s and 1970s, delayed marriage and childbearing outside marriage contributed far more to the growth in single-mother families during the 1980s and 1990s than did divorce (Bianchi, 1995).

Family structures differ significantly among racial and ethnic groups, and the differences in the 1990s were as large as, or larger than, those a generation earlier (Bianchi, 1995). In 1992, 57% of African American families with children were single-parent families, compared with 30%

of Hispanic families and 20% of white families (Norton & Miller, 1992). Though most of the white single-parent families follow divorce, most of the African American single-parent families result from and are headed by unmarried mothers. A major cause of the declining marriage rate among African American women has been the unavailability of marriageable men because of the high mortality rates and the disproportionate rate of incarceration of African American men (N. J. Burgess, 1995; McAdoo, 1998). The declining marriage rate among African Americans has also been attributed to low wages and high rates of unemployment. These circumstances often render black men unable to provide the economic resources for sustaining a marriage (N. J. Burgess, 1995; Jarrett, 1994). Glick (1997), however, maintains that differences between black and white families are narrowing, and that some of the difference may be the result of census misrepresentation and survey misreporting on such subjects as husbands in the household. Similarly, drawing on a national survey data, Heiss (1997) found differences in family and marriage attitudes of black and white women to be very small.

About 65% of divorces involve children under 18 years of age. Of children born in the 1980s, 35% will have experienced, on average, 5 years of life in a single-parent family before reaching their 18th birthday (Glick, 1989; Glick & Lin, 1987).

The vast majority of single-parent families in the United States are headed by mothers. Between 1970 and 1995, the percentage of children living with single fathers quadrupled (from 1% to 4%), with physical custody of the children awarded to mothers in about 85% of the divorce cases (Amato, 2000; Greif, 1995). Joint legal custody, in which parents share responsibility for their children, has become more common in recent decades, and is awarded in 16% of the cases (NCHS, 1989–1990). Single-parent families are often a temporary family configuration, because over half of the single mothers in the United States remarry (Bohannan, 1997). However, 60% of the remarriage also end in divorce, and so remarriage does not necessarily mean the end of the single-parent family.

The term *single-parent family,* though more neutral than the older term *broken family,* suggests, inaccurately, that the noncustodial parent is no longer a part of the family, and it reinforces an attenuating of responsibility toward the noncustodial child. Though the noncustodial parent does not reside with the family, she—or more usually he—forever remains a parent. In many cases, the family is not truly single-parented. This is especially the case for many African American single-parent families, which often include a tight kin network that transcends household boundaries; an array of men, brothers, uncles, grandfathers, friends, and fictive kin often play significant roles in the lives of the children (Hill, 1998). Furthermore, single mothers may have various kinds of relationships with male partners, ranging from cohabitation to an ongoing relationship without sharing residence (Jarrett, 1994).

HISTORICAL BACKGROUND
AND LEGAL ISSUES

The marriage and divorce practices of Western countries can be traced back to conflicting ancient legal traditions. According to early Hebrew law, a wife had no right to divorce her husband (Bohannan, 1997). In the Roman Empire, however, either the husband or wife could terminate the marriage; the law required only a clear indication of the intent to divorce, as set forth in a formal letter (Bohannan, 1997). In the early Christian view, marriage was an indissoluble sacrament. Canon law concerning divorce, which became the law of the Christian countries of Europe during the Middle Ages, could be summarized by the phrase from the marriage ceremony: "What therefore God has joined together, let not man put asunder" (Matthew 19:6).

When Martin Luther broke away from the Roman Church in the 16th century, the Protestants adopted a different view of marriage. They placed marriage under secular jurisdiction and permitted divorce on specific grounds, such as adultery, cruelty, or desertion (Bohannan, 1997). Similarly, after breaking with the Roman Catholic Church, England treated divorce as a legal matter. However, every divorce required a separate act of the House of Lords, making it accessible only to the rich and powerful. This system of legislative divorce continued in England until 1857, when Parliament established the Court for Divorce and Matrimonial Causes (Bohannan, 1997).

The early American settlers brought with them these different divorce practices. Although Virginia and the southern colonies did not recognize divorce at all, by the 1690s Massachusetts recognized seven grounds for divorce (Bohannan, 1997). Until well into the 20th century, the grounds for divorce were strictly limited to adultery, cruelty, or desertion (Phillips, 1997). However, reflecting the patriarchal basis of divorce law, it was only the wife's, not the husband's, adultery that was grounds for divorce. Adulterous wives were dealt with harshly, losing their rights to maintenance and property, even that which they had brought into the marriage, and they often lost child custody and visitation rights as well (Rodger, 1995).

In 1969, California became the first state with a "no fault" divorce law, permitting divorce on the basis of "irreconcilable differences." Since then, nearly all states have added no-fault divorce options to their existing laws (Bohannan, 1997).

At present, divorce is obtained in most industrialized countries through action in a court of law; however, in many other societies, divorce is handled by religious institutions. In some societies, couples draw up a divorce contract that takes effect on the return of the payments made at the time of the marriage (Bohannan, 1997). The liberalized no-fault divorce law has made divorce more accessible for both women and men, and has paved the way to the growing prevalence of divorce in all industrialized countries, and especially in the United States. Nevertheless, divorce remains unavailable to women in many parts of the world.

Despite liberalized divorce law, divorce proceedings usually disadvantage single mothers. Following divorce, women's standard of living declines, whereas that of men rises (Arendell, 1993; Weitzman, 1988). Divorce law generally fails to take into account the economic inequalities between women and men within marriage and in the larger society. In failing to do so, it creates an illusion of gender equality while contributing to the poverty of divorced, single-parent families (Weitzman, 1985). Noncustodial fathers are also subject to ambivalent policies. Though child support requirements and their enforcement clearly favor the fathers over the mothers and the children, fathers who do not pay child support are stigmatized as "deadbeats."

Women almost always want to keep the children, and generally do, thereby assuming the main financial burden of providing for them (Maccoby, 1995). Furthermore, women are rarely compensated in divorce for having facilitated their husbands' education and career, for their own caregiving, and for interrupted work due to homemaking and child care responsibilities. This inequity is compounded by inadequate child support, which leaves most single-parent families with insufficient income (Arendell, 1993).

Single mothers face further discrimination for being poor. Their poverty places them at risk of being considered negligent by state courts for living in substandard conditions. Instead of receiving sufficient government support to maintain adequate living standards, they risk having their children removed from the home and placed in foster care (Steinbock, 1995).

Recently, there has been a growing attempt to restrict the mobility of single mothers by requiring the custodial parent to obtain court permission to move to another state (Walters & Abshire, 1995). The express intention of these laws is to ensure that noncustodial fathers have access to their children. In reality, such laws restrict the ability of single mothers to pursue their careers, to move closer to family, or to follow their husbands if they are remarried. Such restrictions on the custodial mother reflect the courts' tendency to be much more demanding of mothers than fathers, expecting them to subordinate their own needs for the sake of the children (Walters & Abshire, 1995). If the intent of this restriction were solely to guarantee that both parents are accessible to the child, the restrictions would apply to both parents, not just the custodial parent.

SOCIAL-CULTURAL CONTEXT AND POLICY ISSUES

The increase in single-parent families has been a touchstone for heated debate about divorce and unmarried parenthood. Conservatives see the surge in single motherhood as evidence of an eroding social order, a decline of traditional values, and the splitting apart of the "normal" nuclear family (Popenoe, 1992). Others argue that the increase in single parenthood reflects a welcome loosening of social controls over the lives of women. The problem, they argue, is the lack of social supports for single-parent families. Feminist scholars suggest that this lack of supportive social programs constitutes a form of punishment against women who dare to have a family without a man (e.g., Polakow, 1993).

Social and Family Policies
Related to Single-Parent Families

In response to the dramatic increase in divorce and single-parent families, most industrialized countries strengthened their policies to support poor families, including single-parent families (Bowen, Desimone, & McKay, 1995). These policies include universal health care and child care programs, generous family leave provisions, housing subsidies, and substantial welfare payments. The United States, however, is a notable exception, lagging far behind in supportive family policies (Kamerman & Kahn, 1988). As a result, the United States has the highest poverty rate in the developed world. A comparison of 18 industrialized nations found a U.S. child poverty rate of 21.5%, far higher than second-ranking Australia (14%) and more than double most of the other nations. Thirteen countries had child poverty rates under 10%, and of these, eight had rates below 5% (Rainwater & Smeeding, 1995).

This lack of government intervention to ensure the welfare of children and mothers reflects the widespread view in the United States that children's well-being is the responsibility of the parents, not the state. The thrust of social policy in the United States has been not to design policies that protect children and mothers, but rather to protect the state against the supposed danger of dependency, as reflected most recently in the enactment of the Personal Responsibility and Work Opportunity Reconciliation Act of 1996 (PRWORA, Public Law 104-193). As Dowd (1997) observes, "There is concern that these families not be too well supported, because to do so would challenge the social, cultural, political, and ideological position of the heterosexual marital family" (p. 115).

Empirical findings about the effects of public assistance programs show no evidence that they increase the likelihood of divorce or nonmarital childbearing (Kammerman & Kahn, 1988; Moffitt, 1997). Nonmarital births have increased even as AFDC benefits have declined by about half in real value since the 1970s. States with the highest benefits have had the lowest rates of nonmarital births, and other Western countries have provided far more generous income support, housing, and health and child care services for single parents without experiencing higher rates of single parenthood (Jarrett, 1994; McLanahan & Casper, 1994). When welfare benefits were rising, the rate of unwed motherhood fell, and then rose again when welfare benefits were falling. The highest rates of unwed motherhood are found in states and countries with low welfare benefits and high rates of poverty and economic inequality (Coontz, 1997). Furthermore, the increase in single parenthood in the United States has occurred not only among the poor, but among the middle- and upper-income strata as well.

The current emphasis on requiring single mothers to work and forgo public assistance has not ensured that these women will attain economic self-sufficiency. Because of their low wages and the lack of affordable child care, many women find it difficult, if not impossible, to assume full caretaking responsibilities while also working full time (Arendell, 1993; Bowen et al., 1995).

Current policies cause children and divorced mothers to bear the economic brunt of divorce (Brandon, 2000; Weitzman, 1985). The economic status of single mothers in the United States is the lowest of all Western industrialized countries (Strand, 1995). Single mothers (widowed, never-married, or separated) and their children constitute the bulk of the poor population in the United States, resembling the situation in preindustrialized Europe (Phillips, 1997). Polakow (1993) argues that their poverty is a result of a political economy in a wealthy society that denies social responsibility for poor mothers and their children. She states that "to construct a language of women and children in poverty is to speak a shadow language of patriarchy and domestic ideology, of power and control and privilege, which embeds histories of discrimination" (p. 2). Historically, Western Eurocentric tradition has held these families to be deviant, and attributed to them the status of *other*, a view that has dominated public sensibilities and public policy.

The poverty of single mothers is not caused by divorce and lone parenthood, but has its roots in gender inequality in marriage and discrimination in the labor market. For single mothers, their sex rather than marital status is the real key to their poverty (Dowd, 1997). Traditionally, the gender-role allocation of paid work and family responsibilities dictates that fathers work in the wage workforce while mothers care for children and the home without being paid for their work. Although there has in theory been a change in this domestic division of labor, still "men and women think more equally than they act" (Dowd, 1997, p. 57). Regularly, women still do most of the family work. This unequal division of labor is based on gender. Women are the primary caretakers even if they also work outside the home and earn as much as, or more than, their husbands do. When men do participate in household and child care responsibilities, they serve as backup to the mothers while maintaining the power and control over resources (Dowd, 1997). During marriage,

> mothers voluntarily or involuntarily trade parenting for job opportunities and income. Their spouse's income conceals their economic vulnerability during marriage, a vulnerability that becomes apparent with divorce.... The legal structure of divorce functions to perpetuate the economic impoverishment and asymmetric psychological relationships of *de facto* single-parent families that exist within intact marriages. Single parenting exists within marriage—indeed, marriage fosters it—as the result of existing work-family structures and the persistence of gender roles and gender segregation, within and outside the family. (Dowd, 1997, p. xvi)

With divorce, the inequalities within marriage stand out more visibly as the mothers continue to care for the children and their former husbands continue to earn an income while avoiding parental responsibilities (Dowd, 1997). Thus, "the shift from dual to single parenthood is often not a shift from well-being to poverty, but rather a shift from one kind of poverty to another" (Dowd, 1997, pp. 58–59). For some women, single parenthood is a preferable kind of poverty, because as single parents they control the income.

Why Doesn't the United States Have Sufficient Policies to Support Single-Parent Families?

The "cult of domesticity"—whereby the husband is responsible for the financial support and the wife, in return, provides domestic services and child care, and maintains the emotional and family ties—is still the prevailing norm (Springer, 1995). This societal norm is reflected in social policies and legal guidelines for child support awards and for custody and visitation rights that reinforce the caregiving responsibilities of women while failing to provide for their economic security. Divorce arrangements underscore the value placed on men's work outside the household, while excusing them from the daily responsibilities of fatherhood (Springer, 1995; Weitzman, 1985). This patriarchal norm has changed little since preindustrial times. It still serves to restrict women's power and to penalize them should they choose to have a family life without a husband.

Individualism in the United States is expressed in the view that children are a private responsibility and that public support is both unnecessary and an unwarranted intrusion on the family. The deeply rooted belief in the supremacy of the nuclear, two-parent family, with a traditional division of labor between husbands and wives, still holds sway. Any deviation from this mode is viewed as a threat. Single-parent families pose a challenge to the hegemony of the traditional model both because of their increasing prevalence and because they represent a failure of marriage and the breakup of the two-parent family. They are especially threatening because the mothers replace men in their traditional role as the heads of the family. The fact that these families are headed by women makes them a convenient target, one lacking the power and status to contest the stigma of single parenthood. As a matter of social policy, economic and psychic penalties are imposed on what society deems the wrong kind of family (Dowd, 1997). The high rates of poverty experienced by single-parent families can be viewed as a kind of punishment exacted on women who deviate from the norm (Dowd, 1997).

SINGLE-PARENT FAMILIES AND POVERTY

Causes of Poverty

Mother-headed single-parent families are the poorest of all family groups. The median per capita income for children in mother-headed households is less than one third that of two-parent families (Louv, 1993). In 1991, nearly half of these families—47%—were below the official poverty line, compared to only 8% of two-parent families (Lino, 1995).

Several factors contribute to the impoverishment of single-parent families. Women heading single-parent families face the same kinds of disadvantage as other women, including those in traditional two-parent families. As women, they are subject to wage discrimination. As parents, they are disadvantaged in having to reconcile work and child care responsibilities, and are therefore likely to have an interrupted work history. These disadvantages worsen once they are single parents, accentuating the conflict between public, paid work and domestic, unpaid work (Dowd, 1997; Springer, 1995). Single-parent families are uniquely disadvantaged by inadequate child support policies, biased divorce laws, and insufficient and punitive welfare policies. With a lack of affordable child care, many mothers who raise their children—in two-parent and in single-parent families—are forced to sacrifice wage work for unpaid work as caretakers. Those who do work outside the home often have part-time and temporary employment, and may face interruptions in employment because of their caregiving responsibilities.

The difficulty of supporting a family on one income is exacerbated for single mothers because of gender and race discrimination in the wage labor market. Like most women, single mothers most frequently work in service and blue-collar jobs, which are low paying (Dowd, 1997). The constraints of part-time and episodic employment make it difficult to establish careers, acquire needed education, and update skills. Regardless of their family status, women's earnings are generally lower than men's are (Lino, 1995). This is true for "pink collar" workers as well as for women in traditionally male occupations. The reality is that poor single mothers need to combine funds from work in the labor market, support from friends or family members, and government aid to make ends meet (Tilly & Albelda, 1994).

Inadequate child support policies place single mothers in a bind. Estimates show that in the United States, only about half of divorcing fathers who are court ordered to pay child support do so (e.g., King, 1994; Pearson & Thoennes, 1988; Seltzer, 1991). Failure to pay child support forces mother-headed households to live in poverty (Garfinkel & McLanahan, 1986; Wright & Price, 1986), or at least to struggle with economic hardship (Seltzer, 1991). Furthermore, fathers who do pay child support pay very little, particularly to their older children (King, 1994). Based on a national sample, Seltzer (1991) found that the mean monthly contribution of fathers who pay child support is less than $200. When single mothers try to collect child support that has been awarded to them but not paid, they are often viewed as greedy and vindictive (Walters & Abshire, 1995).

Finally, current welfare policies perpetuate poverty by failing to provide an adequate safety net for single-parent families. The 1996 PRWORA stigmatizes single-parent families in general, and never-married single-parent families in particular. It proclaims its goals as "restor[ing] the American family, [and] reduc[ing] illegitimacy" (Dowd, 1997, pp. 3–4). The act also includes significant incentives for states to reduce births to unmarried women, dubbed the "illegitimacy bonus" (Dowd, 1997, p. 4). The financial support is both too little and too limited in duration to ensure a minimum economic standard for children and mothers (Lino, 1995; Springer, 1995). Housing assistance, child care, and health care are woefully limited. The meager financial support that is available is contingent on the mother's working, thus perpetuating the conflict between wage work and nonwage child care for single parents. Mothers are forced to accept whatever low-wage jobs are available while forgoing training and education that would improve their future employment prospects.

Poverty as Deliberate Social Punishment of Single Mothers

In reality, less than full-time work for most women in the United States—and, for many, full-time work—simply does not pay enough to feed and clothe children, make rent payments, or provide child care (Tilly & Albelda, 1994). Yet current social policies consider single motherhood as the cause of its own poverty. They assume it is merely a matter of will for single mothers to work their way out of poverty (Thomas, 1994). In that sense, the new poverty paradigm represents a transition from the culture of poverty to the culture of single motherhood (Thomas, 1994). But this focus on single-parent families and on their hardships obscures the broader public context of gender and family politics, and the social policies that shape their lives (Brewer, 1995; Springer, 1995).

STEREOTYPES AND DISCRIMINATION
AGAINST SINGLE-PARENT FAMILIES

Manifestations of the Stigma

The mother-headed single-parent family is the "other" of family forms, well outside the bounds of the normative two-parent family, subject to derogatory stereotypes, stigma, and discrimination (Sands & Nuccio, 1989). Political debates and popular attitudes cast the single-parent family as a deviant social outcast or, at best, as a needy supplicant (Dowd, 1997).

The public debate about family life in recent years centers on the issue of moral behavior, with a presumption that many nontraditional families are immoral and, therefore, generate maladapted children (Rodger, 1995). Empirical findings, however, show that the variance within different family types (first-married, stepfamilies, single-parent families, and continuously single families) is larger than variance across family types, suggesting that structure itself is not an important measure of well-being (Acock & Demo, 1994; Horowitz, 1995).

There is no evidence to support the common belief that high divorce rates produce social disorganization (Bohannan, 1997). The social effects of divorce depend on the arrangements society makes for the single-parent families following divorce (Bohannan, 1997). Nevertheless, the prevalent perception of the single-parent family is one of deviance and pathology, a danger to society. It has been held responsible for social and psychological ills ranging from juvenile delinquency, and drug and alcohol abuse, to violence against women (Popenoe, 1996; Rice, 1994). For example, Barbara Dafoe Whitehead (1993), who heads the Institute for American Values with David Blankenhorn, has argued that the increasing numbers of single-parent and stepparent families . . . dramatically weakens and undermines society. . . . Indeed, it is not an exaggeration to characterize [family disruption] as a central cause of many of our most vexing social problems . . . poverty, crime, and declining school performance. (pp. 47, 77)

Rather than helping single parents to manage the demands of work and family life, and to provide adequate income support for the children, the United States has relied on increasingly punitive policies. As a result, the most serious consequence of single parenthood is the increased risk of poverty.

The stigma of the single-parent family is embedded within the legal system, lending it the legitimization of the presumed objectivity of the law. "The law fiercely supports the patriarchal nuclear family" (Dowd, 1997, p. 54), hence "as ideology, the law reinforces and validates stigma" (Dowd, 1997, p. 53).

Current divorce laws contribute to single mothers' poverty in the division of property and income, as well as the division of financial and caretaker responsibilities for children (Arendell, 1993; Springer, 1995). The law systematically ignores the economic inequalities between women and men both within marriages and in the larger society (Weitzman, 1985). Legal guidelines for child support awards highlight the way divorce reinforces the caregiving responsibilities of mothers while keeping them from achieving economic security.

Stigma and victim blaming are also apparent in research and intervention models designed for single-parent families (Rice, 1994; Weitzman, 1985). Researchers inadvertently contribute to the deviance image of single-parent families by the selection of variables they choose to investigate (Worell, 1988), emphasizing psychopathology, deficiency, and deficit. In focusing on the deleterious effects of single parenthood, investigators give expression to their own negative stereotypes (Smith, 1997). This stigmatizing view is paradoxical, in that mainstream psychology views women as having a special aptitude for child rearing, yet when women do it alone, it is not considered good enough (Rice, 1994). Furthermore, the stereotype omits any consideration of the positive attributes of single-parent families (Dowd, 1997). For example, single-parent families are less hierarchical and far more cooperative and communal than two-parent marital families (Dowd, 1997). The children are much closer to their mothers. Single mothers, despite their hardship, often experience their lives as liberated from the control and restrictions imposed by husbands; and children of divorced families are often more mature, responsible, and caring than those of two-parent families. However, these strengths are rarely acknowledged, examined, or appreciated.

Stigma as Scapegoating

The United States has a long tradition of finding scapegoats to blame for social and economic problems, attributing to individuals who are considered deviant concerns that are rooted in structural conditions. Single parents are especially apt targets, because they evoke negative myths and stereotypes based on gender and racial prejudice (Dowd, 1997).

The stigma and negative stereotypes of single mothers create a climate for blaming them for their own hardship and poverty, as well as for a host of social problems attributed to single parenthood. They are expected to work extra hard to provide for their children, and to sacrifice their own needs. They are also expected to feel guilty for their poverty, for working and neglecting their children, and for relying on welfare (Worell, 1988). The deficit view of single-parent families, as broken and destined to have problems, engenders guilt in divorcing parents and blame from others for having failed to live in a "normal," two-parent family (Morrison, 1995). They are penalized for asserting independence by the withholding of societal support or sanction (Rice, 1994; Weitzman, 1985). To punish mothers for their "immorality," their children are deprived of decent housing, health services, and basic economic support. This self-defeating strategy puts the children at risk (Dowd, 1997).

Justifications of the Stigma

As a society, we continue to view the stigma of single-parent families as appropriate and justified (Dowd, 1997). Single mothers are stigmatized because many of them are poor, and, in the United States, poverty is considered a moral flaw (Walters & Abshire, 1995). Poor single-parent families are often considered responsible for and deserving of their poverty. Ironically, working does not exempt single mothers from stigma. If they work full time to provide for their children, they may be viewed as not nurturing, and this may be used against them in custody disputes. However, the courts tend to view working fathers more favorably, especially if they are remarried (Walters & Abshire, 1995).

Single-parent families have been thought to be psychologically unhealthy for children, because of the absence of a father. There is a widespread stereotype—frequently internalized by women themselves—that single mothers cannot raise children—especially boys—without a father who provides a masculine role model for identification. This stereotype found expression in the writings of the anthropologist Malinowski (1966) and his Principle of Legitimacy, which stated that "no child should be brought into the world without a man—and one man at that—assuming the role of sociological father" (p. 35). The assumption that fathers are essential to healthy child development has held sway in the academic literature although it is not supported by empirical research. Furthermore, in most two-parent families, parenting is done by the mothers. Contrary to sociologist Talcott Parsons's (1964) classic theory about distinctive gender roles—that mothers perform expressive roles, and fathers instrumental roles—parenting is neither gender specific nor gender related (Dowd, 1997). Furthermore, as rigid gender-role models lead to gender inequality, one may question the desirability of existing masculine role modeling for children.

The stigmatization of single mothers reflects concerns about morality as well as deviation from traditional gender roles (Walters & Abshire, 1995). Women are judged to be "good" based on their commitment to marriage, their sexual behavior within marriage, and their fulfilling the roles of wife, homemaker, and caretaker—all within marriage. Single mothers are blamed for divorcing, for failing to marry, or for having becoming pregnant outside marriage. They are blamed by some if they elect to abort, and by others for electing not to abort. When they give birth, they may face disapproval for relinquishing the children for adoption or for choosing to raise the children on their own (Worell, 1988). Unwed single mothers are depicted as sinful, selfish, immature, and angry. Their children are portrayed as the innocent victims who pay the price for their mothers' narcissism (Rice, 1994). As the stigma is based on belief, it is impossible to undo it with factual information alone. Insofar as it condemns women for having sex outside of marriage, it reflects the patriarchal designation of women as either respectable or "bad."

This kind of victim blaming is paradoxical, because the mothers are blamed for a pregnancy that is conceived by both women and men, and for assuming responsibility for their children—a responsibility that the noncustodial fathers avoid. The noncustodial fathers, who may at best contribute child support while avoiding caretaking responsibility, are exempt from such condemnation.

The Root of the Stigma

Stigma, negative stereotypes, and scapegoating are the representations of fear, hatred, or jealousy. In the case of single-parent families, the two core sources of hatred and fear are racism and sexism.

Most single-parent families are white. However, African American mothers are disproportionately represented among single-parent families, and especially among never-married single-parent families. Marriage is a way out of poverty for most white mothers. This is not as true for African American mothers, because African American men are usually poorer than white men. Therefore, many more African American women choose not to marry. Race pervades policy making, reflecting a long history of devaluing African American families and African American men (Dowd, 1997). The African American family is frequently portrayed as a problem requiring national action, thereby suggesting that African Americans lack appropriate family values (Ziegler, 1995). In reality, however, this picture is both inaccurate and ironic. Research suggests that African American single-parent families are more successful in coping with single parenthood than whites. Their relative success is attributed to their strong social support networks, close communities, and the help and presence of multiple parental figures. A network consisting of grandmothers, neighbors, extended family, and fictive kin serves as surrogate parents and as a highly effective support system. African American single-parent families manage their family situations and poverty through flexibility in role definitions and role performance (Hill, 1998). Finally, African American single-parent families are not subject to stigma within the African American community the way that white single-parent families are in white communities (Jarrett, 1994).

Sexism is also a basis for stigmatizing single mothers. Although the term *single-parent family* is gender neutral, most of the single-parent families are headed by women who are also doing most of the parenting. We equate single-parent families with single mothers, and, overwhelmingly, stigma is tied to the strongly negative images we have of single mothers (Dowd, 1997). As stated by Rich, "woman is one of our most powerful social categories. It wraps women in myth, mysticism, and awe. At the same time, the concept and reality of the single mother generates intense fear, anger, and a threat to men" (in Dowd, 1997, p. 47).

The single-parent family represents a challenge to patriarchy (Dowd, 1997). Men fear women's assertion of independence with respect to reproduction and childbearing. Fathers and husbands may fear that if women are not kept dependent, they will not want to marry men or share children with them because fathers will be regarded as inessential and replaceable (Dowd, 1997, p. 38).

THE EXPERIENCE OF DIVORCE: THE CUSTODIAL MOTHER'S PERSPECTIVE

Divorce can be a devastating experience, because it requires a drastic change in one's life. While the divorce is in progress, and for some time afterward, both parties are likely to feel personally rejected, cheated in the economic arrangements, misrepresented legally, bitter about the coparental arrangements, lonely, and afraid of living alone (Bohannan, 1997). The divorcing couple must separate on several different levels. Financially, single mothers often need to work and become the families' breadwinners. Reduced income following divorce sharply increases the probability that the mother and her children will move to significantly poorer neighborhoods (South, Crowder, & Trent, 1998). And because of their high levels of poverty, women-headed families are at great risk of homelessness. Nationally, between 70% and 90% of homeless families are headed by women (Bassuk, 1990).

If they did not work while married, or if they come from a traditional marriage in which the gender roles were segregated, divorced women are likely to experience the transition to the breadwinner role as particularly stressful (Fassinger, 1989). On the psychological level, each partner must learn to be without a person whose presence has been an everyday part of life. In the social sphere, they frequently have to give up old friends with whom they no longer feel comfortable and make new friends. Economically, they must divide their property and establish separate households. Finally, as most divorces end up with a sole custody of the children, each parent needs to relinquish the two-parent arrangement and respectively assume the role of sole parent and noncustodial parent (Bohannan, 1997).

As the main, and frequently sole, breadwinner and parent, the custodial mothers experience overload in divorce and the transition to single parenthood. At the same time that their income decreases, their parental responsibilities increase. The financial strains, worry about parenting, and juggling a job and child care are especially acute when the former husband withdraws, does not participate in raising the children, and fails to pay child support (Ahrons, 1980; Quinn & Allen, 1989; Riessman, 1990). The strain and overload are often experienced individually as fatigue, depression, and a chronic scarcity of time. Yet they result from social circumstances that are amenable to public policy solutions, including economic support, employment equity, and affordable child care (Worell, 1988). Riessman (1990) found that divorced single mothers are most likely to be depressed when they are under economic strain, when they have difficulties affording food, housing, medical care, leisure activities, and essential household items that need to be replaced. As Riessman describes it, single-parent mothers "transform the public issue—the lack of social provisions for single women and their children—into their own private 'trouble'" (p. 127).

Poverty, which is prevalent among single-parent families and especially among African American single-parent families, has been found to be associated with more depressive symptoms and lower self-esteem among mothers. This, in turn, affects the quality of mother-child relationships (Brody & Flor, 1997). Women also tend to empathize with their children, and if the children are distressed, the mothers carry their sadness, feeling guilty for not being "good enough" mothers, for not being able to do it all (Riessman, 1990).

Additional sources of strain for single parents are the lack of a spouse who shares parental responsibilities and the lack of social support for emergencies, as well as for help around the house, small favors, loaning money, and sharing in decision making and daily talk (Acock & Demo, 1994; Riessman, 1990). The rate of fathers' visitations with their noncustodial children is disheartening. More than half of all children who do not live with their father have never been in their father's home (Furstenberg & Cherlin, 1991). Between 30% and 40% of the children see their noncustodial fathers less than once a year. Only one third of the children see their father at least once a week (King, 1994; Seltzer, 1991).

Despite poverty and hardship, divorce often brings positive benefits for single mothers (Demo & Acock, 1988). Divorce can be experienced as breaking a barrier. Successfully living through it and coping with the daily challenges of single parenthood enhances self-esteem and confidence, which can generalize to other areas of life (Morrison, 1995; Smith, 1997). The divorced women studied by Riessman (1990) reported positive changes in three areas: competence, social relationships, and self-identity. Their sense of enhanced competence came from successfully taking initiative and managing multiple responsibilities. They experienced financial independence and greater control over finances, taking pride in their paid work, which, unlike homemaking, is rewarded with external recognition, status, and a wage. These achievements produced a sense of resilience, pride, and mastery (Riessman, 1990; Smith, 1997).

Separated and divorced women build new intimate relationships and maintain old ones not only better than men, but also better than they themselves did while married (Gerstel, 1988). Gerstel (1988) observes that marriage frequently constrains individuals, and especially women, from developing relationships, while divorce liberates them to do so. Following divorce, women diversify their emotional investments instead of focusing exclusively in the family. This is often accompanied by a growing assertiveness and by establishing a new balance between relatedness and self-reliance (Morrison, 1995; Riessman, 1990; Strand, 1995).

A third area of change women experience following divorce is in their identities. Frequently, women's identity is submerged in marriage and given over to the spouse to manage (Rice, 1994; Riessman, 1990). As Ortiz (1995) notes, women have been defined by men for so long that they do not know how to define themselves. It is therefore not surprising that many women view their divorce and living on their own as powerful vehicles for reclaiming their identity and gaining a fuller sense of who they are (Rice, 1994; Riessman, 1990). The changed identity is bolstered by the sense of competence, confidence, and improved self-esteem (Smith, 1997). As single mothers are forced to take on new responsibilities and roles, they transform their public identity. This, in turn, transforms their private selves (Riessman, 1990). Traditional gender roles are replaced by more egalitarian sex-role attitudes and more positive attitudes toward feminism (Kurdek & Blisk, 1983; Rice, 1994).

The benefits single mothers draw from their situation are especially striking when compared to men. Comparing 177 divorced single mothers and single fathers, Buehler (1988) found the single mothers reported better health and self-esteem than the single fathers. A comparison of divorced single mothers and noncustodial fathers showed that, overall, women are more satisfied with their divorce outcome than are men, including satisfaction with custody, visitation, property, and financial settlements. This greater satisfaction existed despite their worsened financial situation after divorce, and despite their dissatisfaction with child support arrangements (Sheets & Braver, 1996).

For many women, divorce and single parenthood is seen as a mode of resistance against the devaluation and domination they experienced in their marriages (Rice, 1994; Riessman, 1990). Many divorced single mothers have been found to experience the divorce as a liberating experience, identifying divorce with freedom from subordination and control. Indeed, some feminist scholars view divorce as a way of changing the patriarchal relationships between women and men. From this perspective, divorce signifies a transition from passive endurance of oppression to active decision making about the woman's life (Rice, 1994).

Interviews with divorced women and men show that "images of the experience of subordination fill some women's accounts [of their marriages] —being a child, overwhelmed, buried, chained-in, and controlled. Other women remember instances in which they were devalued and discredited— more subtle forms of domination" (Riessman, 1990, p. 58). It is not surprising that women are twice as likely as men to initiate divorce (Kposowa, 1998; Rice, 1994), and that a growing number of women, especially well-educated and economically self-sufficient women, choose to postpone marriage or not to marry at all (Rice, 1994).

IMPLICATIONS FOR CHILDREN

Children are distressed when their parents divorce. Depending on their age, children's reactions include grief, self-blame and guilt, anxiety, sadness, depression, clingingness, sleep disturbances, bed wetting, and fear of separation (Bohannan, 1997; Wallerstein & Kelly, 1980). In the popular view children raised in single-parent families continue having more difficulties than children in two-parent families no matter how long it has been since the divorce. The research, however, is inconclusive.

Numerous studies have found that children raised in single-parent families manifest a host of adverse behaviors, most commonly in three areas: academic performance (e.g., Amato, 1999; Lindner, Stanley, & Cavanaugh, 1992; Roizblatt et al., 1997), social functioning (Dunn, Deater-Deckard, Pickering, O'Connor, & Golding, 1998; Duran-Aydintug, 1997; Parish & Parish, 1991; Robinson, Garthoeffner, & Henry, 1995), and psychological functioning, showing such symptoms as low self-esteem (Bynum & Durm, 1996; Garnefski & Diekstra, 1997; Parish & Parish, 1991), emotional distress (Simons, 1996), anxiety, loneliness, depressed mood, and suicidal thoughts (Garnefski & Diekstra, 1997; McCabe, 1997). In a meta-analysis of 92 studies comparing children living in divorced single-parent families with children living in continuously intact families, Amato and Keith (1991) found that in more than two thirds of the studies, the children with divorced parents had lower levels of well-being than children from intact families.

Though many studies found that boys of single-parent families have more behavioral and academic problems than girls (Dunn et al., 1998; Hetherington, 1989; Kaye, 1989; Wallerstein & Kelly, 1980), a study using longitudinal data from the National Survey of Children found no differences between boys and girls (Furstenberg & Teitlev, 1994), a finding supported by Amato and Keith's (1991) meta-analysis, as well as by Lindner and colleagues (1992).

Other studies did not find significant differences between children of single- and two-parent families (Acock & Demo, 1994; Bohannan, 1997; Demo & Acock, 1996; Young, 1995). Amato (1994) reports that although children who have experienced divorce scored lower on a variety of indicators of psychological, interpersonal, and socioeconomic well-being, overall group differences between children from divorced and intact families are small, with considerable diversity in children's reactions to divorce. Smith's (1995) study of 1,688 7th- and 9th-grade students found no significant effect of parental separation on academic achievement when parental occupation and education were controlled. Similar results were reported by Weisner and Garnier (1992). Adolescents from divorced families also differed little from those of two-parent families in their relationships with parents and peers, and in their psychological well-being (e.g., self-esteem, happiness, depression; Gonzalez, Field, Lasko, & Harding, 1995). Similarly, adults who experienced parental divorce or death as children did not differ in self-esteem or on sense of power from adults who grew up in continuously intact families (Amato, 1988).

A handful of studies compared children from high-conflict intact families with children from single-parent families. Studies conducted by Amato and his colleagues (Amato & Booth, 1996; Amato, Loomis, & Booth, 1995; Amato & Rezac, 1994) suggest that children of divorced families are fairing at least as well as, if not better than, children raised in conflict-ridden two-parent families.

Some studies have found that children benefit from being raised by their single mothers. Single mothers promote more flexible attitudes toward gender roles among their children, as well as fewer gender-role stereotypes, more gender respect, and equality beliefs and practices (Dowd, 1997; Smith, 1997). Single-parent families contribute to the independence of children and their sense of responsibility, autonomy, and maturity (Arditti, 1999; Dowd, 1997; Young, 1995). Finally, many children of single-parent families feel a sense of equality with their single mother and feel close to her (Arditti, 1999).

What accounts for these contradictory findings? It may be that both sets of findings are valid, because "the monolithic concept of the single-parent family is inadequate and misleading . . . as description, explanation, and basis for policy" (Fitchen, 1995, p. 355). Furthermore, some argue that many of the documented negative effects of divorce on children are methodologically biased (Coontz, 1997; Demo & Acock, 1988; Dilworth-Anderson & McAdoo, 1988; Rice, 1994).

Amato and Keith (1991) point to several important methodological issues. Most often, convenience samples have been used. Studies employing larger samples and control variables or matched respondents yielded a weaker effect of divorce. Many research reports give the impression that the differences between divorced and intact families are stronger and more pervasive than the data warrant. Amato and Keith conclude that the view that divorce has profound detrimental effects on children and negatively affects their psychological well-being is not supported by empirical research. More recent studies have yielded weaker effect of divorce than did studies carried out in earlier decades, suggesting that the negative effects of divorce on children's well-being have diminished since the 1950s and 1960s. In addition, there is some evidence that the impact of divorce decreases with time, especially with regard to children's conduct. Therefore, conclusions about the influences of divorce need to be framed within the context of the time that has elapsed since the divorce.

Although single-mother families account for half of all poor families (Brewer, 1995; Lino, 1995; Rice, 1994), the poverty of single-parent families has been frequently overlooked in research on children's adjustment (Ambert, 1982; Hill, 1998; Schnayer & Orr, 1989). Few studies have compared children of divorced families with those of intact families while controlling for family income (Amato & Keith, 1991). Those studies that have done so have found that although children of single-parent families exhibited a consistent achievement decrement in school, these effects were reduced or eliminated when socioeconomic status was controlled (Amato, 1994b; Finn & Owings, 1994; Guidubaldi, Cleminshaw, Perry, & McLoughlin, 1983). For example, Hill (1998) found that, overall, black single-parent families were about as likely to have children in college as black two-parent families (13%). The research has also neglected to include such potentially critical variables as predivorce domestic violence and child abuse in examining the long-term outcomes of children in single-parent families.

The adverse consequences for children raised in single-parent families are attributed to several factors. The most frequently examined explanation is father absence (Bray & Berger, 1990; Popenoe, 1996; Wallerstein & Kelly, 1980). Four related sets of findings cast doubt on this widely accepted theory. First, comparing the impact of father absence due to father's death and parents' divorce, children of divorce have lower levels of well-being than do children whose fathers died (Amato & Keith, 1991). Second, the addition of a father to the single-parent family following the remarriage of the single mother does not "solve" the problems children experience in single-parent families. Children in stepfamilies exhibit more problems, especially in terms of psychological adjustment, than children in single-parent families do (Amato & Keith, 1991). Third, contact with the noncustodial father has been found to be unrelated to children's outcomes, especially for girls (Furstenberg & Cherlin, 1991; Simons, 1996) and for boys if there was conflict between the resident and nonresident parents (Amato & Rezac, 1994). Furthermore, findings regarding the quality of the relationship with the noncustodial father on children's outcomes are inconclusive (Amato & Keith, 1991; Clingempeel & Segal, 1986; King, 1994). Finally, the absence of fathers as active participants in family life is a feature of all family types, including most intact, two-parent nuclear families (Acock & Demo, 1994).

Another explanation attributes children's postdivorce adjustment to the quality of the mothers' parenting (Friedmann & Andrews, 1990; Parish & Parish, 1991; Wallerstein & Kelly, 1980). The distress experienced by the single mother affects her parenting behavior (Hetherington & Hagan, 1995; Simons, 1996). A key reason for this distress is the mothers' poverty. The daily struggle for survival affects the psychological well-being of parents, generating anxiety, depression, and emotional distress. This, in turn, affects their relationship with their children (Acock & Demo, 1994). "Poor parents are stressed parents" (Dowd, 1997, p. 26). Single mothers were found to seek support from their children, hence creating a role reversal (Arditti, 1999; Weiss, 1994). Single mothers also had problems controlling and disciplining their children (Bank, Forgatch, Patterson, & Fetrow, 1993; Weiss, 1994). By focusing on the mother as the cause of children's difficulties, we blame the victim.

Instead, we should consider the number of adults who are parenting the child. By looking at the number of parents available, the focus shifts to such issues as the mothers' burden as the sole or principal breadwinner and caretaker (Wright & Price, 1986).

An investigation of the respective variables examined in studies of fathers' and mothers' involvement with the children following divorce reflects differing expectations of the two parents. Though the quality of the fathers' involvement with their children is evaluated on the basis of the frequency of visitation and the payment of child support, the quality of the mothers' involvement is evaluated on their exercising discipline and control, and on their leaning on their children for help (role reversal). To some extent, these distinctions reflect the fact that the fathers do not parent their children on a daily basis. Nevertheless, these differences also reflect gender expectations. Good fathering means simply seeing the child (without regard for what actually takes place when the father is with the child) and being the breadwinner. Mothers, on the other hand, are expected to have difficulties with such "masculine" tasks as discipline and control, and with managing on their own without the support and guidance of a man, a son, or, if these males are unavailable, their daughters.

Children need at least one responsible, caretaking adult who has a positive and consistent emotional connection with them. The gender of the single parent does not matter in terms of successful or unsuccessful outcomes (Ambert, 1982; Downey, Ainsworth Darnell, & Dufur, 1998; Schnayer & Orr, 1989). Further, Schnayer and Orr (1986) found that socioeconomic status is a better predictor of children's behavior problems than the gender of the single parent. "Neither the sex of the adult(s) nor the biological relationship to the child has emerged as a significant variable in predicting positive development" (Silverstein & Auerbach, 1999, pp. 397–398).

Additional issues examined as possible causes of the adverse outcomes exhibited by children of single-parent families include the degree of conflict or harmony between the previously married parents both prior to the divorce (Ahrons, 1981; Amato & Booth, 1996; Furstenberg & Teitlev, 1994) and following the divorce (Acock & Demo, 1994; Demo & Acock, 1988; Kelly, Emery, Kressel, Kurdek, & Sprenkle, 1988; Simons, Whitbeck, Beamn, & Conger, 1994). These studies show that cooperative coparenting following divorce enhances the children's adjustment

(Ahrons, 1981; Amato & Keith, 1991; Duran-Aydintug, 1997; Stern, 1989), whereas coparental conflict predicted increased behavior problems in the children (Lee, 1997).

VARIATIONS AMONG
SINGLE-PARENT FAMILIES

Although the most prevalent single-parent families are woman-headed families following divorce, single-parent families may be single-father families, foster families, adoptive families, or never-married families, or they may result from the death of a spouse. Foster and adoptive single-parent families were discussed earlier in Chapters 2 and 3, respectively. In this chapter, I consider single-father families, never-married single-parent families, teenage single-parent families, and joint-custody families.

Single-Father Families

Single-parent families headed by fathers are still comparatively rare, but the numbers are increasing (Eggebeen, Snyder, & Manning, 1996). Although the number of father-headed families has tripled since 1974, fathers with full custody of their children represent about 14% of divorced fathers (Hetherington & Stanley-Hagan, 2000). In 19 reporting states, 72% of custody cases were awarded to the wife, 9% to the husband, and joint custody was awarded in 16% of the cases (NCHS, 1989–1990). Though most of the father-headed families are headed by young, never-married men with few children (Eggebeen et al., 1996), there is still considerable diversity in single-father families, which include gay, divorced, widowed, foster, and adoptive single-father families.

In contrast to the stigmatizing of single mothers, men in single-father families are usually viewed with respect and regarded as exceptional parents (Dowd, 1997). This appreciation is reflected in the tendency of children of custodial fathers to verbalize their appreciation for the father, whereas children of custodial mothers do so only rarely (Ambert, 1982).

Father-headed families and mother-headed families face similar difficulties, and most studies find no significant differences between them (Hetherington & Hagan, 1995). Like single mothers, single fathers experience overload, social isolation, and worries about their parenting competence (Hetherington & Hagan, 1995). In a study of 1,132 single-father families, DeMaris and Greif (1997) report that, as with mother-headed families, the key predictors of problems in father-child relationship were difficulty balancing work and child care, and conflict with the former spouse. Factors associated with successful parenting experiences were involvement in child care while married, father's income, social support, and satisfaction with the father's social life.

Father-headed single-parent families generally have more economic resources than mother-headed families (Hetherington & Hagan, 1995). The disproportionately high number of single mothers in poverty, compared with single fathers, is striking. Though almost half of single-mother families are poor, less than 3% of single-father families are poor (Funiciello, cited in Dowd, 1997). The average income of single-mother families, including child support, is less than half that of single-father families (U.S. Bureau of Census, 1989). Yet despite their enjoying greater economic well-being and social approval, the children in single-father families do no better than children in single-mother families (Dowd, 1997). Furthermore, the differences that are found between single-mother and single-father families can be attributed to factors predating their becoming single parents (Downey et al., 1998).

Many single fathers experience active parenting for the first time. Even among those who were married, many had not been actively involved in parenting. As might be expected, single fathers who were not active parents while married face a more difficult transition and have less positive attitudes toward their children than fathers who had been actively involved in their children's care. DeMaris and Greif (1997) found that although most of the fathers in their study (72%) said that they felt comfortable as single parents, 28% were not.

Although not addressed in the research literature, it is likely that single fathers, like single mothers, can gain from their new circumstances. During marriage, women tend to relinquish independence, power, and opportunity, whereas men forgo love, nurturing, and giving (Dowd, 1997). Many single mothers experience divorce and single parenthood as an opportunity to assert their "masculine" selves by earning and gaining status in the labor market, being independent, and making important decisions. At least some men may experience their single parenthood as a source of growth, a chance to get in touch with their "feminine" sides— nurturing, caring, establishing a close and intimate relationship with their children, and homemaking.

Findings about children's adjustment are inconclusive. Adolescents living with single fathers are reported to be more involved in delinquent activities than those living with single mothers; daughters living with single fathers have more adjustment problems, and fathers report having more difficulty dealing with adolescent daughters than adolescent sons; and though school-aged boys living with single fathers have higher self-esteem, exhibit fewer behavior problems, and are more socially competent than those living with single mothers, they lack openness in communication and expression of feelings (Hetherington & Hagan, 1995). Downey and colleagues (1998) found that there was little evidence that children are better off or develop particular characteristics in one household versus the other.

Never-Married Single-Parent Families

Never-married single-parent families, also known as single parents by choice, are families headed by a single woman or a single man who became a parent while not married. These single parents may be foster or adoptive, lesbian or gay, and if they are women, they may have given birth to their children as single women.

Unmarried mothers are less stigmatized and ostracized than they used to be. Nowadays, they do not need to hide their pregnancies, and social norms permit them to keep and raise their children. By 1990, 97% of unmarried women chose to raise their children rather than relinquish them for adoption (Dowd, 1997). Nevertheless, single mothers by choice are stigmatized both because they are single mothers and because their children are legally fatherless. Paternity, which is a critical condition for many legal entitlements including child support, is established for only 30% of nonmarital children (Dowd, 1997). That means that the vast majority of children of unmarried mothers are denied child support payments. In the common law tradition, an unmarried putative (i.e., presumed) father has no legal duties toward his child and is, in effect, a "stranger" to the child (Dowd, 1997).

In the past two decades, there has been a dramatic increase in childbearing among never-married women. In 1994, 37.8% of all births were to unmarried women. Of these, 20.6% were births to women between the ages of 30 and 44 years (U.S. Bureau of Census, 1996). Increasing numbers of educated, financially autonomous single women over 30 years of age choose to bear, foster, or adopt a child.

Teenage Single-Parent Families

Although there is relatively little research on single mothers by choice, especially heterosexual single mothers, there is considerably more scrutiny of single teenage mothers by politicians, social-policy makers, and social scientists. Among the most common themes addressed in the literature on teenage mothers are discouraging sexual activity and preventing pregnancies; the "risk" factors associated with teenage parenting (e.g., Christopher, 1995; Scaramella, Conger, Simons, & Whitbeck, 1988); and the association between teenage pregnancy and race (e.g., Jacobs, 1994; Kaplan, 1997; Trent & Harlan, 1994). Another concern is the negative impact of parenting on the teens' own lives and on their children (e.g., East, 1999; Garrett & Tidwell, 1999; Hetherington, 1997), and especially the poor educational attainment of adolescent mothers (Strand, 1995). Though these negative consequences do indeed occur, most scholars and policymakers acknowledge that the poor outcomes result, to a large extent, from living in poverty (Hetherington, 1997; Strand, 1995) and from lacking financial support, affordable child care, and social support (Campbell, Breitmayer, & Ramey, 1986; Danziger & Farber, 1990). Interestingly, relatively little attention has been paid to the father's role with respect to the mother's pregnancy and adjustment, his role in assuring the child's well-being, and his responsibility toward the mother and the child. This consistent omission shows that teenage pregnancy and parenting is considered a woman's issue, for which women, rather than men, are held responsible. That the stigma of teenage parenting is almost exclusively placed on the mothers seems especially unfair in that more than half of the fathers are adults, not teenagers (Dowd, 1997).

Teenage mothers are even more stigmatized than divorced or older never-married mothers, because they "seem to epitomize all of the worst negatives of single parenting" (Dowd, 1997, p. 8). Although immorality has not disappeared as a basis for stigmatizing teenage mothers, there has been a shift in the stereotype. They are now more likely to be considered stupid rather than sinful, and immature rather than unfit (Dowd, 1997).

The greatest problem teenage mothers face is their disadvantage in the existing economic structure. They enter the workplace early, with few skills and little or no experience. They frequently begin parenting in poverty and are likely to remain in poverty. The nearly insurmountable barriers that most teenage single mothers need to struggle against are "deliberately placed in their path" (Dowd, 1997, p. 8) as a punishment for their being unwed, female, young (Dowd, 1997)—and frequently for being African American.

Joint-Custody Families

Joint physical custody means that the children reside alternately with each parent. With joint legal custody, both parents are responsible for their children regardless of residency arrangements (Walters & Abshire, 1995). Even when joint physical custody is awarded, most children reside almost full time with their mothers. Physical custody decisions are usually made by the divorcing couple, not imposed by the courts (Hetherington & Hagan, 1995). The major advantages of joint custody are that the children are parented by both parents and both parents maintain their parenting roles. Joint-custody families are usually better off financially than single-parent families, because there is greater compliance with child support orders (U.S. Census Bureau, 1994).

Joint custody is usually ineffective and even harmful if there is intense conflict between the parents (Stern, 1989). Joint custody requires that the parents remain in the same location, limiting their mobility. From the children's perspective, possible disadvantages of joint custody are that children need constantly to move between two households. Though this may suit some children, it might be an inappropriate arrangement for others, depending on their age and their lifestyles. Children also may feel a conflict of loyalty between the joint-custody parents (Stern, 1989).

Generally, studies have not found joint physical custody to disadvantage the children, especially where parents are cooperative (Glover & Steele, 1989). The increasing reliance on joint legal and physical custody appears successful when such arrangements are carried out with genuine concerns for the best interests of the children (Springer, 1995; for reviews for and against joint custody, see Folberg, 1991; Sack, 1992).

IMPLICATIONS FOR POLICY

Legal Implications

The circumstances of single-parent families underscore the need for social policies and programs to protect children and their mothers and to mitigate the negative consequences of divorce (Springer, 1995). Most of the adverse consequences of divorce and single parenthood are not the result of divorce per se, but rather reflect external structural circumstances. Foremost is the sexism that pervades the family, the educational system, the media, and the workplace. It is reflected in a gender-based division of household work, an uncompensated domestic labor, a dual labor market, and dual welfare system (Springer, 1995).

Reforms in divorce laws are needed to ensure equity between husbands and wives in terms of property, income, and the division of financial and caretaker responsibilities for children (Arendell, 1993; Springer, 1995). The adversarial legal process exacerbates the intense emotions and antagonism that accompany divorce (Springer, 1995). Divorce laws should provide for mandatory mediation for parents in dispute over child custody, requiring parents to come up with a plan that will safeguard the children's welfare while trying to satisfy the concerns of the parents (Maccoby, 1995). Concern about the emotional and economic costs of conflictual custody proceedings has led to the adoption of mandatory mediation in some jurisdictions (Maccoby, 1995). Springer cautions, however, that mediation can potentially reinforce gender inequality by failing to take into account the unequal circumstances of women and men (Springer, 1995).

There is a need to develop and expand programs to enhance child visitation by noncustodial parents. Some initial steps in this direction have been taken with provisions of the 1996 PRWORA, which encourages states to develop visitation programs. States can apply for grants to provide counseling and mediation to parents in conflict and to offer a safe, supervised environment to maintain the children's contact with the father in instances where there's been a history of violence.

Economic Implications

One can learn from single-parent families about the need for gender equality in families. To achieve gender equality, we need also to bring about economic independence within the marriage so that both partners are economically self-sufficient. This can be achieved through any combination of wages and public income support (Dowd, 1997). To change the gender inequality in families, we also need to redefine fatherhood and motherhood, the division of labor between parents, and their basis of partnership (Dowd, 1997).

We also need to create a healthy balance between wage work and family work. The conflict between work and family exists in two-parent families; they are only more evident and difficult to avoid in single-parent families. At present,

> We continue to pretend that family responsibilities do not exist, or virtually ignore them, while at the same time, those who take parenting seriously often face severe, long-term detriments at work. We demand that parents be invisible in the workplace, but single parents stick out like sore thumbs. Their conflicts between work and family, however, are simply

more evident and difficult to avoid than those of two-parent families. They are harbingers of the dilemmas all families have. (Dowd, 1997, p. xii)

We need to move away from the idea that parents alone are responsible for their child's support and care (Young, 1995), a view that sets the United States apart from other developed nations. Social policies should guarantee that all children and their parents have an adequate income, regardless of family structure. To ensure that no child will live in poverty, primary caregivers should be provided with universal family support regardless of family form (Dowd, 1997).

In the short run, we need to end the link between single parenthood and poverty (Abramovitz, 1994; Dowd, 1997). Single-parent families face many of the same issues as two-parent families (Hanson, Heims, Julian, & Sussman, 1995), but because most of them are headed by women, this must be taken into account in providing services (Strand, 1995). Rather than attacking single-parent families and cutting welfare supports in order to regulate their moral behavior, social policies should provide single-parent families with financial support and services (Abramovitz, 1994; Acock & Demo, 1994; Rodger, 1995). A good model to emulate is the Swedish system, in which all families, regardless of origin or structure, are entitled to universal family support supplemented by needs-based support for housing, child care, and income (Dowd, 1997).

As Arendell (1993) describes it, "Without widespread changes in public policy, . . . marriage is destined to become an institution that [women] cannot afford to support and cannot afford to dissolve" (p. 310). Single-parent families should be provided with sufficient income to support a reasonable lifestyle. This income should be provided by the state as long as they raise children, combining wage and family support as needed. This is essential for the children and the mothers, and is grounded in the commitment of the society to its children, as well as on principles of freedom of choice for adults to live in any family configuration they wish (Dowd, 1997). Single-parent families as well as primary caretakers in other family structures, including two-parent marital families, should be provided with wage replacement for periods of parenting leave, and the paid employment of primary caregivers should be protected while they are on leave for parenting (Dowd, 1997).

The nation needs a central system of child support enforcement that ensures support even if the noncustodial parent is unable or unwilling to pay. The Family Support Act of 1988 (Public Law 100-485) strengthened child support enforcement, mandated presumptive child support guidelines, and made improvements in the process of establishing paternity (Springer, 1995). Though this is indicative of a trend in the United States toward states' adopting legislation to hold fathers accountable for supporting their children (Seltzer, 1994), there is still a long way to go. Social policies should guarantee child support payments from noncustodial fathers, subsidized by the state when income is insufficient (Arendell, 1993). At present, child support awards are not routinely established and, if established, are often inadequate in amount (Springer, 1995). Single-parent families would benefit from an improved system of child support modeled on approaches common in other developed countries where the state provides the support payments and then collects from the noncustodial parent. Under such programs, the children receive support payments irrespective of whether or not the father contributes. A reform along these lines is long overdue in the United States, although norms against anything like a children's allowance—common in other industrialized countries as diverse as Australia, Israel, and Denmark—make this a formidable challenge.

There is a need for economic and employment policies that ensure that working women earn a fair wage. Wage discrimination against women needs to be stopped, both in the lower-paid pink collar sector and in other sectors in which women receive lower wages than men (Arendell, 1993). Vocational education and on-the-job training programs are needed to help displaced homemakers enter the workforce (Abramovitz, 1994; Arendell, 1993; Riessman, 1990).

Social policies need to facilitate a combination of family work and market work for both women and men (Springer, 1995). Policies need to support women's employment by providing workplace flexibility, which includes job sharing, parental leave, and sick leave (Rodger, 1995). Such policies should allow women to give birth and have maternity leave to take care of their children while continuing to earn full salaries for this caretaking and without having to fear losing their jobs. Parents of both genders need to have health coverage during the years they parent children, including the times they are at home. Furthermore, social security contributions should continue to be made on their behalf while they are out of the paid labor force so they do not face a loss of retirement income because of caregiving responsibilities.

IMPLICATIONS FOR PRACTICE

Given the diversity of single parent households, practice interventions will differ depending on their circumstances and their resources. It is important to put aside the deficit model, and to recognize that the anxiety and depression experienced by single parents may be exacerbated by the social environment. Single parents may need help in combating negative self-images derived from societal disapproval. Counseling and groups may be helpful in building self-esteem (Strand, 1995). In addition to therapeutic interventions, single parents may benefit from concrete assistance in improving their education and vocational prospects, securing affordable child care, and negotiating community agencies, schools, and the legal system. They may also need help developing social support networks (Strand, 1995; Worell, 1988).

It has been found that the stability of social networks is positively related to postdivorce adjustment (Aniels-Mohring & Berger, 1984), and that satisfaction with social support, rather than social support frequency, accurately predicts self-esteem, depression, and anxiety (Waggener & Galassi, 1993). Not surprisingly, in contrast to fathers, single mothers were found frequently to base their decision about whether or not to move on the availability of social supports (Asher & Bloom, 1983).

Practitioners dealing with single-parent families need to examine their own beliefs and stereotypes about single-parent families. Intervening in the lives of single-parent families with a deficit model is likely to generate a self-fulfilling prophecy that reinforces guilt and the internalized oppression of single-parent families.

IMPLICATIONS FOR RESEARCH

The deficit view of single-parent families as broken and beset with problems continues to shape the discourse about these families and about the adjustment of women and children to divorce (Rice, 1994). The deficit model has restricted the growth of knowledge about single-parent families (Morrison, 1995). We need instead to examine these families from their own perspective. Researchers who have done so have found strengths and abilities. This new knowledge, although increasing our understanding of single-parent families, can also point to new directions for traditional two-parent families (e.g., Riessman, 1990).

Research is needed on the economic and social consequences for single-parent custodial mothers and fathers, the labor force opportunities for women, the implications of the shortage of affordable child care, and the retirement implications of single parenthood (Lino, 1995). Further research is also needed comparing poor and nonpoor single-parent families to distinguish the effects of family structure from those of economic circumstances. The research should examine the effects of poverty along with other variables of interest. In countries with more adequate family supports, single parenthood does not appear to have the negative effects attributed to it in the United States. Cross-national studies examining the role of these support services can help to broaden the discussion of policy options in the United States.

Given the interest in the implications of divorce and single parenthood for child development, more and better quality research is needed utilizing large, diverse samples with matched respondents and controlling for family income. Longitudinal studies that track the effects of divorce over time are also needed. Studies on the long-term consequences of divorce need to take into account the prior, predivorce history, which may include domestic violence and child abuse.

As joint-custody arrangements are becoming more common, they should be studied to assess the implications for the various parties, and to determine which specific types of arrangements and circumstances work best for the children and parents.

The provision of the PRWORA encouraging states to establish parental visitation programs should be studied to assess its implementation by states, its success in increasing visitation, and the implications for the families and especially for the children.

The advent of welfare reform provides an opportunity to examine potentially critical elements in the circumstances of poor single parents. These include the availability of income support, health insurance, child care, subsidized housing, and low-wage employment. We do not know enough about how families leaving welfare have fared. Time limits, if permitted to take effect, will demonstrate the consequences for families of withdrawing a key component of the social safety net. This must be followed closely.

DISCUSSION QUESTIONS

1. Should public policy seek to discourage the formation of single-parent families? Why or why not? How might this be done? What would be the consequences?

2. How would you assess the social impact of no-fault divorce? On balance, do you think it has been a beneficial development or not? Why? Would you favor any changes?

3. What would it take to make the American workplace more "family friendly"? What role should government play? Employers? Who should bear the costs of such policies?

4. A growing movement contends that people who are childless by choice are unfairly required to subsidize other people's children. They point to their tax dollars, which go for such things as educational benefits, health and social services for children, and tax deductions for the parents. They also complain that they are required to cover for coworkers who are excused from work and given greater flexibility in assignments to meet parenting obligations. They argue that because the parents made the choice to have children, they should not expect others to help provide for them. What are the assumptions that underlie both this argument and the opposing view? What is your opinion? Why?

5. In your own experience, how do gender-role norms affect the nature of your family relationships and responsibilities?

6. What do you think accounts for the persistence of gender inequalities in family responsibilities? What would it take to change these inequalities?

SUGGESTIONS FOR FURTHER READING

Crosbie-Burnett, M., & Lewis, E. A. (1993). Use of African American family structures and functioning to address the challenge of European-American postdivorce families. *Family Relations, 42,* 243–248.

Morrison, N. C. (1995). Successful single-parent families. *Journal of Divorce & Remarriage, 22*(3–4), 205–219.

Rice, J. K. (1994). Reconsidering research on divorce, family life cycle, and the meaning of family. *Psychology of Women Quarterly, 18*(4), 559–584.

Riessman, C. K. (1990). *Divorce talk: Women and men make sense of personal relationships.* New Brunswick, NJ: Rutgers University Press.

Sands, R. G., & Nuccio, K. E. (1989). Mother-headed single-parent families: A feminist perspective. *Affilia, 4*(3), 25–41.

Schein, V. E. (1995). *Working from the margins: Voices of mothers in poverty.* Ithaca, NY: Cornell University Press.

Weitzman, L. J. (1985). *The divorce resolution: The unexpected social and economic consequences for women and children in America.* New York: Free Press.

Chapter 5

STEPFAMILIES

Stepfamilies are created by marriage or cohabitation following the divorce or the death of a spouse. The stepfamily comprises the remarried or cohabiting couple and the children of each partner from the previous relationships, as well as a network of relatives, or quasi-kin (Bohannan, 1970). These include the former spouses, the former parents-in-law, the spouses of former spouses, and the families of origin (Messinger, 1984). This complexity, the disruption of previous family constellations, and the addition of new members poses unique challenges. Stepfamilies are a thriving family structure that offers the potential for satisfying the developmental needs of both children and adults.

HISTORICAL BACKGROUND AND
THE SOCIAL-CULTURAL CONTEXT

Although stepfamilies have existed throughout history, the causes for remarriage and the structure of stepfamilies have changed in recent times. Stepfamilies were common in preindustrial Europe. In the 17th and 18th centuries, about one in six households in England was a stepfamily (Phillips, 1997). This prevalence of stepfamilies reflected the high mortality rate and the centrality of the family as an economic unit requiring that all family members contribute to its survival. The death of a spouse had a dramatic effect on the domestic economy, and the widowed partner was under considerable pressure to remarry. Remarriage often occurred within several months following the death of the spouse (Phillips, 1997).

Since the second half of the 20th century, most remarriages occur following divorce rather than the death of a spouse. This marks a significant departure from past remarriages. The formation of stepfamilies while both parents are alive means that current stepfamilies are adding rather than replacing a parent. Thus, contemporary stepfamilies constitute a new family structure with unique dynamics.

Modern stepfamilies are the result of trends that include high rates of divorce in Western societies, especially in the United States (Cherlin, 1992; Cherlin & Furstenberg, 1994). Remarriage following divorce also reflects changes in the status of women, with women being acknowledged to be independent, self-sufficient, and entitled to choose their family status. The current divorce and remarriage rates also reflect a contemporary perception of the family as formed principally to provide love, nurturance, and care to its members rather than as an economic institution. In the Western world, stepfamilies, like first-marriage families, are usually created by the love and mutual decision of the spouses, with love being regarded as a normative reason for establishing a family.

PREVALENCE AND DEMOGRAPHIC CHARACTERISTICS OF THE STEPFAMILY

One out of three Americans is now a stepparent, a stepchild, a stepsibling, or some other member of a stepfamily, and more than half of Americans today have been, are now, or will eventually be in one or more step situations during their lives (Larson, 1992). Stepfamilies will outnumber first-marriage families by about 2007 (Bray & Kelly, 1998). Nevertheless, the rate of remarriage in the United States reached its peak in the late 1970s. Since then, although the divorce rate has remained fairly constant, the rate of remarriage has declined as part of an overall declining marriage rate. Currently, about 50% of all first marriages in the United States end in divorce. Whereas in the 1960s three fourths of the women and more than four fifths of the men remarried, at present about two thirds of the women and three fourths of the men remarry (Cherlin & Furstenberg, 1994).

Divorce and remarriage have increasingly become a normal event in a person's life (Cherlin, 1992). About 40% of all marriages are remarriages for one of the adults. About 65% of remarriages involve children from the prior marriage, thus creating stepfamilies.

In 1990, 5.3 million married-couple households contained at least one stepchild under the age of 18, and one of six children under the age of 18 was a stepchild (Norton & Miller, 1992). Sixty-five percent of children living with a stepparent in 1990 lived with a stepfather. At present rates of remarriage, 35% of all children born now can expect to live in a stepfamily household.

Formal remarriage is more prevalent among whites than it is among Hispanics and African Americans (reflecting the lower rates of remarriage among poor people). Non-Hispanic whites make up 80% of the stepfamilies in the United States (Cherlin & Furstenberg, 1994).

LEGAL AND POLICY ISSUES

Public policies have not kept pace with the increasing prevalence of stepfamilies. The law regarding stepparenting is confusing and contradictory (Bernstein & Haberman, 1981). There is no legal relationship between stepparent and stepchild (Kompara, 1980), so that, to date, stepparents have no legal right to "parent" their stepchildren. They have no legal authority to act on behalf of children; they cannot legally discipline a stepchild, sign school report cards or other administrative school forms, or approve emergency medical treatment; and they have no rights or obligations following divorce or death of a spouse (Chambers, 1990; Duran-Aydintug & Ihinger-Tallman, 1995). Under U.S. common law, marriage does not oblige stepparents to support their stepchildren. The rights and duties assumed by a stepparent are voluntary unless the stepparent has intentionally assumed parental responsibilities as *in loco parentis* or by adoption. In the past, *in loco parentis* meant taking the child into the stepparent's home. Currently, *in loco parentis* is defined more broadly to include "psychological parenthood" as well (Duran-Aydintug & Ihinger-Tallman, 1995). The courts determine *in loco parentis* relationships on a case-by-case basis, and, under common law, the *in loco parentis* relationship and its corresponding financial responsibility can be terminated at any time by either the stepparent or the stepchild (Mahoney, 1994a, 1994b).

All U.S. states have legislation or case law pertaining to child support, custody, visitation, and stepparent adoption. There is, however, considerable variation among the states regarding child support. States differ on whether stepparents are obliged to support the stepchild after the marriage is terminated or when the stepchild lives in a separate household. There are also differences with respect to whether the stepparent's income should be considered in determining the amount of child support the birth parent must pay (Duran-Aydintug & Ihinger-Tallman, 1995).

There is also considerable ambiguity regarding a stepparent's visitation and custody rights. In both custody and visitation, the courts tend to hold stepparents to more stringent standards than parents in order to protect the rights of the parent (Duran-Aydintug & Ihinger-Tallman, 1995; Mahoney, 1994b).

There are also numerous inconsistencies among the 50 states and in federal policy with regard to the rights of stepchildren to legal benefits. These include the provisions allowed children under worker's compensation, wrongful death statutes, insurance policies, inheritance, Social Security, immigration law, and welfare programs (Duran-Aydintug & Ihinger-Tallman, 1995).

VARIATIONS AMONG STEPFAMILIES

Stepfamilies may be classified as simple or complex. Simple stepfamilies consist of an adult (usually a mother), children from a previous marriage, and a stepparent (usually a father). Complex stepfamilies also include the stepparent's children from previous marriage. Additional variations include stepfamilies that are constituted following divorce (the most common structure) or following widowhood, and families that have children from previous marriages. Other factors affecting the stepfamily are the number of marriages prior to the current remarriage; whether or not the couple are married or cohabiting; the similarity or difference in the respective former status of the remarried couple (e.g., one being widowed and the other divorced; one being divorced and the other never-married); and age differences. Finally, stepfamilies may also be gay, lesbian, foster, and adoptive families.

With the aging of the population, remarriage of older persons is a growing trend. Remarriage among the elderly is distinguished from remarriage among younger persons, first and foremost, by the absence of residential children. The new marriage resembles first marriages in some aspects, because the couple can focus on their new relationship rather than on establishing a family. The elderly couple is likely to have some unique issues to deal with, such as provisions for care in case of illness and disability, financial arrangements, and the reactions of the couple's grown children and their social network (Rothstein & Erera, 1994). Further, although women were found to remarry quickly if they are young, men remarry quickly if their marriage ends when they are old (Wu, 1994).

For many adult stepchildren, the marriage of a parent is a complicated situation fraught with emotional difficulties as the existing family structure, roles, and relationships are realigned. For adult stepchildren, a parent's marriage and the upheaval it generates can also mobilize long-buried feelings of anger, betrayal, and resentment, as well as a sense of deprivation (Prilik, 1998).

FAMILY STRUCTURE

Several unique structural features of the stepfamily set it apart from the traditional nuclear family. These include their (a) being created by the joining of an additional family member, (b) being created following the disruption of previous families, (c) having residential and nonresidential family members, (d) having multiple parental figures, and (e) being composed of several distinct subsystems.

Families Created by the Joining of an Additional Family Member

Stepfamilies are systems created by the joining of a stepparent. At times, the stepparent brings his or her children from a previous marriage. Both the joining stepparent and the "absorbing" family have their own family connections, rituals, and habits, representing what Bray and Kelly (1998) describe as a merger of two cultures. Stepfamilies, at least in their early stages, comprise two distinct subsystems: the "veteran" or absorbing family members, and the "newcomer." The absorbing subsystem, usually the residential mother, may, in some cases, form a coalition with "her" children, protecting them from the newcomer (Anderson & White, 1986; Hobart, 1987; Visher & Visher, 1988).

Families Created Following the Disruption of Previous Families

Stepfamilies are created out of the disruption of previous families following divorce or widowhood. The loss of family members sets them apart from nuclear families. Remarried persons often describe a painful divorce or separation process, accompanied by feelings of revenge and hostility toward the previous spouse. On the other hand, successful stepfamilies can help heal the scars of divorce (Bray & Kelly, 1998). Hunter and Schuman (1980) identify four characteristics that accompany the loss of the previous marriage and family: (a) grieving for the for-mer family unit; (b) conflicted loyalties, with children often viewing loy-alty to the "new" family as disloyalty to the "old" family; (c) negative self-concept; and (d) a sense of threat by the "shadow" of the former spouse, including feeling jealous about the former love and marriage of the spouse. For example, Messinger (1984) observes that,

> in marriage, most people look for exclusivity of love and loyalty invested in each other. In remarriage, there can be exclusivity in the marital love of the couple, but the family life cannot be exclusive. It is necessarily linked, through the children, to the former marriage and family. Many new part-ners feel threatened by these ties. They feel that the former marriage is not finished, and they frequently want proof that the new marriage is a new be-ginning. (p. 157)

Indeed, several studies have found that remarried couples are most satis-fied when they do not adhere to expectations of loyalty and family bound-aries typical for first marriages (Bray, Berger, Siverblatt, & Hollier, 1987; Hetherington & Clingempeel, 1992; Kheshgi & Genovese, 1997).

Residential and Nonresidential Family Members

The residential family members include the parent and the stepparent, his and/or her children, and shared children born into the stepfamily. The nonresidential members include a parent and, at times, also an additional stepparent (the current spouse of the nonresidential parent), as well as siblings and stepsiblings (of the current spouse and of the nonresidential parent), and quasi-kin (former in-laws and former grandparents, aunts, uncles, etc.).

The residential family is a unique combination in which one adult—the stepparent—is not the parent of the stepchild. The different family members, although sharing the same household, may maintain different surnames, a practice that may contribute to maintaining separate identi-ties and loyalties (Messinger, 1984).

With both residential and nonresidential family members, stepfamily membership extends beyond the family's household (Furstenberg & Spanier, 1984). The physical boundaries are incongruent with the psy-chological boundaries (Pasley, 1987; Pasley & Ihinger-Tallman, 1989), a situation defined by family theorists as *family boundary ambiguity* (Boss & Greenberg, 1984; Pasley & Ihinger-Tallman, 1989).

Multiple Parental Figures

Stepfamilies usually include more than two parental figures. There are two residential parents (parent and stepparent) that perform their parental role on a daily basis, and frequently there is a nonresidential parent, who may act as a partial parent. When there is a nonresidential parent, especially if he or she is involved in the children's lives, residential parents must share parental responsibilities and authority. This may lead to conflict, especially if the respective parties have different goals and priorities (Ahrons & Wallisch, 1987; Ambert, 1986; Visher & Visher, 1983). Some relations between residential and nonresidential family members are charged with tension (Hobart, 1988; Messinger, 1984), as well as with conflicting and ambiguous expectations (Ahrons & Wallisch, 1987; Ambert, 1986). For example, Ahrons (1981) found that following divorce, both men and women tended to perceive themselves as more accommodating than their former spouses, and this attitude appears to be an important source of conflict in postdivorce relationships. Ahrons also found that most former spouses continued to interact with one another, and that former spouses who interacted most frequently were usually supportive and cooperative coparents. Over time, when coparental relationships are constructive, multiple parents can be an asset to the remarried couple and for the children who have three or four adults who love and care for them (Ahrons, 1981; Bray & Kelly, 1998).

Subsystems in the Stepfamily

With the expansion of the nuclear family system following remarriage, stepfamilies can be seen to comprise several subsystems. Here, I consider four subsystems: (a) the remarried or cohabiting couple, (b) the residential parent and his or her child, (c) the nonresidential parent and his or her nonresidential child, and (d) the siblings subsystem.

The Remarried or Cohabiting Couple (Parent and Stepparent). The remarried or cohabiting couple is the most central dyad in the stepfamily (Visher & Visher, 1983, 1988). Based on an analysis of the literature, Vemer, Coleman, Ganong, and Cooper (1989) and Ihinger-Tallman and Pasley (1997) conclude that, overall, remarried couples enjoy similar levels of marital satisfaction as first-married couples. Furthermore, the quality of the marital relationship does not appear to be related to the family's structure, to whether or not it is a stepmother or a stepfather family, or by the presence or absence of residential children (Ihinger-Tallman & Pasley, 1997; Spanier & Furstenberg, 1982; Vemer et al., 1989). What does affect marital satisfaction is the way in which the couple interacts regarding the stepparent's role (Bray, Berger, & Boethel, 1995; Bray & Kelly, 1998; Fine & Kurdek, 1995) and the couple's attitude toward the marital relationship (Ganong & Coleman, 1994; Ihinger-Tallman & Pasley, 1997). Consequently, the marital relationship is enhanced by working out mutually satisfying step relationships (Brand & Clingempeel, 1987; Bray et al., 1995; Crosbie-Burnett, 1984), as well as equitable arrangements for child care and household tasks (Guisinger, Cowan, & Schuldberg, 1989). Nevertheless, it is important that the remarried couple not be so carried away with parenthood issues that they do not make time for nurturing the marriage (Bray & Kelly, 1998; Ganong & Coleman, 1994; Hetherington & Stanley-Hagan, 2000).

Remarried women and men tend to believe that, when there is a conflict of interest between the spouse and the stepchildren, primary allegiance should be given to the spouse (Goetting, 1983; Hetherington & Jodl, 1994). Although it is important to strengthen the couple bond, it is vital that it not be at the expense of the children's needs and well-being, or of the parent-child relationship (Ganong & Coleman, 1994; Hetherington & Jodl, 1994). It is also important that the remarried couple recognize and accept that instant love between the parents and the stepchildren, as well as instant family cohesion, are not possible (Visher & Visher, 1990).

The Residential Parent and His or Her Child. The residential parent and his or her child established a relationship before the arrival of the stepparent, and share a special history and intimacy. There is a potential, especially in the early stages of the remarriage, for the stepparent to be regarded as an outsider and intruder in this subsystem (Bray & Kelly, 1998). In some families, the residential parent, usually the mother, assumes the bulk of the parenting responsibilities, a model described by Bray and Kelly (1998) as a matriarchal stepfamily.

The Nonresidential Parent and His or Her Nonresidential Child. Ahrons and Wallish (1987) coined the term *binuclear family* to describe the two households created following the parents' divorce. In most cases, the nonresidential parent is a father. However, nonresidential mothers are twice as likely to visit with their children than nonresidential fathers (Hetherington & Jodl, 1994). Nonresidential fathers are more likely to disengage from their children following divorce, and when they do visit with their children, the fathers tend to assume a recreational rather than a parental role (Furstenberg & Cherlin, 1991; Hetherington & Jodl, 1994; for additional discussion of the relationship between the nonresidential parents and the children, see Chapter 4).

In addition to the nonresidential parent, the stepfamily often includes nonresidential children. In most cases, these are the stepparent's children from a previous marriage who reside with their mother. This subsystem is often "forgotten," and frequently is the most marginal subsystem in the family (Hobart, 1987), because the children reside elsewhere and when they join the family they usually do so through visits. Nevertheless, the nonresidential children are an important part of the stepfamily. The stepfamily needs to work out how to handle the visitation of the nonresidential children to the satisfaction of all involved. The family needs to decide whether the nonresidential children should be "compensated" and spoiled during their visits, treated as guests, or integrated into the family although they do not share the family life on a daily basis.

The Siblings Subsystem. The siblings subsystem includes full siblings, half-siblings (children who share only one parent), and stepsiblings (when each adult brings children from previous relationships).

THE MAKING OF THE STEPFAMILY

The creation of any family takes time, and for stepfamilies it can take even longer. Here, I consider some of the challenges that stepfamilies face. Stepfamilies have been found to be more conflictual and less cohesive than first-marriage families (Barber & Lyons, 1994). However, this relatively low level of cohesiveness can be healthy for a well-functioning family (Hetherington & Clingempeel, 1992; Ihinger-Tallman & Pasley, 1997). As Messinger (1984) points out, in the first years of the newly formed stepfamily, "Children frequently complain, 'We're a bunch of people living together. We live in a house, not a home'" (p. 161). The task of establishing a sense of a family is complicated by the multiple parental figures, including residential and nonresidential family members, veterans, and newcomers who have joined the family. Although it had been estimated to take two to five years for stepfamilies to develop a sense of family with their own customs, rituals, and history (Dahl, Cowgill, & Asmundsson, 1987; Messinger, 1984), more recent studies assert that this process takes even longer, usually between five and seven years (Papernow, 1993). After these first years, however, successful stepfamilies appear to exhibit intimacy and satisfaction similar to first-marriage families (Berger, 1988; Ganong & Coleman, 1994; Kheshgi & Genovese, 1997).

Despite their increasing prevalence, stepparents have no clear behavioral guides, norms, or models to look to in their performance of the stepparental role (Ahrons & Wallisch, 1987; Clingempeel, Brand, & Levoli, 1984; Ihinger-Tallman & Pasley, 1987). Stepfamilies introduce such unusual roles as stepparents and stepchildren, "his" and "her" children, shared children, nonresidential parents and their new spouses, and half-brothers and half-sisters. These unusual roles, in turn, require unusual and distinctive role performances. For example, parenting is divided both between residential and nonresidential parental figures, and between parents and stepparents. These constellations necessitate sharing tasks and authority, which may expose the remarrieds to ambiguous or conflicting expectations (e.g., Ahrons, 1981; Ahrons & Wallisch, 1987; Ambert, 1986; Visher & Visher, 1983). Cherlin (1992) described this ambiguity as showing the stepfamily to be an "incomplete institution." Ihinger-Tallman and Pasley (1997), however, suggest that with the increasing prevalence and legitimacy of stepfamilies, this no longer holds true.

Family boundaries present another challenge in establishing a stepfamily. Family boundaries define who belongs in the family and what functions they perform (Minuchin, 1974). Boundary ambiguity occurs when family members are uncertain who is "in," who is "out," and who is to carry which responsibilities (Boss, 1987). Gaining clarity about boundaries is a major task for stepfamilies (Dahl et al., 1987; Larson & Allgood, 1987). Living as a family while trying to learn how to become a family, members tend to experience confused identities, split loyalties, and conflicts about affiliations and distance (Kheshgi & Genovese, 1997). They may apply inappropriate, idealized models derived from the traditional first-marriage family where roles are well defined and family members know who they are expected to be to one another.

Establishing intergenerational and interfamilial boundaries is an additional challenge. The stepfamily provides new kin ties that may replace those lost through divorce. Our society both accepts and encourages the establishment of ties with quasi-kin created out of remarriage, and the acceptance of the new partner's kin can facilitate the integration of the stepparent into the family (Berger, 1995; Furstenberg, 1981; Hetherington & Jodl, 1994).

Stress and Strengths in Stepfamilies

Stress and conflict are a normal part of reconstituting a family, especially in the early stages. Messinger (1984) observes that "stress and discomfort are bound to rise in a family that comes together in remarriage with no taken-for-granted life style, with no common history, customs and traditions" (p. 161). Stepfamilies may also experience stress related to the aftermath of divorce, with conflicts over child support and visitation. There is often a sense of overload, calling forth a great investment of effort, patience, and time (Dahl et al., 1987), as well as economic pressures. Financial problems may be more intensively felt by remarried men, who also have child support responsibilities for their nonresidential children, than for remarried women, who may be better off financially following the remarriage (Dahl et al., 1987).

In the first stages of stepfamily formation, the remarried couple may also feel discomfort at living in "someone else's home," or not having enough space for the children (Dahl et al., 1987). Each household brings to the new marriage its own previously established rules, patterns, and rituals, and this, too, may be a source of conflict (Larson & Allgood, 1987; Visher & Visher, 1988).

Close to 60% of remarriages end in divorce—about 10% higher than the rate of first divorces (Glick, 1989). Redivorce among stepfamilies may be reflective of the higher proportions of age-heterogeneous marriages (Booth & Edwards, 1992), greater willingness to leave the marriage, and relatively low commitment to make adjustments and sacrifices (Booth & Edwards, 1992; Furstenberg, 1980). As stated by Hunter and Schuman (1980), "The notion of 'and if it doesn't work out' expresses the attitudinal orientation generally found among chronically reconstituting families, just as 'till death do us apart' expressed the primary attitudinal orientation of the traditional families" (p. 447). Nevertheless, Clarke and Wilson (1994) found that although remarriages dissolve earlier than first marriages in the early years of marriage, the situation reverses with time.

The most stable stepfamilies are those in which the stepparent is a full member highly involved in raising the children (Bray & Kelly, 1998; Hetherington & Jodl, 1994). Uninvolved stepparents are regarded by the birth parent and his or her children as peripheral. In Erera's (1994) study, successful remarriages were characterized by a strong sense of partnership, togetherness, and closeness between the spouses, because in most cases the reason for remarriage was love and partnership rather than the need to share parental responsibilities.

Persistent negative characterizations of remarriage are another source of stress for stepfamilies (Ganong & Coleman, 1997). Comparisons between first-marriage families and stepfamilies are still biased by sociocultural prejudice (Zeppa & Norem, 1993). The negative stereotypes suggest that stepfamilies are deviant and deficient, and that stepfamilies are an incomplete institution (Ganong & Coleman, 1997). This stigmatic view is reflected in the belief that stepfamilies are prone to incest because they experience loosened sexual boundaries (Bray, 1995; Ganong & Coleman, 1997), as well as the persistent myth of the wicked stepmother. Research findings, however, show that biological caretakers, in both stepfamilies and biological families, were more likely to engage in serious physical abuse than stepparents were (Malkin & Lamb, 1994).

FAMILY DYNAMICS

Some members occupy a more central role in the stepfamily, and this has implications for how they interact. Hobart (1987) rank ordered family members according to their centrality or marginality as follows. The most central figure is the mother, who assumes most of the parenting responsibilities. The stepfather is the more marginal parent. The shared children are the least marginal among the children, the wife's children are more marginal than the shared children, and the stepparent's children are more marginal than the wife's children, especially if they are not residing with the stepfamily. The more marginal the child, the weaker the relations with his or her parent, as well as with the stepparent (Hobart, 1987). In addition, shared children had the most positive effects on the spousal relationships, followed by her children, and, finally, by his children (Hobart, 1987).

This section examines how the various stepfamily members relate and interact with one another as they become a family, and how position in the family, gender roles, and parenting styles influence stepfamily dynamics. I consider (a) stepparent and stepchild relationships, (b) parenting styles of stepparents, (c) the relationships between the residential parent and his or her children, (d) the relationships between nonresidential parent and his or her children, (e) sibling relationships, and (f) the relationships with grandparents and extended family members.

Stepparent and Stepchild Relationships

The centrality of the relationship between stepparents and stepchildren is reflected in the term *stepfamily* as well as in numerous studies about step relationships. Typically, the literature focuses on the difficulties involved in the stepparent role that may inhibit closeness with stepchildren. One source of difficulty is the need to share parental responsibilities not only with a spouse, but also with the nonresidential parent. Stepparents may be perceived as a threat to the exclusive bond between the nonresidential parent and his or her child, a bond established before the remarriage (Giles-Sims & Finkelhor, 1984). From the stepchildren's perspective, being raised by a stepparent while their parent lives elsewhere may cause both an idealization of the parent (Kompara, 1980) and a sense of divided loyalty. Children tend to view loyalty to the stepparents as disloyalty to the nonresidential parent (Erera, 1994; Ganong & Coleman, 1994; Hetherington & Jodl, 1994). When the nonresidential parent is deceased, the "invisible" figure of the parent may create unique complexities (Grinwald & Shabat, 1997).

The involvement of stepparents in their stepchildren's lives has been found to be influenced by the expectations and behaviors of four key persons: the stepchild, the spouse, the nonresidential parent, and the stepparent (Erera, 1996). The younger the stepchild at the time the stepparent entered the family, the closer the eventual stepparent-stepchild bond (Crosbie-Burnett, 1984; Erera, 1996; Ganong & Coleman, 1992). The child's gender does not appear to be a significant predictor of the quality of the stepfather-stepchild relationship (Marsiglio, 1992). The most important determinant of the quality of the stepfather-adolescent relationship was found to be the agreement between the stepfather and mother about raising the adolescent child (Skopin, Newman, & McKenry, 1992).

The stepmother-stepchild relationship is generally more stressful than that of the stepfather with the stepchild (e.g., Ahrons & Rodgers, 1987; Ihinger-Tallman & Pasley, 1997; Kleinmann, Kuptsch, & Koeller, 1996). A major reason for this difference is that stepmothers spend more time with their stepchildren (Ambert, 1986; Hobart, 1987). Regardless of whether they are mothers or stepmothers, they are still expected to be the primary caretakers who provide nurturance and caring (Hetherington & Stanley-Hagan, 2000; Ihinger-Tallman & Pasley, 1997; Levin, 1997), which contradicts the more distanced step role (Levin, 1997). Men are less likely to confront such a dilemma, because both their step role and male role sanction more distance from their children.

The research findings are inconclusive about the effect of relationships within a stepfamily on the well-being of the various family members. Several studies found that the quality of the step relationship is strongly associated with the satisfaction and happiness of family members (Bray & Berger, 1993; Crosbie-Burnett, 1984; Fine & Kurdek, 1995; Visher & Visher, 1989), and Hobart (1988) suggested that step and spousal relationships are mutually influenced: the step relationship influences the spousal bond, and the quality of the spousal relationship influences the step relationship.

Parenting Styles of Stepparents

Confusion abounds about the role of the stepparent. Should he or she act as a full parent, with all rights and obligations toward the stepchildren, or as a partial parent? Or, is he or she an intruding outsider who has no business "bossing" the children (Fine, Coleman, & Ganong, 1998; Ihinger-Tallman & Pasley, 1997; Marsiglio, 1992)? In contrast to this lack of stepparenting role models is the "model" of the wicked stepmother from such fairy tales as *Cinderella, Snow White,* and *Hansel and Gretel.* This motif of the cruel stepmother and the helpless children has continued to shape the current negative perceptions of the step situation, contributing to the view that step is less (Bernstein, 1994).

Five different stepparenting styles were identified in Erera's (1996) study: (a) the birth-parent style, in which the stepparent adopts a biological-parent style, viewing step and biological parenthood as identical; (b) the "supergood stepmom" style, reflecting an attempt to behave as a "supergood" mother in reaction against the wicked-stepmother stereotype; (c) the uncertain style, reflecting the stepparent's doubt and uncertainty about the "proper" behavior as a stepparent; (d) the detached style, in which the stepparent is minimally involved in the stepchildren's lives; and (e) the friendship style, in which the stepparent acts as a friend or companion to the stepchildren.

The stepparenting styles are essentially developmental (Furstenberg, 1987; Ganong & Coleman, 1992), with stepparents "trying on" different parenting styles during the marriage. In Erera's (1996) study, some step-parents parented their stepchildren on the basis of carefully thought-out plans and decisions about what they considered appropriate behavior, whereas others relied on their intuition, common sense, and previous experiences. Some stepparents felt very comfortable with the stepparent-ing style they adopted, whereas others were more critical about their parenting style.

Most studies have found that stepfather-stepdaughter relations are more conflictual and negative than stepfather-stepson relations, espe-cially when the stepfather has brought his own birth children into the household (Hetherington, 1991; Ihinger-Tallman & Pasley, 1997). Step-daughters were found to be at greater risk of behavioral and emotional problems than stepsons are (see the following section on "Implications for Child Development").

Relationships Between the Residential Parent and His or Her Children

The residential parent, and especially the mother, tends to form coali-tions with his or her children and protects them from the stepparent's care (Anderson & White, 1986; Visher & Visher, 1989). Hobart (1988) sug-gests that the mother protects her child from a position of centrality in the home, whereas the husband's relative marginality dampens his ability to protest his wife's treatment of his child. In either case, the residential parent tends to feel caught between the needs of his or her child and those of the spouse (Erera, 1994). This is especially so when the conflict involves the more central parent (i.e., the mother) and the most marginal child (i.e., the father's child; Hobart, 1987).

The stepparent may be perceived as a threat to the exclusive bond, established before the remarriage, between the parent and his or her chil-dren (Hobart, 1987; Messinger, 1984). This is further accentuated when the remarriage disrupts the sense of stability that has been achieved in the single-parent household, requiring yet another adjustment (Hobart, 1987; Messinger, 1984).

Some mothers prefer to maintain the exclusive bond with their chil-dren and establish a matriarchal stepfamily in which they assume the major responsibility for raising their children (Bray & Kelly, 1998). Oth-ers prefer to establish a more egalitarian two-parent stepfamily in which the stepfather assumes responsibility and is actively involved in parent-

ing. As long as both the parent and the stepparent share the same prefer-
ences, the remarriage is largely healthy and mutually satisfying (Bray &
Kelly, 1998).

Relationships Between the Nonresidential
Parent and His or Her Children

Visitation and the payment of child support may provide for coparental involvement with the child's well-being. It may also be a source
of conflict between the residential and nonresidential parents, as well as
between the residential parent and the stepparent. Studies of the involvement of nonresidential fathers with their children after divorce show that
both the payment of child support and the frequency of visitation
decrease over time (Dudley, 1991; Seltzer & Bianchi, 1988). About half
of the fathers do not pay any child support (King, 1994; Seltzer, 1991),
and fathers who do pay child support pay very little, particularly to their
older children (King, 1994). In 1991, the mean monthly contribution of
fathers paying child support is less than $200 (Seltzer, 1991).

Nonresidential fathers tend to have infrequent contact with their children. Only one third of the children see their father at least once a week,
and between 30% and 40% do not see their nonresidential fathers as frequently as once a year (King, 1994; National Commission in Children,
1991; Seltzer, 1991). More than half of all children who do not live with
their father have never been in their father's home (Cherlin & Furstenberg,
1994). By and large, the relationship fathers maintain with their nonresidential children can be characterized as primarily recreational, whereas
the residential parent has the primary caretaking responsibility (Bray &
Kelly, 1998; Pasley & Ihinger-Tallman, 1988).

The relationship of children to their nonresidential parents may affect
the bond between the children and their stepparents. The direction of this
influence seems to depend on such factors as the gender of the nonresidential parent, or whether the contact is measured by frequency or by
quality (Ahrons & Wallisch, 1987; Santrock & Sitterle, 1987). Several
studies found that good relations with the nonresidential parent, regardless of the stepparent's gender, support the stepparent-stepchild bond
(Pink & Wampler, 1985; Santrock & Sitterle, 1987). Others found that
the frequency of contact with the nonresidential father had no effect on
the relations between stepfather and stepchild, but that frequent contact
with the nonresidential mother was associated with less positive stepmother-stepchild relations (Clingempeel & Segal, 1986; Furstenberg,

1987). Clingempeel, Brand, and Segal (1987) suggest that close contact with the nonresidential parent reduces the child's fears that the step-parent is a parental replacement, and therefore generates a positive step relationship.

The formation of a stepfamily requires reassessment of the former coparenting to accommodate the structure of the new stepfamily (Bray, 1995; Papernow, 1993). Still, the goal is not to allow the remarriage to cause the nonresidential parent and the child to lose each other (Bray & Kelly, 1998). The newly remarried spouse may expect the stepparent to maintain a positive relationship with the children's nonresidential parent in the best interest of the children. The stepparent, on the other hand, may feel jealous or antagonistic over the children's attachment and visits with the nonresidential parent, and may prefer to maintain only minimal con-tact (Bray & Kelly, 1998). This seems to be more of a challenge if the for-mer husband remarries (Hetherington, Cox, & Cox, 1982).

The new partner and the nonresidential parent may become caught in a triangular power struggle over the children. The stepparent may want to extend warmth and guidance in a parental way to the children, which may threaten the nonresidential parent. Relatively few nonresidential parents are able to accept that the stepparent must have a role in the child's life (Messinger, 1984). Nevertheless, Ahrons (1981), Ahrons and Wallisch (1987), and Masheter's (1998) studies show that former spouses are not necessarily hostile or competitive, and in many cases they establish sup-portive and friendly coparenting relationships.

Sibling Relationships

The nature of half-sibling relationships is contingent on a host of factors, including the age and number of children, the age differences between the siblings, the stepparent's gender, whether the stepfamily is simple (stepmother or stepfather) or complex (both adults are steppar-ents), the custody arrangement, and the amount of conflict in inter-household relationships (Bernstein, 1997; Hetherington & Jodl, 1994).

Evaluating the influence of stepsiblings on the stepfamily system, Ganong and Coleman (1993a) found that the relationships were rela-tively positive, although stepsiblings' interactions were marginally less positive than those of half siblings and biological siblings. Hetherington and Jodl (1994) found that relationships between half siblings are warmer and more supportive over time, and suggest that these relationships may buffer tensions in the stepparent-stepchild relationships.

Over half of the stepfamilies have children with their new spouses, which adds half siblings to the family (Hetherington & Stanley-Hagan, 2000). The birth of a shared child no doubt affects the stepfamily's dynamics, though precisely how is in dispute (Ihinger-Tallman & Pasley, 1997). Some studies found that the birth of a child tends to strengthen the family and enhance its stability, because the new child "glues" the family together, helping it move from a binuclear constellation into a family (Erera, 1994; Hobart, 1988; Wineberg, 1992). Others, however, did not find that the birth of additional children cemented or enhanced the bond between the couple (Ganong & Coleman, 1988). Both stepfathers and stepmothers experienced the relationships with their stepchildren as less satisfying following the addition of a child into the family, especially if this was their first shared child (Kleinmann et al., 1996; MacDonald & DeMaris, 1994).

Relationships With Grandparents and Extended Family Members

The contemporary postdivorce family frequently includes three or four parental figures and several grandparents, as well as numerous other family members. The relationships with the former in-laws and their families can range from lack of contact to formal, sporadic contacts (e.g., Christmas cards), from remote and frustrating relations to close and warm relations. Closer relationships tend to occur more frequently when the former marriage ended as a result of widowhood rather than divorce, when the residential parent values the in-laws' involvement with their grandchildren, when the current remarriage is satisfying, and when the new partner, his or her children, and the new, shared children are integrated into these family relationships. In remarriage following divorce, relationships with the former in-laws may fall into two possible extremes: an uninterrupted closeness or an abrupt discontinuation resulting in total estrangement. Maintenance versus discontinuation is likely to be a result of the in-laws' reaction to the act of divorce and the quality of the previous ties. Often, those who maintain warm relationships with their former in-laws also maintain close relationships with their former spouses, though close contact with former spouses does not necessarily guarantee closeness with former in-laws (Erera, 1994).

IMPLICATIONS FOR CHILD DEVELOPMENT

Although numerous studies have documented behavioral and emotional problems experienced by children living in stepfamilies, most studies found that, on average, the adjustment of children in stepfamilies did not differ significantly from that of children in first-marriage families, especially if measured several years following divorce (Books-Gunn, 1994; Bray & Berger, 1993) and when children are raised in stepfather households with low conflict between the parents (Hanson, McLanahan, & Thomson, 1996). The meta-analysis of Amato and Keith (1991) and review of the empirical literature by Ganong and Coleman (1984, 1993b) show that children in stepfamilies resembled children in first-marriage families in psychological functioning, including self-sufficiency, dominance, psychosomatic complaints, self-esteem, self-acceptance, and well-being; behavioral measures, including delinquent behavior, associating with delinquent companions, crime involvement, drug use, and number of days absent from school; cognitive functioning, including school grades, academic achievement, and I.Q. scores; social functioning, including relationships with friends, involvement in school and community activities, and social adaptation; and general mental health, including positive attitudes toward parents, school, and marital roles.

Several studies found that the remarriage of the residential parent and living with a stepparent, particularly for boys, ameliorates the negative outcomes of divorce (Peterson & Zill, 1986; Santrock, Warshak, Lindbergh, & Meadows, 1982). The parent's remarriage decreases depression and withdrawal of both the stepsons and stepdaughters, and for stepsons, living with a stepparent also decreases their levels of antisocial behavior and impulsive or hyperactive behavior (Peterson & Zill, 1986). Living with a stepfather also improves the social development and well-being of boys, whereas living with a stepmother improves the social development of girls (Amato & Keith, 1991; Hetherington & Jodl, 1994; Santrock et al., 1982). Based on data collected from the National Survey of Families and Households, Demo and Acock (1996) found that stepfamilies report higher levels of mother-adolescent disagreement and lower levels of parental supervision and mother-adolescent interaction than both intact first-married families and single-parent families. Positive stepparent-stepchild relationships were associated with lower aggression rates for both stepsons and stepdaughters, and with higher self-esteem for stepdaughters (Clingempeel & Segal, 1986). Furthermore, children in stepfather families with low conflict did as well as children in two-parent households (Hanson et al., 1996).

On the negative side, children in stepfamilies scored lower than children in first-marriage families in their general sense of psychological well-being and in their reported closeness to their parents (Ganong & Coleman, 1984; Hetherington & Jodl, 1994). Remarriage, parental separation, and divorce increase the risk of adolescents' depression, stress, and suicidal behavior (Hetherington & Jodl, 1994; Rubenstein, Halton, Kasten, Rubin, & Stechler, 1998). Young children (aged 6 to 8) in stepfamilies manifested more behavioral problems, more stress, and lower competency than children in first-marriage families did (Amato & Keith, 1991; Bray & Berger, 1993). Children of stepfamilies tend to leave their homes sooner than children from first-marriage or single-parent families do (Aquilino, 1991; Kiernan, 1992; Mitchell, Wiser, & Burch, 1989), possibly trying to avoid conflictual relationships in the stepfamily (Aquilino, 1991; Mitchell et al., 1989).

Usually, stepfather families have more negative effects on girls than on boys (Ihinger-Tallman & Pasley, 1997). Compared with boys, girls tend to have more difficulty interacting with stepfathers (Hetherington & Jodl, 1994; Vuchinich, Hetherington, Vuchinich, & Clingempeel, 1991), are more withdrawn (Vuchinich et al., 1991), and are more likely to have behavioral problems (Lee, Burkan, Zimiles, & Ladewski, 1994). Garnefski and Diekstra (1997) found that girls from stepfamilies had lower self-esteem, more symptoms of anxiety and loneliness, more depressed mood, more suicidal thoughts, and more suicide attempts than adolescents from both one-parent and two-parent first-marriage families, and more so than boys in stepfamilies.

Comparing boys from stepparent and single-parent families, we find that boys from stepparent families had more emotional problems and a higher rate of suicide attempts (Garnefski & Diekstra, 1997). Furthermore, Pagani, Tremblay, Vitaro, Kerr, and McDuff (1998) found that boys between the ages 12 and 15 raised in stepfamilies are at greater risk for theft and fighting than their peers in first-marriage families are.

Generally, the younger the stepchildren at the time the parent remarries, the better the children adjust to the stepfamily (Bray, 1992; Hetherington, 1989; Visher & Visher, 1993). Though young adults who were raised in divorced and stepfamilies may exhibit prolonged behavioral, emotional, and interpersonal problems (Amato & Keith, 1991; Hetherington et al., 1982; Hetherington & Stanley-Hagan, 2000), the negative impact of remarriage usually occurs in its early stages and is considerably reduced when the adjustment of children preceding the marital transition is controlled (Block, Block, & Gjerde, 1986, 1988; Cherlin et al., 1991; Hetherington & Jodl, 1994). Over time, most children are well adapted and well functioning (Hetherington & Stanley-Hagan, 2000). Overall, the average differences between children of divorced and stepfamilies and children of first-married families are small, but with a substantial overlap between the two groups and considerable diversity of outcome within each family type (Amato & Keith, 1991; Hetherington & Stanley-Hagan, 2000). Finally, given the small effect sizes and the diversity in outcomes, it is questionable whether social scientists should continue to investigate children's outcomes as resulting from different family structure (Amato, 1994a).

IMPLICATIONS FOR POLICY AND PRACTICE

Marriage does not in itself confer rights or responsibilities to stepparents, and state laws vary considerably on matters pertaining to child support, visitation, and eligibility for public benefits (Austin, 1993). The erosion of the social safety net, stagnating wages for the less-skilled jobs, and the passage of the 1996 Personal Responsibility and Work Opportunity Reconciliation Act (PRWORA, Public Law 104-193) ending welfare entitlements place additional stress on all low-income and poor families, including stepfamilies.

Helping professionals are not always well prepared to deal with the unique issues in stepfamily relationships (McIvor, 1998). Examining what parents found helpful and unhelpful in stepfamily therapy, Visher, Visher, and Pasley (1997) found that nearly half (48.6%) of those who found therapy unhelpful reported the problem as the therapist's lack of knowledge of stepfamily dynamics and issues. Therapy with remarried couples should address the emotional consequences of separation, the presence of children in the new relationship, finances, and dealing with the lack of guidelines and role models for stepfamilies. It should be noted, however, that conflict is equally present in both successful and dysfunctional marriages. Conflict is an inevitable part of human association that keeps social units as disparate as nations and families from collapse (Galvin & Brommel, 1982). Moreover, conflict can be constructive. From a conflict perspective, the focus is not on the differences, but

rather on the ability of family members to deal with them (Sprey, 1969).
If we alter our assumptions about the role of conflict in the family and
remarriage, we could help this new family system survive with fewer
frustrations and expectations that are more realistic.

Stepfamilies need reassurance that it takes time to develop a sense of
cohesion, integration, and emotional closeness between family members
(Bray & Kelly, 1998; Hetherington, 1991). Social workers and family
counselors should view the new family pattern as a work in progress in
order to appreciate fully what is happening to the family and to evaluate
the consequences. Stepfamily couples could benefit from an understanding of the relationship between current and former spouses (Gold,
Bubenzer, & West, 1993). In addition, children should be permitted to
mourn the absence of the nonresidential parent at their own pace
(Kompara, 1980).

It is important to create physical space and permission for privacy and
time alone for the respective members of the newly blended family. It is
also important that the couple discuss their mutual expectations regarding household and financial arrangements. The couple may wish to consider making a prenuptial agreement regarding their respective posses-
sions and savings, and a will stipulating their wishes about inheritance.

The stepparent needs to allow for the gradual process of gaining the
access and trust of the stepchildren, rather than choosing one of the less
constructive measures of either forcing one's presence, "invading" the
family unit, or being a detached outsider. Tension and conflicts with the
stepchild may ensue when the stepparent attempts to act as if he or she is
the parent. Stepparents should probably avoid assuming total parental
responsibilities, particularly when the stepchild is older and has a close
and warm relationship with the nonresidential parent; when the spouse is
overly concerned about the step relationship; or too early in the remarriage (Visher & Visher, 1990).

On the other hand, stepparent detachment may lead to animosity and
alienation between stepchild and stepparent, and this can threaten the
entire stepfamily. In view of the research suggesting that the detached
stepparent may be motivated by negative feelings toward the stepchild,
stepparents should attempt to acknowledge and deal constructively with
these negative feelings.

Though the wicked-stepmother stereotype cannot be totally ignored,
stepmothers who react against it by attempting to be "supergood" may
undermine their parenting role by failing to set appropriate limits or

enforce necessary discipline. This can, in turn, result in emotional burn-out and resentment toward both stepchild and spouse, who may be held responsible for the stepmother's overexertion. Stepmothers must acknowledge this cultural stereotype, but they would do well to resist reacting against it (Bernstein, 1994).

Although norms do appear to be developing regarding the stepparent role (Ihinger-Tallman & Pasley, 1997), stepparents, their spouses, and the stepchildren should seek to clarify their expectations of each other. The stepparent, parent, and children may wish also to acknowledge openly their respective feelings toward the nonresidential parent. These may include unresolved feelings of loss, anger, abandonment, rejection, divided loyalties, and the psychological splitting between "good" parent and "bad" stepparent. Following this mutual clarification of feelings, stepparents and stepchildren should be encouraged gradually to estab-lish a parent-child dyad. A repertoire of shared activities may also facili-tate a bonding between stepparents and stepchildren.

Though some stepparenting styles may seem more effective than oth-ers, there is no one stepparenting style that suits all. Stepparents should be encouraged to explore the parenting style that best suits their own per-sonality, the expectations of their spouse and stepchildren, the stage in the remarriage, the age and gender of the stepchildren, and the nature of the bond between the stepchildren and the nonresidential parent (Bray & Kelly, 1998; Erera, 1996; Ganong & Coleman, 1994; Visher & Visher, 1990). Family life educators, social workers, and counselors can discuss alternative stepparenting styles with stepfamilies, helping stepparents avoid the least beneficial alternatives. Such discussions can be most effective with support groups for remarried couples where the facilitator can use modeling, role play, simulation, and the processing of real-life situations.

Several studies show that the degree of stepfather involvement in parenting the stepchildren tends to vary with the stage of the stepfamily, with stepfathers being less involved with their stepchildren in early re-marriage (Bray & Berger, 1993; Cherlin & Furstenberg, 1994; Schwebel, Fine, & Renner, 1991). This partial involvement is constructive and desirable (Bray et al., 1987; Hetherington & Clingempeel, 1992), and should be encouraged.

It is important to encourage the remarried couple to cultivate and nourish their marriage through shared activities, including time away from the children.

Following remarriage, children and grandparents may sometimes be deprived of their relationship, even forbidden to see one another. Culturally, it is essential that we change our attitudes to make it possible for divorced persons who remarry to accept the reality that only the partners are divorced, not the children or grandparents. In addition, we must move beyond the view that the only "real" family is the birth family. Remarried partners come to each other with their own families. For the new group to coalesce into a family, the extended kin, past and present, must have their place in the remarried family (Ganong & Coleman, 1994).

IMPLICATIONS FOR RESEARCH

To this day, the extensive research on stepfamilies has almost exclusively examined white, middle-class stepfamilies. Future studies should be based on samples more reflective of the U.S. population and of the diversity to be found among stepfamilies. There is a great need for research on stepfamilies from culturally diverse backgrounds, whether formally married or not, especially African Americans, Hispanics, and immigrant populations.

I know of no study that has examined the association between children's specific behaviors and stepparents' parental involvement. In addition, the influence of the spouse, in his or her capacity as a parent, on the stepparent-stepchild bond needs further study. The developmental process of adopting different stepparental roles, although frequently mentioned (e.g., Ganong & Coleman, 1994; Miles, 1984; Visher & Visher, 1990), also needs further examination. Longitudinal studies are needed that examine changes in the stepfamilies over time. We also need to explore more purposively the unique characteristics of well-functioning stepfamilies (Coleman & Ganong, 1997).

Studies of stepfamilies following widowhood and of remarriage among the elderly, and of partners who differ considerably in age, are also needed. Additional studies are needed on remarriage with adopted and foster children, gay and lesbian stepfamilies, and comparisons between first, second, and serial remarriages. Finally, we need more studies on the effects of inconsistent policies on the rights of stepchildren to various benefits.

DISCUSSION QUESTIONS

1. How do you account for the increasing prevalence of stepfamilies today? How and why have the reasons for stepfamily formation changed today, as compared with earlier times?

2. Given the fact that stepfamilies have become so common, how do you account for the lack of clear stepparenting models for remarried couples to emulate and draw on in forming the new family? What are the implications of this lack of stepparenting guidelines? What could be done to correct this situation?

3. In what ways are stepfamilies similar to and different from traditional, first-marriage families? Do you think such comparisons are valid or useful? Why or why not?

4. How do socially prescribed gender roles influence the way stepparents parent?

5. What challenges does a newly formed stepfamily face? What issues might they confront? What can they do to facilitate the transition to becoming a family?

6. What advice would you offer a newly remarried couple about parenting the stepchildren? About maintaining relationships with former spouses? What information would you want to know before offering your suggestions?

SUGGESTIONS FOR FURTHER READING

Ganong, L. H., & Coleman, M. (1994). *Remarried family relationships.* Thousand Oaks, CA: Sage.

Messinger, L. (1984). *Remarriage: A family affair.* New York: Plenum.

Pasley, K., & Ihinger-Tallman, M. (Eds.). (1994). *Stepparenting: Issues in theory, research and practice.* Westport, CT: Guilford.

Visher, E. B., & Visher, J. S. (1988). *Old loyalties, new loyalties: Therapeutic strategies with stepfamilies.* New York: Brunner/Mazel.

Chapter 6

LESBIAN AND GAY FAMILIES

Lesbians and gay men are still fighting for acceptance and recognition for a very basic human right: that of sexual orientation. It is only recently that a significant number of lesbian and gay families have come out of the closet, that lesbian and gay couples are claiming the right to live as a family, and that lesbian and gay couples have openly given birth to, adopted, and fostered children, all within the lesbian or gay family unit.

Lesbians and gay families have received little attention in the social work and family studies literature. When discussed in the gender, lesbian and gay, and queer studies literature, it has often been to refute negative stereotypes, addressing such issues as the impact gay and lesbian parents have on their children's sexual, psychological, and social development (Belcastro, Gramlich, Nicholson, Price, & Wilson, 1993; Falk, 1989; Golombok & Tasker, 1996; Victor & Fish, 1995), and the rights of lesbian mothers to legal custody, visitations, and adoptions (Brienza, 1996; Duran-Aydintug & Causey, 1996; Erlichman, 1988; Rubenfeld, 1994; Sears, 1994). Furthermore, attention has been focused on the more pressing issues of oppression, coming out, and living in a homophobic society (Laird, 1993; Neisen, 1990; Oles, Black, & Cramer, 1999).

Though reliable data are lacking, it is estimated that as many as 80% of gay men and lesbians live as couples and in families (Laird, 1993), and that about 3 million gay men and lesbians in the United States are parents (Allen, 1997). Yet gay and lesbian families are rarely mentioned in the literature. This omission implies that the terms *gay, lesbian,* and *family* are, by definition, mutually exclusive, and that their families are not "real" families.

Gay men and lesbians become parents through a variety of means. These include having a child while in a heterosexual relationship, or through adoption, donor insemination, or foster care as a single parent or as a lesbian or gay couple (Pies, 1989). In those instances where a child is born into a heterosexual relationship and the mother or father subsequently enters into a relationship with another woman or man, the partner becomes a stepparent. The majority of lesbian and gay families raising children are lesbian stepfamilies (Lewin, 1993). However, the numbers of lesbian and gay couples electing to have children together is steadily increasing (Flaks, Ficher, Masterpasqua, & Joseph, 1995; Pies, 1989).

Lacking a standard terminology to describe these various family arrangements, I refer to families in which a child is born in the context of a previous heterosexual relationship, followed by the parent's forming a gay or a lesbian couple, as *lesbian/gay stepfamilies*. Families in which a child is born or added to an existing gay or lesbian relationship are referred to as *coparent lesbian or gay families* (see Rae, 1995). Another note about terminology: Strictly speaking, there are no lesbian or gay families, only families with lesbian and gay members. When I refer to lesbian or gay families, this should be understood as a shorthand way of saying "families headed by lesbians or gay men."

HISTORICAL BACKGROUND AND THE SOCIAL-CULTURAL CONTEXT

Historically, homosexuality has been regarded as a deviance, as a sin, and as a form of mental illness (Cabaj, 1998). Gay men and lesbians have been burned, beheaded, institutionalized, subjected to lobotomy and electroshock treatment, and placed in concentration camps during the Holocaust (Laird, 1993). In recent years, they have been subject to violent hate crimes, discrimination, isolation, humiliation, and stigmatization (e.g., DePoy & Noble, 1992; DiPlacido, 1998; LaSala, 1998). Their families of origin may disown them. Their relationships are not legally sanctioned, and they are under threat of having their children taken away. They lack many of the protections and benefits that heterosexual persons take for granted (Laird, 1993). Nevertheless, gay and lesbian families have always existed, though not as visibly as today.

Despite deeply rooted prejudices against lesbians and gays, such attitudes are not universal. For example, in Afro-Caribbean religions, such as Santeria, gays and lesbians are regarded as having greater spiritual potential (Morales, 1996). In the past, in ancient Greece and Rome, same-sex sexuality was openly practiced among men. In some Mexican indigenous religions, Inez is a goddess that makes love to women (Morales, 1996). Similarly, several gods in Buddhism are represented as androgynous, and the Swiss psychologist Carl Jung, who was influenced by Buddhism, argued that all people are both masculine and feminine.

Until very recently, the study of gay men and lesbians focused on the etiology of homosexuality, and on whether or not gay and lesbian individuals, lesbian and gay couples, lesbian and gay families and their children are as mentally healthy and socially well adapted as heterosexuals. This reflected a view of lesbian and gays as being unnatural, dysfunctional, and pathological in some ways. The belief in a deviant etiology drew from a variety of sources, including psychoanalysis, learning theory, genetics, and family theories. Psychoanalytical theory regarded homosexuality as an unresolved Oedipal or Electra complex, as a masculine protest (for gay men), or as confused identity (for lesbians). Other theories viewed homosexuality as the result of inappropriate role models; of being raised in a family constellation of a weak father and a dominant mother (for gay men); or of genetic, chemical, hormonal, and brain disorders (Green, 1982; Laird, 1993). These theories made it impossible to regard gay and lesbian parenting as a normal and healthy option (Green, 1987). In a heterosexist world, virtually all public displays of sexuality or family life are depicted with heterosexuality in mind (Green, 1987).

A major change has occurred over the past three decades, both in lesbian and gay consciousness and in the way society views gay men and lesbians. This change has largely been the result of lesbian and gay activism, as reflected in the lesbian and gay liberation movement, symbolized by the 1969 Stonewall riots in which gay men fought back against police who harassed them, and in the activities of organizations like Queer Nation and Act-Up. In addition, the AIDS epidemic has brought gays and lesbians together in a common cause (Laird, 1993).

These developments have brought forth a growing lesbian and gay culture and greater visibility of lesbian and gay families as evidenced by their inclusion in films, television shows, and professional books on family life, and in the behavior of lesbians and gays themselves. There has been increasing visibility of lesbian and gay cultural symbols, organizations, periodicals, newspapers, plays, and activities like the Gay Pride marches. Nevertheless, we have also witnessed increased physical violence and hate crimes against lesbians and gays, challenges to lesbian and gay people's right to parent, and the denial of legal protections that are taken for granted by heterosexuals (Allen, 1997). There has also been an increase in state antigay legislative initiatives, usually disguised as promoting "family values" (Hartman, 1996).

LEGAL AND POLICY ISSUES

Most of the discussions about legal and policy issues relate to lesbian mothers, because most of the families are lesbian rather than gay. The majority of lesbian mothers have custody of children born within a heterosexual marriage. In contrast, gay fathers who had children within a heterosexual marriage, and then later divorced, usually do not have custody. In this sense, gay men and lesbians are like heterosexual men and women in that custody is usually awarded to the mother.

Courts and judges are influenced, like all of us, by dominant social attitudes that stigmatize lesbian mothers. Although most lesbian mothers are awarded custody of children born within a marital relationship, many are denied custody based on the discriminatory assumption that their sexual orientation renders them unfit for motherhood (Falk, 1989; Patterson & Redding, 1996; Polikoff, 1986; Rubenfeld, 1994). Rand, Graham, and Rawlings (1982) found that the courts repeatedly deny a mother custody and visitation if she expresses her lesbianism through involvement or cohabitation with a female partner, is affiliated with a lesbian community, or discloses her sexual orientation to her children. A Florida judge awarded custody of an 11 year old girl to her father, who had been convicted of murdering his former wife over a child custody dispute and who allegedly molested the daughter of the wife that he killed, instead of awarding the custody to the girl's lesbian mother (Brienza, 1996). Interviews with a sample of district court judges and other legal service professionals found that, in many cases, judges decide against lesbian mothers solely based on their sexual orientation without taking any evidence into account (Duran-Aydintug & Causey, 1996). Like lesbians, gay men also face discrimination in court proceedings (Sears, 1994). However, gay men encounter less discrimination than lesbians do, probably because in most cases they are requesting visitation rather than custody, which may appear to judges as less threatening.

Four states have laws deeming gays and lesbians unfit to be parents (Henry, 1993). Only one jurisdiction, the District of Columbia, bans the use of sexual orientation as the basis for custody rulings (Rubenfeld, 1994). Despite continuing discrimination, the situation is slowly changing. There are more and more court decisions that uphold gay and lesbian rights. For example, a Brooklyn family court judge, granting custody to a lesbian stepmother, ruled that sexual orientation and race are not valid reasons to determine which nonrelative of a child should have custody (Brienza, 1996).

One area in which discrimination remains firmly entrenched is that of marriage. Gay and lesbian couples are not legally able to marry in the United States. However, in July 2000, Vermont adopted a Civil Unions Law establishing a legal framework parallel to marriage, whereby same-sex couples can go to their town clerk to obtain a civil union license, just as different-sex couples obtain marriage licenses. The civil union is certified by a justice of the peace, judge, or member of the clergy, as is the case with marriage. Partners seeking to dissolve their unions will have to go through the family court, just as divorcing couples do, although their breakup will be called a dissolution rather than a divorce. Civil union partners gain all of the benefits the state confers through marriage, such as making medical decisions on behalf of partners or the right to inheritance. Stopping just short of actual marriage, this law still puts Vermont far ahead of any other state in recognizing commitments between lesbian and gay couples. In 1999, the Hawaii Supreme Court upheld a 1998 amendment to the state constitution against gay and lesbian marriages, although lesbian and gay couples in Hawaii can share medical insurance and state pensions. More than 30 states have banned same-sex marriages; some have added laws specifying that they will not recognize same-sex unions legal in other states. For example, in response to the Vermont law, the top policy-making body of the U.S. Presbyterian Church has approved an amendment to the church's constitution forbidding ministers from conducting same-sex unions. Similarly, the federal Defense of Marriage Act (DOMA), which defines marriage as a union only between one man and one woman, prohibits states from being forced to recognize same-sex marriages (Allen, 1997).

The Netherlands legislature provided for same-sex couples to marry in civil ceremony in 1998, and France legalized same-sex unions with passage of the Civil Solidarity Pact, or Pacte Civil de Solidariti (PACS), in 1999. Though it will be much easier to dissolve PACS than a marriage and though the dissolution will not require a lawyer, unmarried French couples, including same-sex couples, will be able to register unions at courthouses and get most of the rights of traditional married couples. Under the French legislation, after three years of their civil union, unmarried couples may file tax forms jointly and claim rights of married couples, such as simultaneous vacation time from employers and lighter inheritance taxes (Alternatives to Marriage Project, 2000). Several countries, including Denmark, Norway, Iceland, and Sweden, permit registered partnerships that extend to the partners almost all the legal provisions relevant to married couples, including inheritance (Goransson, 1998). Similar legislation is currently under consideration in Australia, Brazil, Canada, the Czech Republic, Spain, and Switzerland (Goransson, 1998).

Nevertheless, gays and lesbians cannot marry or form legal unions in most of the world and the United States, and so there is no divorce, nor is there a body of law pertaining to separation, custody, visitation, or child support of lesbian and gay stepparents and coparents. This policy vacuum requires the separating couple to handle a complicated issue, at a time of distress, by improvising their own settlement (Hartman, 1996).

Another issue coming before the courts is adoption. Despite the solid evidence that children of lesbian and gay parents do not differ from children of heterosexual parents in their academic, social, and psychological functioning or sexual orientation, continued debate about the morality of homosexuality has kept most public adoption agencies from formulating explicit policies regarding adoption by lesbians and gays. To date, only three U.S. states—Rhode Island, New York, and New Mexico—have legislation or regulations permitting gay and lesbian adoptions, and two states—Florida and New Hampshire—explicitly prohibit gays and lesbians from qualifying as foster or as adoptive parents. Although Nevada's regulations permit the placement of children with gay and lesbian individuals, state law does not allow adoption by unmarried couples (Reilly, 1996).

Most of the other states have a "don't ask, don't tell" policy with regard to adoption by lesbians and gays (Hartman, 1996), and agencies yield considerable discretion to caseworkers on whether to grant lesbians and gays the right to adopt (Falk, 1989). If gays and lesbians are considered as adoptive or foster parents, their application is usually assessed according to different criteria than those applied to heterosexual applicants. This lack of specific policies contributes to inconsistent and often unjust decision making (Reilly, 1996).

Except in Connecticut, gays and lesbians may adopt a child only as single persons, regardless of whether they are coupled or not (Hartman, 1996). This hypocrisy forces coupled gays and lesbians who wish to adopt or foster a child to deny the true nature of their relationship and remain closeted, living in fear of being found out (Muzio, 1996). If the lesbian or gay partner wishes to adopt the child later, the procedure is called second-parent adoption. Except for a few states that officially prohibit placing children in homes where unmarried adults are living together (e.g., Arkansas, Florida, Utah, and Mississippi), in most U.S. states, these policies against second-parent adoptions are not official laws. Though this ban includes unmarried opposite-sex couples, it clearly targets gay and lesbian parents.

In May 2000, the Connecticut legislature approved a bill allowing for second-parent adoptions by unmarried partners, becoming the first state to do so and putting it ahead of Denmark, Norway, and Sweden. Although these countries permit adoption by unmarried, nongay adults living together, they do not allow joint legal adoption by gay or lesbian couples (J. Trost, personal communication, November 11, 1998). Second-parent adoption is especially significant in that it provides legal recognition, rights, and security to these families.

HOMOPHOBIA, STEREOTYPES, AND DISCRIMINATION

Lesbian and gay families are subjected to homophobic stereotypes, heterosexism, prejudice, and discrimination (Rothblum, 1985). The most common prejudices have to do with raising children—that children raised in lesbian and gay families are likely to be emotionally harmed, molested, or impaired in their gender-role development (Falk, 1989). Such prejudices are expressed in a legal system that denies lesbian and gay parents child custody and visitation rights (e.g., Brienza, 1996; Duran-Aydintug & Causey, 1996; Rubenfeld, 1994; Sears, 1994), and in persistent beliefs, contrary to empirical evidence, that being raised in a lesbian and gay family will produce lesbian and gay children (Belcastro et al., 1993; Falk, 1989; Golombok & Tasker, 1996; Green, 1982; Tasker & Golombok, 1995). Homophobic stereotypes also assume that being raised in a lesbian and gay family will hinder the child's psychological development and social adjustment (Belcastro et al., 1993; Gibbs, 1988; Victor & Fish, 1995). Lesbian mothers are considered unfit, emotionally unstable, and unable to assume a maternal role (DiLapi, 1989; Falk, 1989; Gibbs, 1988; Robson, 1992), and lesbian and gay couples are thought to be less stable than heterosexual couples, and therefore not likely to provide a stable family life (Gallagher, 1993; McVinney, 1988). Other common beliefs are that gay men molest children; that a child needs two parents, a male and a female; that boys need a male role model in order to develop into healthy adults; and that it is not fair to children to be raised by gays (DiLapi, 1989; Hargaden & Llewellin, 1996; Wright, 1998).

Anti–lesbian and gay stereotypes view lesbians and gays as deviant, unnatural, and immoral (DePoy & Noble, 1992; Hargaden & Llewellin, 1996), as violating acceptable gender roles, and as being inferior altogether (Madon, 1997). Fear of AIDS has generated additional stigma, attributed mostly to gay men. Not until 1973 did the American Psychiatric Association (APA) remove homosexuality from its list of psychiatric disorders. Prejudice and homophobia are not limited to laws and social policies: They are also expressed by family members, friends, and colleagues.

Behaviorally, these prejudices, based on homophobia, are expressed in anti–lesbian and gay violence (DiPlacido, 1998) and in derogatory nicknames (Morales, 1996). Gay and lesbian couples experience countless forms of discrimination at the workplace, in housing, in the military, in immigration policies, and in laws criminalizing sexual contact between people of the same sex (sodomy laws), as well as in the discriminatory policies of schools and social welfare and health agencies (DePoy & Noble, 1992; Hartman, 1996; LaSala, 1998; Rivera, 1991).

Discrimination and intolerance are usually greater in white suburban environments, and in communities and cultures that place high value on religion and segregated gender roles. Under such circumstances, gays and lesbians tend to be more closeted and less visible, and do not develop a distinct lesbian and gay culture (Morales, 1996; Patterson, 1996).

Gays and lesbians who are from ethnic and racial groups are a minority within a minority (Morales, 1996). In addition to experiencing homophobic prejudice from the mainstream, heterosexual society, they are often subject to discrimination from their ethnic communities. Ethnic minorities tend to exert pressure for unity and homogeneity as a means of surviving oppression. In doing so, they tend to reject, stigmatize, and oppress lesbians and gays of color (Walters, 1988). In addition to being discriminated against because of their sexual orientation, lesbians and gays of color are often also subject to racism within the lesbian and gay community (Carrier, 1992; Icard, 1986; Morales, 1996; Walters, 1988). The gay liberation movement has been predominantly white, middle class, and Anglo. Consequently, lesbians and gays of color are less likely to have the same social support that is available to white gays and lesbians (Walters, 1988). Relatively, urban, white, educated, middle-class gay men experience lower levels of discrimination and homophobia than ethnic minorities and less educated working-class gay men (Laird, 1993).

FAMILY STRUCTURE

Most of the literature on lesbian and gay family life addresses lesbians rather than gay men. This is probably because most of the children raised in gay or lesbian families are raised by lesbian couples. Consistent with this thrust, I focus primarily on lesbian rather than gay families.

Though this section considers the unique aspects of the gay/lesbian family, it should be noted that lesbian and gay families resemble heterosexual families in many ways, particularly in relations with partners, raising children, and interactions with the extended family and community (Green & Bozett, 1991). Studies show that lesbian and heterosexual families are similar in the quality of parents' relationship (Flaks et al., 1995), in parenting experiences (Green, Mandel, Hotvedt, Gray, & Smith, 1986), and in childrearing attitudes and lifestyle (Kirkpatrick, 1987). For both lesbian and heterosexual mothers, motherhood is the most salient factor in the mothers' identity (Mitchell, 1996).

Here, I discuss three significant structural features of gay and lesbian families: (a) being step- and coparent lesbian and gay families, (b) having residential and nonresidential family members, and (c) the lack of legal marriage.

Step- and Coparent Lesbian and Gay Families

The two major types of gay and lesbian families are step- and coparent families. In lesbian and gay stepfamilies, the children were conceived in previous heterosexual marriages, whereas in coparent families, the children join an existing lesbian or gay couple. To date, most lesbian and gay families are lesbian stepfamilies (Allen, 1997), and, with few exceptions (e.g., Flaks et al., 1995; Mitchell, 1996), most of the existing research is on this family structure.

Lesbian and gay stepfamilies are like heterosexual stepfamilies in key aspects (Erera & Fredricksen, 1999; Wright, 1998). Like heterosexual stepfamilies, lesbian and gay stepfamilies are systems created by the joining of a stepparent to a single-parent household. The joining stepparent and the previously established family often constitute, at least in their early stages, two distinct subsystems: the veteran or absorbing family members, and the newcomer (Erera & Fredricksen, 1999). These two subsystems may be further divided by the possible formation of a coalition between the residential birth parent and her or his birth children, "protecting" them from the stepparent (Kirkpatrick, 1987; Wright, 1998).

In both gay and lesbian stepfamilies, children may have difficulty accepting the stepparent (Bigner, 1996; Kirkpatrick, 1987), and the stepparent may feel excluded (Crosbie-Burnett & Helmbrecht, 1993). The stepparent usually needs to define his or her role as a parent. Often, the stepparent develops unique parental roles based on his or her special strengths and characteristics, the interests of the child, and on the expectations of the biological parent (Wright, 1998). In many cases, the stepparent and the biological parents need to negotiate power and control issues related to parenting (Crosbie-Burnett & Helmbrecht, 1993; Wright, 1998). Furthermore, lesbian and gay stepparents and, to some extent, coparents lack clearly defined behavioral guides about their relationships with their partner's children (Muzio, 1993; Patterson & Chan, 1997; Rohrbaugh, 1992). This is reflected in the lack of agreed-on terms for the lesbian and gay step- and coparents (Hare & Richards, 1993; Muzio, 1993; Pies, 1989).

In addition to having to establish parental roles, the stepparent has no legal rights with respect to the child. Consequently, regardless of whether or not the stepparent was actively involved in raising the child, if the couple separates, the court usually denies the stepparent custody and visitation rights. Nevertheless, in some cases courts have granted stepparents parental rights. For example, a New Jersey Superior Court judge granted a former stepmother joint custody because she "has been able to show that she stands in the shoes of a parent to the child and should be accorded the status of parent" ("Lesbian Ex-Partners," 1998).

Lesbian coparent families are formed through the conception of one or both of the lesbian mothers, usually through donor insemination, adoption, or foster care (Pies, 1989; Rohrbaugh, 1992). This lesbian family style is becoming more common (Flaks et al., 1995; Hare, 1994; Pies, 1989). Coparent families of gay men are usually formed through adoption or fostering. At times, there may be a surrogate mother who bears a child conceived using a sperm of one of the gay partners. Gay men may also conceive and raise children jointly with a woman with whom the man is not sexually involved. For example, a gay male couple and a lesbian couple might undertake parenthood together, with a sperm of one of the men used to inseminate one of the women (Patterson & Chan, 1999). For both gay men and lesbians, having children within the context of an existing lesbian and gay relationship is on the increase (Patterson, 1995).

In some gay and lesbian coparent families, both parents are biological parents, although not of the same child. For example, both lesbian mothers can conceive a child through a donor, or both gay fathers can be donors of children born to a surrogate mother. Similarly, children in coparent families can be siblings related by blood, half brothers and sisters, or biologically unrelated.

Coparent lesbian and gay families resemble in many ways first-married heterosexual families, because the addition of the child signifies a transition from being a couple to becoming a family (Hare & Richards, 1993). Nevertheless, in first-married heterosexual families, both parents are biological parents, whereas in gay and lesbian families, at least one parent (the coparent) is generally not a biological parent. In other coparent lesbian and gay families, neither of the residential parents are biological parents. This is true of adoptive and foster families, the most common type of coparent families involving gay men.

Residential and Nonresidential Family Members

In addition to residential family members, both lesbian and gay stepfamilies and coparent families also include nonresidential family members. In lesbian and gay stepfamilies, as in heterosexual stepfamilies, the nonresidential member is the former spouse or partner of the biological parent, usually a father. The nonresidential father may be involved in the lives of the children through visitation (Hare & Richards, 1993). Lesbian mothers tend to have more congenial relations with their previous husbands than divorced heterosexual mothers (Hare & Richards, 1993; Kirkpatrick, 1987). Nevertheless, documentation of custody and visitation trials involving lesbian mothers suggests that, at least in some cases, fathers try to prevent the lesbian mother from having custody and deny her visitation rights (Brienza, 1996; Duran-Aydintug & Causey, 1996; Sears, 1994). These cases suggest that, as with stepfamilies, visitation and custody may generally be an arena for antagonism, tension, and competitiveness between the lesbian mother and her former spouse. Lesbian mothers are vulnerable in this because of the discrimination they face.

In contrast to stepfamilies, in coparent lesbian and gay families, the nonresidential parent is often a donor. The donor may be unknown, a friend, or an acquaintance. The literature on heterosexual families suggests that when the nonresidential parent is inaccessible, the children may develop fantasies about the father, idealize him (Kompara, 1980), or view him as a "parent in the shadows" or as a ghost member of the family (Kadushin & Martin, 1988; Silin, 1996).

In foster and adoptive lesbian and gay families, the nonresidential family members are the child's parents. Again, these biological parents may be involved in the family's life through visits with the child, or they may be inaccessible or unknown.

Lack of Legal Marriage

By not being able to marry, lesbian and gay families are often viewed as a cohabiting couple rather than a family (Gallagher, 1993), and, based on heterosexist assumptions, the bond between the partners is expected to be less stable than in a heterosexual relationship (McVinney, 1988). Not having the protection of legal marriage or other forms of legally recognized union denies the lesbian and gay partners such rights as joint tax filing, joint property rights, dependent social security benefits, and custody and visitation rights in case of separation (Pies, 1989; Rohrbaugh, 1992).

Gay and lesbian couples may face a denial of their relationship from their families, who may refuse to acknowledge the partner and may be antagonistic toward him or her, even after many years (Laird 1993; LaSala, 1998). In such cases, the partner may feel left out, and the couple may feel that the relationship is neither acknowledged nor sanctioned.

Some studies find that gay and lesbian couples often develop long-lasting stable relations (Bigner, 1996; Mackey, O'Brien, & Mackey, 1997; Weston, 1994), and that lesbians are deeply committed to creating strong families, emphasizing emotional closeness, love, and security (Hare, 1994; Rothblum, 1985). Others suggest that lesbian and gay couples break up more frequently than heterosexual couples (e.g., Gallagher, 1993; Kurdek, 1998), and that many gay male couples are not sexually exclusive (Blumstein & Schwartz, 1983; Kurdek, 1995; Laird, 1993). These mixed findings reflect a mixed situation. If lesbian and gay couples are less stable than heterosexual couples, it is likely that this reflects internalized homophobia and stereotypes of a lesbian and gay lifestyle that portray lesbians and gays as less committed in relationships than heterosexuals (McVinney, 1988). In addition, it is possible that the inability to marry may inhibit stability in the relationship. Marriage is certainly no guarantee of a lasting relationship, as evidenced by the high divorce rate among heterosexual couples; however, not being able to marry and lacking social sanction, recognition, and the privileges attached to marriage may affect the relationship, contributing to a greater likelihood of breakup (McVinney, 1988; Pearlman, 1988; Townsend, 1998).

Though denied legally sanctioned marriage, many lesbian and gay couples design marriage-like ceremonies (Haldeman, 1998) incorporating demonstrations of love and shared history, and symbols of enduring solidarity (Laird, 1994; Muzio, 1996; Weston, 1994).

FAMILY DYNAMICS

There are several features that significantly affect the dynamics of the lesbian and gay family: (a) same-sex parents, (b) families affected by losses, (c) coping with homophobia and discrimination, (d) the lesbian and gay community and social support, and (e) the consequence of being different from the traditional family.

Same-Sex Parents

Because lesbians and gay men are stigmatized for having children, the decision to parent, especially in coparenting families, is generally a deliberate choice that reflects a strong commitment to raising children (Benkov, 1994; Flaks et al., 1995). Studies have found that lesbian mothers exhibited more parenting awareness than matched heterosexual couples (Flaks et al., 1995), had strong child development orientation (Miller, Jacobsen, & Bigner, 1981), and provided their children with greater emotional resources and a richer family life than single, heterosexual mothers (Kirkpatrick, 1987). On the other hand, a review of 56 studies concluded that lesbian and heterosexual mothers do not differ in their parenting skills (Victor & Fish, 1995).

Parenting, for some noncloseted lesbians, may be, in part, both a social statement and an assertion of basic rights. Some lesbian mothers view motherhood as a means of effecting social change by raising politically aware, open-minded children. They endeavor to impart feminist values and to raise their children's consciousness about sexism, racism, and lesbian and gay rights (Ainslie & Feltey, 1991; Wright, 1998).

Because most gay men who have children are noncustodial fathers (Allen, 1997; Crosbie-Burnett & Helmbrecht, 1993), most of the research on lesbian and gay parenting concerns lesbian mothers. Nevertheless, a few studies have addressed parenting by custodial gay fathers. One study found that custodial gay fathers are highly invested parents whose parenting style incorporates considerable emotional expressiveness and nurturing (Bigner, 1996). Compared with heterosexual fathers, the gay fathers went to greater length in promoting their children's cognitive skills, consistently emphasizing the importance of setting and enforcing limits. They were found to be more responsive to their children's needs and more prone to offer resources for activities with their children (Bigner & Jacobson, 1989).

Research shows that once they establish families, same-sex couples differ from heterosexual couples in their high level of cohesion and flexibility (Green, Bettinger, & Zacks, 1996). Although lesbian couples were found to be the most cohesive, gay couples were also more cohesive than heterosexual couples. Furthermore, both lesbians and gay men were found to be significantly more able than heterosexual couples to change the power structure, role relations, and rules regarding the relationship in response to stress. Compared with heterosexual couples, lesbians and gay men tend to relate to each other more as friends or peers, emphasizing companionship, sharing, and equality in power and status in the relationship (Demo & Allen, 1996; Kurdek, 1995; Peplau, 1991). Most lesbians and gay men actively reject traditional gender roles (Blumstein & Schwartz, 1983; Peplau, 1991), and have a more egalitarian division of household and child care labor (Bigner, 1996; Hare & Richards, 1993; Kurdek, 1995; Mitchell, 1996; Patterson & Chan, 1997; Sullivan, 1996).

Lesbian parents and their children report higher levels of satisfaction when the child care responsibilities are evenly distributed between both parents (Chan, Brooks, Raboy, & Patterson, 1998; Patterson, 1995; Sullivan, 1996). Conversely, when the responsibilities are not evenly distributed, birth parents may feel dissatisfied, perceiving themselves as single parents who are living in a two-parent family (Hare & Richards, 1993; Muzio, 1993; Pies, 1989).

Despite the tendency of the lesbian couple to share household tasks and decision making, the biological mother is generally more involved in child care than the comother (Chan, Brooks et al., 1998; Hare & Richards, 1993; Kirkpatrick, 1987; Patterson, 1995; Rohrbaugh, 1992; Sullivan, 1996). This unequal involvement in child care is attributed to financial considerations, with higher-earning mothers spending more time in paid employment and less time with the children (Sullivan, 1996); to internalized heterosexual cultural norms, where only one parent serves as a primary caregiver (Pies, 1989; Rohrbaugh, 1992; Sullivan, 1996);

and to biological ties between mother and child (Hare & Richards, 1993; Kirkpatrick, 1987). Birth mothers in stepfamilies tend to assume more parental responsibilities than the stepmothers, whereas parenting in coparent families tends to be more equally shared, regardless of whether one or both of the mothers are biological mothers, or how the child was conceived (Hare & Richards, 1993).

Although the division of labor of gay male parents is more egalitarian than that of heterosexual couples (Bigner, 1996), it is usually less so than that of lesbian couples (Kurdek, 1995). Benkov (1994) suggests that this is due to the way they were socialized: Males tend to ascribe personal success to achievement in work roles rather than in relationships and domestic roles.

Regardless of how the lesbian and gay family was formed, lesbian and gay parents may choose how to parent their children from a wide variety of parenting styles, from the patriarchal, which they are likely to reject, to the egalitarian (Kirkpatrick, 1987; Muzio, 1993; Pies, 1989; Rohrbaugh, 1992).

Families Affected by Losses

Lesbian and gay stepfamilies, like heterosexual stepfamilies, are created following the dissolution of the heterosexual marriage in which the children were born. Hence the newly established lesbian and gay family experiences a loss of family members (Kurdek, 1997). Many lesbian and gay families also experience losses from the AIDS epidemic. Multiple losses of people to whom they are close, common among HIV-infected gay men, chronically exacerbates their emotional distress (Gluhoski, Fishman, & Perry, 1997). Finally, like heterosexual families, gay and lesbian families may experience loss following the breakup of the family. As lesbians and gays are not permitted to marry, the fact that the breakup of the lesbian and gay family can be as traumatic as the divorce of the heterosexual family is often not acknowledged. This lack of recognition deprives "divorced" lesbians and gays of the legitimization to mourn and process the separation.

Coping With Homophobia and Discrimination

Unlike racial minorities, most lesbians and gays not yet aware of their sexuality grow up absorbing the prejudice against lesbians and gays without yet experiencing it directed toward themselves (Green, 1987). Although racial and ethnic minorities are usually raised by parents who are of the same ethnicity and who can help them learn how to cope with discrimination, lesbians and gays are almost exclusively raised by heterosexual parents. Similarly, lesbian mothers who have had their children while in heterosexual relationships may face an emotional hurdle as they come to terms with their own sexual orientation.

One of the primary fears of gay and lesbian parents is that they will lose custody of their children because of their sexual orientation (Polikoff, 1986; Wright, 1998). They are also concerned about potential social difficulties their children may face resulting from the stigma associated with lesbian and gay parenthood (Hare, 1994; Wright, 1998). Indeed, lesbians and gays who are raising children need to develop ways of coping with the prevailing homophobia and heterosexism. They may choose to maintain secrecy, especially with people or institutions considered to be unsafe, and to be very selective in forming friendships (DiPlacido, 1998). Secrecy, however, may also create additional stress in the form of emotional inhibition and internalized homophobia (DiPlacido, 1998). If lesbians and gays decide to live openly as a couple or as a family, they are vulnerable to the stresses resulting from heterosexism, prejudice, and discrimination (DiPlacido, 1998; Mitchell, 1996). Lesbian identity, feminist activism, and a strong social support network help lesbians cope with stress. Lesbian mothers who expressed their lesbianism openly to their employer, former husband, and children have been found to be psychologically healthier than those who do not (DePoy & Noble, 1992; Levy, 1992; Rand et al., 1982).

The Lesbian and Gay
Community and Social Support

Gay men and especially lesbians often have a close network of fellow lesbians and gays whom they regard as an extended family, who provide validation and emotional, social, and material support (Hare, 1994; Hunter & Mallon, 1998; Lott-Whitehead & Tully, 1993). This support is especially valued as a means of coping with the oppression experienced by gays and lesbians (Aronson, 1996; Lott-Whitehead & Tully, 1993; Pies, 1989; Slater & Mencher, 1991). Based on choice and mutual agreement, these extended families perform many of the same functions as networks based on marriage and kinship (Ainslie & Feltey, 1991; Weston, 1994). The lesbian and gay community is often a more reliable and consistent support than families of origin (Crosbie-Burnett & Helmbrecht, 1993; Demo & Allen, 1996; Green et al., 1996).

Nonetheless, although the lesbian and gay community buffers stress, it is not always supportive of lesbian mothers (Laird, 1993; Lott-Whitehead & Tully, 1993). Hare (1994) suggests that lesbian mothers are not always accepted by the lesbian community, because they resemble and identify more with heterosexual families than with child-free lesbians.

The "extended" lesbian family may also include males. Many lesbian families consciously "adopt" male friends as male role models for their children. Lesbian mothers generally have more men participating in the lives of their children than do single heterosexual mothers (Hare & Richards, 1993; Kirkpatrick, 1987).

Other members of the extended gay and lesbian family include step- and biological grandparents, who may be quite involved with their grandchildren. Grandparents tend to "forgive" the lesbian and gay child his or her deviance, and the birth of a grandchild "helps to soften family homophobia, linking the family of blood to the family by choice" (Laird, 1993, p. 303).

The Consequence of Being Different From the Traditional Family

Gay and lesbian families are perceived, and may perceive themselves, as different, marginal, or deviant, especially in comparison with the idealized template of the heterosexual, nuclear family (Allen, 1997). This model does not correspond to their own life experiences (Green et al., 1986; Kirkpatrick, 1987). Because these families lack role models to guide them in their daily lives, such comparisons may increase their sense of marginality (Ainslie & Feltey, 1991; Pies, 1989).

Based on clinical observations, Pies (1989) concluded that same-sex parents arouse questions in the community as to which of the two is the "real" mother or father. This, in turn, can add to the coparents' uncertainty about the appropriateness of their parental roles (Rohrbaugh, 1992).

IMPLICATIONS FOR CHILD DEVELOPMENT

There has been extensive research on the sexual, psychological, and social development of children of lesbian mothers. The most striking finding is how similar these children are to children raised by heterosexual parents. The research confirms that homosexuals are effective parents who provide a home life at least as good as that of heterosexuals. The parent-child bond may be even closer than in traditional families (Green & Bozett, 1991).

In discussing the implications for child development, I consider the sexual orientation of the children; their psychological, social, and behavioral functioning; and some possible advantages of being raised by same-sex parents.

In contrast to commonly held assumptions, there are no differences between children of lesbian and gay parents and children of heterosexuals with regard to their sexual orientation or gender development. The great majority of children of gay and lesbian parents grow up to be heterosexual adults (Gibbs, 1988; Green, 1982; Green et al., 1986; Patterson & Redding, 1996; Tasker & Golombok, 1997; Victor & Fish, 1995).

Furthermore, children of gays and lesbians do not differ from children of heterosexuals with respect to their emotional health or psychosocial development (Gibbs, 1988; Patterson & Redding, 1996; Tasker & Golombok, 1997; Victor & Fish, 1995). Children raised by lesbian mothers function well in adulthood in terms of psychological well-being, family identity, and relationships (Patterson, 1996; Patterson & Redding, 1996; Tasker & Golombok, 1995, 1997), and do not differ from children of heterosexual mothers in their self-esteem or behavioral adjustment (Huggins, 1989; Patterson, 1995; Patterson & Redding, 1996; Tasker & Golombok, 1997). Finally, children raised by same-sex parents do not differ from children raised by opposite-sex parents in their personality characteristics, academic achievement, or socioeconomic status (Chan, Raboy, & Patterson, 1998; Flaks et al., 1995; Green et al., 1986; Patterson, 1996; Powell & Downey; 1997; Tasker & Golombok, 1997; Victor & Fish, 1995).

Children of lesbians do differ from children of heterosexuals in their coping mechanisms. In order to avoid stigma related to their parents' homosexuality, children are careful in selecting to whom they disclose their parents' sexual identity (Bozett, 1980, 1987; Wright, 1998). Lesbian and gay parents frequently teach their children skills in handling the stigmatized identity (Wright, 1998).

Being raised by gay or lesbian parents may also bring some advantages. Lewis (cited in Victor & Fish, 1995) reports that for most children of lesbian mothers, their mothers' coming out as lesbians gave them permission to consider nontraditional roles and avoid conventional pathways. Being raised by lesbian and gay parents, children can learn to stand up for their choices and convictions, and to respect, empathize, and value diversity (Bigner, 1999; Laird, 1993; Patterson, 1996). They have an opportunity to experience flexible gender behaviors and the freedom to engage in egalitarian relationships (Allen, 1997; Bigner, 1999; Blumstein & Schwartz, 1983; Patterson, 1996; Patterson & Redding, 1996). They may also benefit from the strong ties within the lesbian and gay community and the support it can offer to family members (Allen, 1997; Weston, 1994).

VARIATIONS AMONG GAY AND LESBIAN FAMILIES

Although the family context into which a child is born or adopted has important implications, the diversity of gay and lesbian families has not been sufficiently acknowledged. Lesbian and gay families differ significantly on such dimensions as gender, generation, age, race, and ethnicity (Demo & Allen, 1996). Furthermore, the involvement of step- or co-parents in the children's lives may vary, depending on whether the children were born during an earlier heterosexual relationship, whether they were conceived through insemination and born into a lesbian family, or whether they were adopted (Allen, 1997; Hare & Richards, 1993). Although the most prevalent gay/lesbian families are lesbian step-families, gay and lesbian families come in all the variations found among heterosexual families, and then some (Green, 1987; Lewin, 1993). They may be single-parent or two-parent families; their children may have been produced through a donor within the context of a lesbian and gay couple or in a heterosexual relationship; they may be a stepfamily or a coparent family; they may be adoptive or foster families; and they may be families that "came out" or did not.

Single-Parent Gay and Lesbian Families

Like heterosexual single mothers, lesbian single mothers encounter discrimination in housing, employment, and child custody, though to a greater degree than heterosexual single mothers do (Pagelow, 1980).

Adoptive Gay and Lesbian Families

For more on adoptive gay and lesbian families, refer to the section "Legal and Policy Issues" earlier in this chapter.

IMPLICATIONS FOR POLICY

Gay men and lesbians lack legal protection against discrimination in employment, housing, and education. Extending basic civil rights guarantees against discrimination on the basis of sexual orientation is an essential first step toward normalizing the status of gay and lesbian families. Beyond this, gay men and lesbians should be granted the legal right to marry or to have legal recognition of their relationships as is now available in Vermont. This will serve to legitimize their status, their relationships, and their families. It will also facilitate application of appropriate laws regarding divorce, custody, and child support, as well as inheritance and eligibility for public benefits. It should be noted, however, that the issue of marriage is controversial among lesbians and gays. Some consider marriage to be a heterosexist institution that has no applicability to the gay and lesbian experience.

Court decisions regarding child custody and visitation should be based solely on parental abilities rather than on the parents' sexual orientation. Courts have sent mixed messages with respect to the legal protection of gay and lesbian parental rights. The prejudice and discrimination encountered by gay and lesbian parents in the legal system need to be eliminated by law and through the promulgation of objective legal standards (Rubenfeld, 1994; Sears, 1994). Lawyers and judges need to be educated about the realities of homosexuality and the implications of lesbian and gay parenting. As with heterosexual family issues, mediation should be available as an alternative or adjunct to court adjudication (McIntyre, 1994).

Laws and explicit policies about adoption and fostering by gays and lesbians are also needed. Basically, these policies should not differ from those applied to both single and coupled heterosexual applicants.

IMPLICATIONS FOR PRACTICE

As lesbian and gay families have few role models and guidelines on how to negotiate their unique family life, they are likely to need information, guidance, and social support from other lesbian and gay families and knowledgeable social service professionals (Pies, 1989). The focus of professional help should be on the provision of information and mutual exchange rather than counseling, per se. First and foremost, to render effective assistance, practitioners need to come to terms with their own homophobia and stereotypes (Oles et al., 1999).

Lesbian and gay parents, stepparents, previous spouses, and their children may also need assistance in clarifying their relationships and expectations of one another. They may also wish to acknowledge openly their respective feelings toward nonresidential parental figures, addressing the respective expectations and feelings toward one another. This may bring forth unresolved feelings of loss, anger, abandonment, rejection, and divided loyalties. Lesbian and gay stepparents and their stepchildren should be encouraged to establish a close parent-child dyad, if this has not already occurred. A repertoire of shared activities may facilitate the bonding between coparents and non–birth children.

Studies of heterosexual stepfamilies suggest that although some coparenting styles seem more effective than others do, different styles may suit different personalities (Erera, 1996; Visher & Visher, 1989). Social workers can discuss these alternative parenting styles with gay and lesbian families, helping the parents identify what works best for them. Such discussions can be most effective with support groups for gay and lesbian couples, where the facilitator can use modeling, role play, simulation, and the processing of real-life situations.

In coparent lesbian and gay families, the partners should also be encouraged to discuss their parenting roles and responsibilities. The parents and, when old enough, the children should be given the opportunity to express their feelings regarding unknown donors who may be part of the family's and children's identities. Children may also benefit from group discussions about their lives and their parents' sexual orientation (Kirkpatrick, 1987).

Practitioners should, if necessary, help lesbian and gay couples to strengthen the intergenerational, emotional boundaries to protect their relationships from parents' and in-laws' disapproval and hostility (LaSala, 1998). More generally, social workers can help empower these families through groups that address issues of lesbian and gay identity development, homophobia, and family concerns (Morrow, 1996).

IMPLICATIONS FOR RESEARCH

Most of the research on gay and lesbian families is based on small, nonrandom samples of white, well-educated, North American, urban respondents (Demo & Allen, 1996; Oerton, 1997). With few notable exceptions (e.g., Allen, 1997; Allen & Demo, 1995; Bozett, 1980, 1987; Green & Bozett, 1991), most of the studies focus on lesbian rather than gay families. Studies based on samples that are more representative are needed to capture the diversity among gay and lesbian families.

Although in the early stages it was important to compare gay and lesbian families with heterosexual families to understand the similarities and differences, it is time to move on, to understand the lesbian and gay family in its own right, with its diverse styles and structures.

The research also needs to move beyond issues of custody, visitation, and the impact of lesbian and gay parents on their children's development, and to examine the dynamics of the lesbian family. Research should consider the impact of different methods of impregnation on the family; the differing parental styles of lesbian and gay stepfamilies and coparent lesbian and gay families (see, for example, Crosbie-Burnett & Helmbrecht, 1993); the role of the coparent vis-à-vis the non–birth child; and the implications of diverse lesbian and gay family arrangements for the division of domestic labor (Oerton, 1997). Additional research is also needed on the variations of gay and lesbian families, including adoptive families, foster families, single-parent families, and childless families. Only then will we begin to understand and appreciate the family lives of gays and lesbians in all their complexity.

Given the extent of homophobia, it is important to examine how institutions such as the courts, schools, social agencies, and health facilities treat gay and lesbian families. As states adopt new legislation—such as, for example, those in Vermont—the effects should be studied for their policy implications. Similarly, the experiences of the Nordic countries and the Netherlands should be followed carefully.

DISCUSSION QUESTIONS

1. Which of the characteristics of gay and lesbian families reflects intrinsic characteristics, and which reflect the response of these families to external pressures stemming from the mainstream, heterosexual society?

2. Will changing society's laws, policies, and attitudes change the family dynamics of the gay or lesbian family? How?

3. Research findings show that some lesbian mothers view their parenting as part of a social statement, consciously educating their children about combating oppression. What could be the reasons for this attitude?

4. Would you favor or oppose legalizing gay and lesbian marriage? Why? What are the principal arguments for and against such a policy? What about civil union, as exists in Vermont and some European countries?

5. In what ways are gay and lesbian families like heterosexual families? How are they different? Is it valid to make such comparisons?

SUGGESTIONS FOR FURTHER READING

Allen, K. R. (1997). Lesbian and gay families. In T. Arendell (Ed.), *Contemporary parenting: Challenges and issues* (pp. 196–218). Thousand Oaks, CA: Sage.

Laird, J. (1993). Lesbian and gay families. In F. Walsh (Ed.), *Normal family processes* (2nd ed., pp. 282–328). New York: Guilford.

Laird, J., & Green, R. J. (Eds.). (1996). *Lesbians and gays in couples and families: A handbook for therapists.* San Francisco: Jossey-Bass.

Mallon, G. P. (Ed.). (1988). *Foundations of social work practice with lesbian and gay persons* (pp. 145–182). New York: Haworth.

Patterson, C. J., & Chan, R. W. (1999). Families headed by lesbian and gay parents. In M. E. Lamb (Ed.), *Parenting and child development in "nontraditional" families* (pp. 191–219). Mahwah, NJ: Lawrence Erlbaum.

Wright, J. M. (1998). *Lesbian step families: An ethnography of love.* New York: Haworth.

Chapter 7

GRANDMOTHER-HEADED FAMILIES

This chapter examines caregiving in skipped-generation families—
families in which grandchildren live with one or more grandparents in
the absence of the parents. The chapter focuses on grandmother-headed
rather than on grandparent-headed families. Although 76% of grandparent-headed families are married (Sands & Goldberg-Glen, 2000), and
though grandfathers, too, are involved in raising grandchildren, grandfathers usually do so as secondary caregivers who share caregiving with
the grandmothers (Chalfie, 1994; Dressel & Barnhill, 1994; Fuller-
Thomson, Minkler, & Driver, 1997). Use of the gender-neutral term
grandparent obscures the critical role of gender in understanding these
families.

PREVALENCE AND
DEMOGRAPHIC CHARACTERISTICS
OF THE GRANDMOTHER-HEADED FAMILY

A recent and significant development in women's caregiving has been
the rapid increase in the number of grandmothers who are raising their
grandchildren. About 1 in 10 grandparents have raised a grandchild for at
least six months at some point in their lifetime (Fuller-Thomson et al.,
1997). In 1997, 5.5% of American children—about 5.5 million—resided
in households with a grandparent. This is an increase of over 40% since

---

AUTHOR'S NOTE: This chapter was coauthored with Dr. Laura Landry-Meyer.

1980 (Jendrek, 1993; Minkler & Roe, 1993). The increase in the number of children in grandparent-headed households was fueled chiefly by the increase in the number of skipped-generation families. Of the 5.5 million children residing in households with a grandparent in 1997, 1.4 million lived in homes headed by grandparents where no parent was present (U.S. Bureau of the Census, 1999a).

Estimates of the ethnicity of grandparent caregivers differ according to the measures that are used. Informally adopted children may not be included in official statistical reports. Chalfie (1994), using unpublished data from the 1992 Current Population Survey, found that 58% of grandparent-headed families are white, 29% black, 10% Hispanic, 2% Asian or Pacific Islanders, and 1% American Indian. Although most grandparent-headed families are white, proportionately, African Americans are about twice as likely as whites to be grandparent caregivers (Chalfie, 1994; Sands & Goldberg-Glen, 2000), and African American grandchildren are three times more likely to live with grandparents than white grandchildren (Giarrusso, Silverstein, & Bengston, 1996; Littlejohn-Blake & Darling, 1993).

Analyzing the 1989 Census Bureau Population Reports, Billingsley (1992) found that 1.2 million, or 16.5%, of all black children were informally adopted by and lived with grandparents. However, extended kinship households are often included in informal adoption figures. Saluter (1992) reports that, in 38% of these informal adoptions, the grandparents were the sole caregivers, 56% had the child's mother present, 2% had the child's father present, and 4% had both parents present.

HISTORICAL BACKGROUND AND
THE SOCIAL-CULTURAL CONTEXT

In the past, older women served as parental surrogates primarily because the children's mothers had entered the workforce (Neugarten & Weinstein, 1964). Currently, most grandmothers assume the parental role when the mothers are deemed unfit parents (Apfel & Seitz, 1991; deToledo & Brown, 1995). Being an unfit or unavailable parent has been linked with a number of conditions, many associated with poverty. These include the increased incarceration of women (Dressel & Barnhill, 1994), the drug and AIDS epidemics (Burton, 1992; Minkler & Roe, 1993), divorce (Cherlin & Furstenberg, 1986; Johnson, 1985), nonmarital childbearing

(Apfel & Seitz, 1991), mental illness, and the lack of affordable child care (Jendrek, 1993; Presser, 1989).

Caregiving by grandparents is especially prevalent among African Americans, and the influence of grandmothers is highly regarded in the African American community (Burton, 1992; Burton, Dilworth-Anderson, & Merriwether-deVries, 1995; Dressel & Barnhill, 1994; Minkler & Roe, 1993; Minkler, Roe, & Price, 1992). When it comes to their grandchildren, African American grandparents are less likely to adopt majority norms of noninterference, and are more likely than their white counterparts to be actively involved (Longino & Earle, 1996; Pearson, Hunter, Ensminger, & Kellam, 1990).

The grandmother's decision to provide care to her grandchild is influenced by previous familial and cultural history. For African Americans, extended kinship systems, consisting of blood relations or fictive kin (e.g., non–blood "relatives" granted the status of family members), gained prominence under the impact of slavery (Billingsley, 1992; Wilkinson, 1993). It is within this system that the informal adoption of grandchildren takes place (Crosbie-Burnett & Lewis, 1993). Historically, poor African American households have been able successfully to absorb into their families relatives and friends in need (Fine, Schwebel, & James-Myers, 1987; Littlejohn-Blake & Darling, 1993). Informal adoption has been seen as a normative way to adapt to adverse circumstances (Littlejohn-Blake & Darling, 1993), and as a way to circumvent involvement with a legal system that is viewed with suspicion (Crosbie-Burnett & Lewis, 1993; Littlejohn-Blake & Darling, 1993). The fluid caregiving roles (Billingsley, 1992; Littlejohn-Blake & Darling, 1993) and the ability to define caregiving functionally rather than biologically reflect norms of interdependence, communal cooperation, and mutual support (Littlejohn-Blake & Darling, 1993). Regardless of race and ethnicity, informal rather than legal arrangements are preferred by many grandmothers. Like African Americans, Hispanics are less likely to rely on formal services than whites (Dilworth-Anderson & Williams, 1996; Hildreth & Williams, 1996), and prefer caregiving by family members to institutional care (deToledo & Brown, 1995; Minkler & Roe, 1993).

Grandparent caregivers, especially single grandmothers who head households, are the poorest of all nontraditional households (Chalfie, 1994). About 60% of skipped-generation grandparent-headed families live in poverty (U.S. Bureau of the Census, 1999a). The 1992 median income of grandparent caregiver households was $18,000, about half that of traditional nuclear families (Chalfie, 1994). Women of color from the lower socioeconomic brackets who provide care to family members over their life span are at greatest risk for being impoverished in later life. African American women have the highest employment rate throughout their lives, but are the least well off when compared to other groups, such as Hispanic women and white women (Ozawa, 1995).

In Burton's (1992) study, 80% of the grandmothers reported that they needed financial assistance to provide care for their grandchildren, compared with 50% of the grandfathers in the study. Minkler and Roe (1993) found that, before assuming care, about one fourth of grandmothers in their study were not doing well financially, whereas after assuming care of their grandchildren, 87% reported significant financial difficulty. In a study of grandparent caregivers in which 92% of the sample was female, Lai and Yuan (1994) found that 83% reported their income to be inadequate. Many grandmothers are unable to access financial assistance, because legal custody is frequently a condition for receiving support and legal recognition is often difficult for grandparents to obtain (Purnell & Bagby, 1993). The parents may be missing or not willing to cooperate in relinquishing the parental role. The process is time-consuming, emotionally difficult, and potentially costly. Some families who apply to be foster parents are refused because of their substandard housing arrangements (Mizio, 1983).

For many grandmothers, the cost of providing care in the short term is a loss of wages. Grandmothers often take leaves of absence from jobs, reduce work hours, pass up promotions, or quit (Burton, 1992; Minkler & Roe, 1993). Most women have interrupted and/or reduced earnings throughout their lives due to caregiving, which has a negative effect on their social security benefits (Kingson & O'Grady-LeShane, 1993). Women who dedicate their entire lives to caregiving and do not enter the workforce do not receive compensation for their work as caregivers.

A long-term cost associated with caregiving is inadequate income in the retirement years. Women's interrupted or delayed work histories are associated with lower earnings for social security, employment in secondary sector jobs that pay less, and jobs that do not have pensions. Women retirees confront grave economic problems, with many of them living below poverty level (Richardson, 1993). Many grandmothers assume care of their grandchildren during these retirement years, which adds considerable economic stress to these families.

Some financial assistance has been available through AFDC and foster care programs. With the enactment of the 1996 Personal Responsibility and Work Opportunity Reconciliation Act (PRWORA, Public Law 104-193), the AFDC entitlement has been abolished and replaced with federal block grants to the states. Welfare reform, with its workfare requirements and a lifetime five-year limit for receipt of aid, places grandmother caregivers at even greater risk of poverty. This law assumes that grandmothers and other relatives will be available to assume child-care responsibilities for their grandchildren while the mothers work. Though grandparent caregivers over age 60 are exempted from the work requirement and time limits, younger grandmothers are not. The median age of grandparents heading skipped-generation families is 57 (Chalfie, 1994). The lack of basic child care, health care, and family supports in the United States places added stress on the family, often thrusting on older women caregiving responsibilities that elsewhere are provided by the welfare state (Kamerman & Kahn, 1995).

Policymakers have viewed relative or kinship care as expected and economical. According to Guberman, Maheu, and Maille (1992), in some instances, social service workers pressure relative caregivers to assume unpaid or poorly compensated caregiving roles. Unless the grandparents are officially registered, they are not paid for their care-taking. If they are registered as formal foster parents, their monthly payment ranges between $350 and $500 (C. Gerring, personal communication, August 2000; C. Shaffar, personal communication, August 2000).

The inadequacy of institutional and community resources has also contributed to women's caregiving burden. Many grandchildren are being raised by grandmothers as a result of the middle generation's drug addiction, typically to crack cocaine. There is a decided lack of drug treatment programs to help these parents overcome their addiction and assume responsibility for their children. A growing number of women are being incarcerated for nonviolent, drug-related offenses involving their male partners (Dressel, 1994). The drug wars of the 1980s and 1990s, coupled with the trend toward longer sentencing, have contributed to the incarceration of a growing proportion of the population, again disproportionately poor and of color. Under welfare reform, women convicted of a drug-related felony are no longer eligible for Temporary Assistance to Needy Families (TANF) or food stamp benefits. An estimated 32,000 women are raising their grandchildren because of their daughters' incarceration, and that figure was expected to more than double at the turn of the century (Dressel & Barnhill, 1994).

STIGMA

Grandmother-headed families are "likely to be deemed deviant if not pathological" (Burnette, 1997). Being disproportionally older women of color, these family heads are often subject to ageism, sexism, and racism. This triple stigma is expressed in discrimination and in their being cut off from social, political, and economic resources (Burnette, 1997; Fuller-Thomson et al., 1997).

Rather than being respected and rewarded for raising their grand-children, grandmothers in grandmother-headed families are often blamed for the problems of their children and viewed as incompetent or inferior parents (Burnette, 1997; Nisivoccia, 1996). This kind of victim blaming reinforces the exploitation of these grandmothers. If they are somehow responsible for their children's inability to take care of the grandchildren, it is only fitting that the grandmothers assume that responsibility. The society at large is thereby absolved.

Grandmothers are often considered too old to parent young children. Such sexist and ageist views reflect negative stereotypes of women, of older women, and of caregivers, who are almost exclusively women. The grandmothers often act as voluntary surrogate parents without any finan-cial compensation. Some argue that grandmothers should not get paid for caring for their grandchildren, because this is what extended families are supposed to do anyway (Nisivoccia, 1996). If they are compensated as foster parents, the stipend they receive is well below the poverty level. They frequently lack health care, housing assistance, public welfare, and social services for the children they raise. They may face eviction from senior housing for taking in the grandchildren (Chalfie, 1994; Minkler & Roe, 1993). Many are also unable to work, being full-time caregivers, because of their caregiving responsibilities, and because their age limits their ability to secure employment.

The grandmothers most often lack legal sanction for their caregiving. Most prefer not to adopt the grandchildren, because this may set them against their own children. Lacking legal guardianship constrains their ability to make decisions and interact with social service, health, and educational institutions on the child's behalf (Burnette, 1997; Jendrek, 1993; Karp, 1996). They cannot, for example, enroll the child in a dif-ferent school, sign or obtain medical or educational records, include the child in their medical insurance, or obtain special-needs adoption subsidies.

CAREGIVING: A WOMEN'S ISSUE

At the beginning of the 20th century, women spent approximately 19 years raising children and 9 years caring for a parent (Foulke, Alford-Cooper, & Butler, 1993). Women may now expect to spend on average 17 years raising children and 18 years caring for a parent (Foulke et al., 1993; Kaden & McDaniel, 1990). For many women, the caregiving of children and parents overlaps. A woman's caregiving of children and elderly parents potentially spans 35 years of a 78-year life expectancy. With the added burden of caring for grandchildren, a growing number of women will spend most of their adult lives in caregiving roles, most often without adequate material and social support.

Caregiving is a major contributor to the feminization of poverty. Women—especially those in later life, living in poverty, and of color—are more likely to have caregiving responsibilities thrust on them. The lack of publicly supported, affordable child care and elder care, inadequate family leave policies, and the gendered assumption that women relatives can and will voluntarily undertake caregiving responsibilities contribute to the increasing caregiving burden and poverty of older women.

Grandmothers also provide day care. Relatively few grandmother day care providers are paid (Jendrek, 1994; Presser, 1989). Approximately one third of grandmothers who provide care for grandchildren are also employed, but work different hours than the mother (Presser, 1989). For them, grandchild care is an uncompensated second job. Most mothers who rely on the grandmothers for child care do so because of their own low wages (Presser, 1989). The uncompensated contribution to the economy of grandmother child care has been estimated at between $17 and $29 billion per year (Bass & Caro, 1996, p. 19).

Grandmother caregiving can best be understood in the context of the inequality of caregiving responsibilities between men and women. Ninety-three percent of all single grandparent caregivers are women (Chalfie, 1994). For those grandmothers who are married, the burden of raising the grandchild typically falls on the grandmothers (Minkler, Roe, & Robertson-Beckley, 1994). Almost all of the grandfather caregivers are married and are sharing caregiving with a grandmother (Chalfie, 1994). The typical caregiver for grandchildren, like the typical caregiver for the elderly, is an unpaid female in her late 50s (Chalfie, 1994; Foster & Brizius, 1993). Because more women are caregivers and give more care, this reinforces the belief that women are natural caregivers and that caregiving is unnatural for men (Walker, Pratt, & Eddy, 1995).

Gender-role expectations exert pressure on women to assume caregiving responsibilities (Alford-Cooper, 1993; Doress-Worters, 1994; Guberman et al., 1992). Institutional sexism perpetuates traditional gender and caregiving roles that victimize women (Hartman, 1990). Women tend to view the tensions between work and family responsibilities as a personal rather than as a social problem, thereby accepting the caregiving role throughout the life cycle (Alford-Cooper, 1993). Women's own definition of caregiving generally excludes those responsibilities they consider integral to their role as wife, mother, and grandmother, such as household work and meal preparation (Dwyer & Seccombe, 1991; Walker et al., 1995). Hence they do not see caregiving responsibilities as unusual or unfair. Nevertheless, for many grandmothers, caring for grandchildren isolates them in the home, reduces their employment opportunities, and restricts their time and ability to perform other roles (Doress-Worters, 1994).

The reasons women become caregivers are generally linked to internal, subjective feelings. Women cite love, maternal feelings, family ties, a need to help others, duty, and obligation as reasons for providing care to dependent adults (Guberman et al., 1992). Similarly, grandmothers mention family relationships and the need to provide the grandchild with a nurturing environment. As a result, grandmother caregivers do not want the child in foster care (Burton, 1992; Minkler & Roe, 1993; Minkler et al., 1992), day care (Jendrek, 1993), or other care arrangements (Johnson, 1985). Despite the amount of stress many of these grandmothers face, Burton (1992) found that the majority of grandparents in her sample expressed a strong commitment to raising their grandchildren and identified themselves as the only one to care for the grandchild. In Minkler and colleagues' 1992 study, the grandmothers feared that their grandchildren might be placed in foster care, and this overshadowed their own physical and emotional health concerns. Many expressed an "intense desire to protect the children . . . by down playing their own health problems" (Minkler et al., 1992, p. 759).

Women tend to be viewed as dependent or financially nonautonomous (Guberman et al., 1992). They are paid less in the labor force, and their work is viewed as secondary to a family's income. This reinforces pressures on women to assume unpaid caregiving responsibilities. The increasing caregiving burden on women is also exacerbated by public policies that consider women's caregiving as a private matter and a cost-saving strategy (Alford-Cooper, 1993; Barusch, 1994; Bass & Caro, 1996; Walker et al., 1995). The PRWORA, in failing to provide for sufficient day care, assumes the availability of grandmothers and other relatives to fill in the caregiving gap.

Though men are compensated for fulfilling their gendered obligations, the nonwaged, reproductive labor that women perform is not recognized as work (Meyer, 1990). The uncompensated cost of caregiving is distributed over a woman's lifetime, starting with bearing and rearing children and continuing with the provision of care for elderly parents. "Poverty and caring, for many women, are two sides of the same coin. Caring is what they do; poverty describes the economic circumstances in which they do it" (Minkler & Roe, 1993, p. 211). Being female, being old, and being non-white places women at triple jeopardy for poverty (Minkler & Stone, 1985). Women make up 58% of the elderly population (i.e., those over age 65) and 74% of the poor elderly (Ozawa, 1995; Richardson, 1993).

FAMILY STRUCTURE AND DYNAMICS

The literature identifies two key characteristics of grandmother-headed families: that they are skipped-generation families and that they are developmentally "off time." These two characteristics have significant implications for the grandmother, as well as for the relationships between grandmother and grandchild and between grandmother and daughter or son. A discussion of these issues follows.

Skipped-Generation Families

Families consisting of grandparents and grandchildren with parents absent from the home have been characterized as skipped-generation (Burnette, 1997; Goldberg, Sands, Cole, & Cristofalo, 1998) or missing-generation families (Dressel & Barnhill, 1994). These families have unique multigenerational patterns and family structures (Burnette, 1997), and can be compared with the "sandwich" generation, in which middle-aged daughters care for both their children and their aging parents. According to Dressel and Barnhill (1994), skipped-generation families and the sandwich generation share in common the following characteristics: the daily caring is done almost exclusively by women; the added caregiving responsibilities can negatively impact the caregivers' employment and can produce caregiver stress; the caregiving can produce psychological rewards for the caregivers; and both exemplify caregiver "careers." Skipped-generation families, however, do not have the same material and psychological resources and assistance that the sandwich generation has (Dressel & Barnhill, 1994), nor do they have adequate structural supports (Jendrek, 1993).

Developmentally Off-Time Families

From a developmental perspective, families headed by grandmothers are assuming parental roles off time; that is, they are unable to perform the expected roles that they have been rehearsing (Burton, 1996; Jendrek, 1993), and the timing of their caregiving is incongruent with the grandmothers' developmental stage (Goldberg et al., 1998). Developmental theories suggest that when role transitions occur off time, individuals may experience role overload and stress, and their personal development may be hindered (Burton, 1996; Burton et al., 1995). One manifestation of this off-time experience is the combination of losing the traditional grandmother peer group while not being able to associate with young mothers either (Jendrek, 1993; Kelley, 1993; Woodworth, 1996). There is, in addition, a marked change in the grandmothers' lifestyle following the grandchild's entry into their lives. These lifestyle changes occur in three major areas: marriage and family relationships, the friendship network, and self-care. In a study of grandmothers who are surrogate parents, Jendrek (1993) found the following lifestyle changes: the need to alter routines and plans, having less privacy, having less time for themselves, having less time to get everything done, having less time for and giving less attention to their spouses, having less contact with friends, having less time for recreation and fun activities, and having less money. The grandmothers also were more tired, emotionally drained, and worried. Others have reported that grandmothers experience depression, strain, and deteriorated health (Kelley, 1993).

Most grandmother caregivers are at the age when many people are close to retirement. Raising children at this age is physically and emotionally difficult (Burton, 1992; Kelley, 1993; Minkler et al., 1992), particularly if other family members also require care. Grandmothers are usually at the "role exit" (Blau, 1973) or the "disengagement" developmental stage (Cummings & Henry, 1961). At this age, people retire and decrease their activities, experience diminished physical strength and stamina, encounter a decline in cognitive abilities, and are more prone to acute and chronic illnesses (Pinson-Milburn, Fabian, Schlossberg, & Pyle, 1996).

The grandmothers may also be off time in terms of the age at which they become grandmothers. The majority of African American women, for example, become grandmothers (not necessarily assuming parenting responsibilities) either before they are 40 or after age 60, traditionally off-time periods for this life transition (Szinovacz, 1988). If the surrogate grandmothers are middle-aged, they may have minor children of their own who are still living with them. This creates a unique parenting situation. While parenting the different children, their parenting is regarded as mothering for their own birth children and as grandmothering for the other children. If they have children of their own, they tend to rely on those children for help in taking care of the grandchildren. These parental children may resent the added responsibilities and be jealous of the time their mother devotes to the grandchildren (Jendrek, 1993; Minkler et al., 1994).

The Impact of Caregiving on Grandmothers

Many grandmothers who find themselves rearing grandchildren believe that they are the only ones in this situation. They often feel isolated, frustrated, and angry; sometimes, they feel ashamed (deToledo & Brown, 1995; Woodworth, 1996). Grandparents who are raising their grandchildren were found to experience decreased contact with family and friends (Jendrek, 1993; Kelley, 1993; Minkler et al., 1994; Pinson-Milburn et al., 1996), a lack of social and institutional support (Kelley, 1993; Minkler, Driver, Roe, & Bedeian, 1993), difficulties with the restrictiveness and lack of relief from the parental role (Kelley, 1993; Pinson-Milburn et al., 1996), a decline in marital satisfaction (Minkler et al., 1994), and psychological distress from stressful relationships with both the grandchildren and the grandchildren's parents (Kelley, 1993). In their cross-sectional study of 129 skipped-generation grandparent-headed families, Sands and Goldberg-Glen (2000) found a positive and significant correlation between the grandchildren's psychological and physical problems and the grandparents' stress. Similarly, based on panel data from the National Survey of Families and Households, Szinovacz, DeViney, and Atkinson (1999) found that grandchildren's move into the household increases depressive symptoms among grandmothers. Conversely, grandchildren's leaving the grandparents' home was associated with reduced well-being among grandfathers.

The costs of providing care at an off time in one's life are compounded by economic pressures. Providing care for grandchildren (and other kin) drains a family's resources (Burton, 1992). Most grandmother caregivers report that they are unable adequately to meet their needs on their current incomes (Lai & Yuan, 1994; Minkler & Roe, 1993). Furthermore, grandmothers may put themselves at risk for future economic vulnerability by choosing to provide care.

Despite the added responsibility and stress, grandmothers raising grandchildren may also find that this new role has rewards. These include having another chance to raise a child right, nurturing family legacies through the lives of their grandchildren, receiving the love and companionship of a child (Burton, 1992; Burton et al., 1995; Goldberg et al., 1998), keeping young and active, and having a greater sense of meaning and purpose in living (Jendrek, 1993).

The Grandmother-Grandchild Relationship

From the grandmother's standpoint, being the child's grandmother and acting as his or her parent requires a new definition of roles (Strom & Strom, 1993). While adjusting to the new role, surrogate grandmothers may experience a loss of the traditional grandparenting role, with its joys and relative lack of responsibilities (Kelley, 1993). The grandmother faces a number of difficult issues. To what extent should she act as grandmother and to what extent as parent? Is she expected to act as an extension of the child's parents? Should she attempt to follow the parents' parenting style? In cases were the parents' interests conflict with those of the child, with whom should she ally? If the parent is incarcerated or using drugs, the grandmother may regard the parent's behavior as evidence of her own failure as a parent. In that case, how should she parent the grandchild? Should she parent the child the same way she parented the child's mother or father? What should she tell the grandchildren about the circumstances that required her to assume the parental role?

Grandmother caregivers may be out of touch with child and adolescent development in a contemporary context (Strom & Strom, 1993). Because of the generation gap, grandchildren, especially adolescents, may find themselves socializing their grandmothers to the realities of their daily lives outside the home. In doing so, the grandchildren may interpret, explain, and teach their grandmothers the informal rules of their environment.

Grandmother caregivers also need to monitor social and academic development (Strom & Strom, 1993); keep up with school, social, and physical activities of their grandchildren (Burton et al., 1995); learn about available resources (Burton et al., 1995; Strom & Strom, 1993); and, at times, deal with the grandchild's psychological-physical problems (Sands & Goldberg-Glen, 2000).

The Grandmother-Parent Relationship

By assuming surrogate parenting, grandmothers are faced with a need to reestablish the relationship with their daughters or sons who are the grandchildren's parents. Grandmothers may feel resentment toward their children, whose own problems necessitated their taking over the parental role. As one grandmother put it, "I feel much resentment toward my daughter who can do whatever she wants, whenever she wants [while] I have to plan ahead and get a sitter if I want to go out" (Kelley, 1993, p. 336). Another strain in grandmother-parent relations may be the role reversal they experience (deToledo & Brown, 1995). As one grandmother said, "I resent the fact that I can't be his grandmother in the traditional sense. It feels like my daughter and I have reversed roles!" (deToledo & Brown, 1995, p. 336).

Grandmothers may also resent the parents for the harm they inflicted on their children because of substance abuse, physical abuse, abandonment, or neglect (Kelley, 1993; Sands & Goldberg-Glen, 2000). Feelings of shame or failure about their son's or daughter's inability to care for the children may stand in the way of maintaining a close relationship with them (Nisivoccia, 1996).

If the parent is involved in the child's life, the surrogate grandmother needs to cooperate with the parent and share responsibility for providing care (Strom & Strom, 1993). This may be difficult when there are intergenerational differences in parenting styles between the parent and the grandmother. Furthermore, sharing responsibility may cause tension, because the grandmother and the mother or father are not just two caregivers, but also mother and daughter or son. In some cases, the grandmother may be resented for replacing the parent, especially when the parent is not actively involved with the child. Parental substance abuse is often a major antecedent to children being raised by grandparents and a source of stress in the grandparent-parent relationship (Kelley, 1993; Sands & Goldberg-Glen, 2000). The conflict between parent and grandmother can be especially intense in those instances where the parent wants to regain custody of the child, but is opposed by the grandmother (Doucette-Dudman & LaCure, 1996).

The possibility that the child will return to his or her parent can be the grandmother's fondest dream and worst nightmare. As deToledo and Brown (1995) describe it,

> The dream is that the adult children [the parents] will shape up and become active, responsible parents, that the grandchildren will be safe, and that you [the grandparent] can resume your role of occasional baby-sitter and doting grandparent. The nightmare is that the children will go back before the parents have their lives in order, before it is truly safe. (p. 133)

IMPLICATIONS FOR GRANDCHILDREN

Making the transition from the care of the parent to the care of the grand-mother can be traumatic for the grandchildren, especially in view of the difficult circumstances that caused their having to move in with their grandmother (deToledo & Brown, 1995). Although moving in with a relative is less traumatic than moving in with nonkin, the grandchildren may undergo adjustment problems analogous to those experienced by foster and adoptive children. They may experience a sense of abandonment and grief over the loss of their parents and their parents' home (deToledo & Brown, 1995), and they may feel embarrassed that they live with their grandmother (deToledo & Brown, 1995). They may also experience divided loyalties, feeling that they are caught in the middle between their parents and grandparents, especially when the parents and grandparents have an adversarial relationship (Doucette-Dudman & LaCure, 1997) or when the parents are immature and keep frustrating the children with unfulfilled promises (deToledo & Brown, 1995). When the parent and grandmother are involved in legal conflicts over the child's custody, the child is bound to feel tension, stress, and confusion (deToledo & Brown, 1995). The grandchildren may be particularly vulnerable if they experienced some kind of maltreatment before moving in with their grandmothers.

VARIATIONS AMONG
GRANDMOTHER-HEADED FAMILIES

Like other families, grandmother-headed families come in many different variations. They may be single-grandmother-headed families, two-grandparent families, and families that raise their own children in addition to raising grandchildren. Grandmother caregivers may be informal surrogate parents, foster parents, legal guardians, or adoptive parents. Grandmother-headed families also vary by race and ethnicity, and according to the ages of the grandmother and grandchildren.

Grandmothers are also caregivers in extended households in which both the parent(s) and the grandparent coexist and act as parental figures. Though grandmother-headed families are nuclear, two-generation families, extended households are multigeneration families consisting of multiple residential parental figures. In multigeneration families, the grandmothers are either sharing responsibility and authority with the child's parents, or are acting as the sole caregivers.

IMPLICATIONS FOR POLICY

Because many grandparents act as surrogate parents without having the legal guardianship of the grandchildren, they have difficulty obtaining any available financial, medical, and educational services, and are hindered from acting on the grandchildren's behalf. The legally sanctioned forms of kinship care—custody, guardianship, and adoption—complicate relationships between parent and child, and may create a hostile family environment. Furthermore, they may involve complex, time-consuming, and costly court hearings that many caregivers are unequipped to handle (Karp, 1996). An alternative is the enactment of consent legislation, whereby access to state services is granted through simple documentation (Karp, 1996). In addition, kinship adoptions can be structured to allow parents to relinquish their parental rights while maintaining some supervisory and visitation rights (Karp, 1996). Policy changes are also needed to ensure that kinship caregivers will not be evicted from their homes once they assume responsibility for their grandchildren.

Most important, on a broad policy level, we need to address the conditions that have given rise to grandmother caregiving. This calls for a reexamination of our criminal justice policy, the provision of adequate day care services, drug- and alcohol-treatment programs, and financial assistance. We need to reinstate a social safety net that supports family development while protecting families from the ravages of poverty.

IMPLICATIONS FOR PRACTICE

Grandmothers who act as caregivers for their grandchildren often experience hardship, and may be exploited legally, physically, and financially. The sharp increase in grandmother caregiving may be seen as a marker of the poverty and stress that affect the family structure. Human service professionals are often involved in decisions that result in grandmothers assuming caregiving responsibilities for their grandchildren. At times, the interests of the social welfare agency may be at odds with those of the grandmother. Professionals should consider carefully whether the proposed arrangements adequately compensate the grandmother and whether sufficient support services are available.

If children need to be placed out of the home, grandparents and other relatives should be considered and may be a far better alternative to nonrelative foster care or institutional placement. At the same time, grandmothers' caregiving should be appropriately acknowledged, supported, and compensated. Furthermore, it should be undertaken only by choice. Grandmother caregivers should receive supportive and ancillary services to allow them some respite time to pursue their own interests and needs, and to learn about child and adolescent development in today's society.

Grandmother caregivers may benefit from participation in a support group, where they can talk about their situations with others who are in similar circumstances. In addition to reducing their sense of isolation, the group may be an important source of information about resources, as well as a validation of their caregiving role. There are close to 400 support groups nationwide, and there is a national grandparents information center in Washington, D.C.

IMPLICATIONS FOR RESEARCH

Grandmother-headed families have received increasing attention from scholars. However, the studies tend to be descriptive, focusing on demographic characteristics and the stress experienced by grandmothers. The more conceptual literature considers such issues as welfare eligibility, race, gender, caregiving, and reversing the feminization of poverty. With few exceptions (Billingsley, 1992; Gattai & Musatti, 1999; Goldberg et al., 1998), the literature has so far neglected grandparent-headed families as families. Further research is needed that considers these families as social systems, examining interactions between grandmothers and parents, grandmothers and grandchildren, and parents and grandchildren (Giarrusso et al., 1996). From the perspectives of the grandchildren, we need to learn more about the transition to the grandmother's household and the implications of being raised by a grandmother rather than a mother and a father. There are a host of issues focusing on the grandmother that merit further study. These include the grandmothers' relations with the children's parents, the implications of assuming off-time responsibilities, their coping with role reversal, the experience of the missing generation, and the ways they parent. Research is needed on the differences between parents' and grandmothers' parenting, and between grandmother-headed families and traditional grandmothers who visit with their grandchildren.

There is also a need for research examining the variations within the grandmother-headed family, including the influence of different cultural, ethnic, and racial norms. Other important variables are class and income, the ages of the grandmothers and grandchildren, the circumstances leading to the grandmothers' assuming caregiving responsibilities, and whether or not the parents are involved with the child. In order to design better support services, we need to know more about how grandmother-headed families relate to the social environment, including the role of extended family and the children's parents, and encounters with social and community services. Especially important are the implications of informal versus formal caregiving roles, such as foster care and adoption.

More research is needed that considers the conditions related to the increase in grandmother caregiving and the policies—drug treatment, alternatives to incarceration, public assistance, child care—that help parents perform their parenting obligations. Continued research attention should be focused on the economic plight of grandmother caregivers and how this affects the family. Barriers to grandmothers obtaining legal sanction for their caregiving bear further examination. Finally, we need to continue examining the implications of the gendered division of caretaking responsibilities. Cross-national studies of policies that support caregiving and help families combine caregiving and employment are also needed.

DISCUSSION QUESTIONS

1. What accounts for the increases in grandmother caregiving over the past two decades?

2. In what respects can the increasing prevalence of grandmother caregiving be considered as a marker of poverty and stress on the American families? How is it related to the feminization of poverty?

3. What are the causes and consequences of stigma against grandmother caregiving?

4. In what ways do grandmother-headed families resemble and differ from families headed by one or both parents?

5. Some consider that grandmother caregiving offers a good solution to a serious social problem. Others argue that it represents a problem in itself rather than a solution. What are the arguments on each side of the issue? What do you think? Why?

6. What issues should practitioners consider when working with grandmother-headed families?

SUGGESTIONS FOR FURTHER READING

Burnette, D. (1997). Grandparents raising grandchildren in the inner city. *Families in Society, 78*(5), 489–499.

deToledo, S., & Brown, D. E. (1995). *Grandparents as parents: A survival guide for raising a second family.* New York: Guilford.

Minkler, M., & Roe, K. M. (1993). *Grandmothers as caregivers: Raising children of the crack cocaine epidemic.* Newbury Park, CA: Sage.

Chapter 8

UNRAVELING THE FAMILY
What We Can Learn From Family Diversity

As the experience of each family in this book demonstrates, nontraditional families pay a price for being different. The privileged status of the one "right" family—first-married, heterosexual—persists despite it being just one of a number of diverse family forms. It is marketed as the desirable family, the template and default model (Laird, 1993). As a result, families that are different may feel marginalized and vulnerable to prejudice and discrimination. Some, such as single mothers, are subject to moral regulation through punitive public policies.

Family structure has become a central issue in social policy discourse. Conservatives attribute any number of social ills, including the creation of an underclass, to the breakdown of the traditional nuclear family (Jarrett, 1994; Rodgers, 1995). Politicians, by obsessively focusing on family structure rather than on the quality of family relationships, reveal their agenda: to support the idea that the economic support of families is most appropriately met by the "best" family arrangement—the first-married two-parent, nuclear family (Rodger, 1995). Blaming nontraditional families, and especially single-parent families, for their own hardship and poverty, as well as for generating a multitude of social problems, gives politicians and policymakers a rationale for neglecting to support children and families (Jarrett, 1994; Rodger, 1995).

In this chapter, I discuss the implications of family diversity for our understanding of family, and I consider some of the advantages of family diversity. I look at the ideology embedded in the traditional family model, and examine why it is defended so vehemently. I discuss the need to reconsider some of our assumptions about family relationships in view of what diverse families can teach us. I consider implications for research and policy, and conclude with a framework for understanding family diversity.

FAMILY DIVERSITY: THE ADVANTAGES OF DIFFERENCE

Despite the bias against nontraditional families, these families enjoy some unique advantages, which stem from their being different. As Coontz (1997) points out, each type of family has its own particular strengths, as well as its own vulnerabilities. Lesbian couples, although risking that their children will experience social disapproval, score high on parenting skills and produce children as well adjusted as other families. Single-parent families have only one parent within the home, but more often involve other adults in mentoring children. The complexity of stepfamilies is especially challenging, but it can also provide children with additional adult models and help them develop flexibility in dealing with roles and relationships. Two-earner families have trouble finding time for family relationships, but have the advantages of greater role sharing, equality, and income. Instead of seeing family weaknesses as the problem, we should be seeing family strengths as part of the solution. Families have shown great resilience and creativity in coping with current social realities (Coontz, 1997).

Diverse families are, in a sense, multicultural, because they live in both a traditional world and in a world of difference (Laird, 1993). They are part of the mainstream society and, at the same time, they belong to a distinct "culture." Many members of nontraditional families have at some point in their lives identified themselves as members of traditional families, and have behaved accordingly. However, on establishing a different kind of family, they may then be considered deviant (Allen, 1997). Though accorded an inferior status, their position as outsiders gives members of diverse families a dual perspective on the social environment. As "others," they are able to see that which is invisible to those with power and privilege in the social system (Laird, 1994). They are better equipped to reflect on and examine critically social values, norms, and expectations. As Laird (1994) suggests with respect to lesbian families,

The marginal position provokes certain kinds of questioning, a heightening of certain kinds of consciousness. When one knows that the dominant social discourse is wrong about oneself and one's community, one is more likely to question other powerful social narratives that shape one's life. (pp. 284–285)

Diverse families can lay claim to the innovative possibilities that derive from being different (Allen, 1997). Lacking rules about how a family should be, they are free to make up their own rules, choosing from the best of both traditional and diverse lifestyles (Laird, 1993; Wright, 1998). As many nontraditional families are established on socially constructed kinship rather than on blood ties, they have the latitude to choose family members. They can choose whom they wish to include or exclude among former spouses and lovers, their relatives, and friends, thereby contradicting the saying that "you can't pick your relatives" (Laird, 1993).

CHALLENGING THE HEGEMONY
OF THE TRADITIONAL FAMILY

Families Headed by Women

Most of the families in this book—single-parent, grandmother-headed, lesbian, and many foster and adoptive families—are headed by women. Despite the negative stereotypes, the fact of the matter is that most of these families provide a home and a haven, food, shelter, security, loving care, and guidance. That caretaking is often done under adverse conditions, without society's support and approval, is testimony to the strength and resilience of women-headed families.

The success of women-headed families is threatening to a patriarchal social order that insists that families, firms, organizations, and states be headed up by men. Whitehead (1993) suggests that

family diversity in the form of increasing numbers of single-parent and stepparent families . . . dramatically weakens and undermines society. . . . The new families are not an improvement on the nuclear family, nor are they as good, whether you look at outcomes for children or outcomes for society as a whole . . . family change represents a stunning example of social regress. (pp. 77, 80)

This negative portrayal reflects a normative patriarchal prescription for marriage, family life, and gender roles (Rice, 1994). Viewing nontraditional families through a deficit lens, many politicians, policymakers, and scholars have seen only deficiency and pathology. As Rice (1994) suggests,

> A deficit comparison model is applied to situations where the dominant family form differs from the so-called normative one, that is, intact, white, middle-class, and male-headed, as in the study of black families headed by women and divorced families headed by single-parent mothers. Such a model generally informs the discourse whenever women, by choice or circumstances, live without men. (p. 560)

The deficit model does not comprehend that women would choose to be alone. The data confirming this phenomenon have for the most part been ignored. As early as 1976, reports began to appear that, in addition to a steady increase in women who chose to divorce, a growing number of women chose not to marry, to postpone marriage, to have fewer children, and to become single heads of households (Rice, 1994). Leaving a husband and a conventional, approved family life is for many women an act of resistance to oppression (Rice, 1994).

The traditional family is a bastion of patriarchy and oppression for women (Bograd, 1988; Rice, 1994). Men's oppression of women within the family takes many forms. At the extreme is wife abuse, disguised under the gender-free term of "domestic violence." There are many other, more subtle forms of oppression, experienced by the vast majority of married women, including control over money and decision making, and forms of emotional abuse that sustain the man's supremacy, control, and power (Riessman, 1990). The half of all married women who divorce, along with those women who choose not to marry, make a powerful statement: that marriage and traditional family life are oppressive for them. So much so, that risking poverty and experiencing the hardship of raising their children on their own are considered better than marriage, which is socially sanctioned and secure. Indeed, two of three divorces are now initiated by women (Rice, 1994).

The Myth of Motherhood and the
Gendered Domestic Division of Labor

A great deal of the prejudice against nontraditional families stems from the dominant view of motherhood. It holds that women, by nature, are maternal and possess some special abilities that make them uniquely suited to perform the principal roles of parenthood. According to this paradigm, the biological experiences of pregnancy and breast-feeding generate a strong, instinctual drive in women to nurture. Therefore, mothers are more "natural" caregivers than fathers. Because they are without these experiences, men are said to lack the instinctual drive to nurture infants and children (Silverstein & Auerbach, 1999).

In reality, what transforms women into mothers is the daily responsibility they assume for their children. This responsibility, the countless hours spent with the child, the work and caring involved in raising the child, produce a growing awareness of the child's needs and an intimate connectedness between the child and the mother (Lamb, 1987; McMahon, 1995).

Both men and women have the same biological potential for nurturing, and the gendered division of labor in any culture is defined by the requirements of that culture's specific bioecological context (Silverstein & Auerbach, 1999). Lamb (1987) found no differences in parenting behaviors of mothers and fathers during their children's infancy. Neither mothers nor fathers were natural parents. However, because mothers tended to spend so much more time with their infants, they became much more familiar with their biological rhythms, and visual and behavioral cues. When observations were repeated a year later, mothers appeared to be much more competent caregivers than fathers. Many subsequent studies have shown that when fathers assume the primary caretaking role, they are as competent and as sensitive as mothers (Lamb, 1997; McMahon, 1995).

The concept of natural mothering, which is heavily laden with values, myths, and legends, places women on the altar of motherhood. However, this altar, glorified as it may be, is also a strait jacket. It places high expectations on women to give birth to children, raise them, and take care of them as their principal occupation while subordinating their own needs and ambitions. Furthermore, as this caretaking role is an all-consuming and uncompensated responsibility, mothers who assume full-time caretaking roles are dependent on the income of their husbands. This ties women to marriage and to traditional family lives, and places them in a situation of subordination to men (Allen, 1997).

In nontraditional families, where the parental figures who raise the children are frequently not birth parents, the motherhood myth stigmatizes non–birth parents, usually the women caretakers, as second best, inherently inferior to "real" mothers. Current social norms view married heterosexual women as the most appropriate to parent children. These so-called natural mothers, in turn, are the template for defining whether women are appropriate, only marginally appropriate, or inappropriate as mothers (DiLapi, 1989). Within this motherhood hierarchy, lesbian mothers are viewed as inappropriate, and the motherhood mythology rationalizes antilesbian conduct. Robson (1992) argues the category "mother" operates to domesticate lesbian existence, as it becomes difficult to think of women beyond the category "mother."

Like lesbian mothers, adoptive mothers, foster mothers, stepmothers, and grandmothers who raise their grandchildren are also the subject of negative stereotypes. Their motives for wanting to parent children that they did not bear are viewed with suspicion; their parenting is considered "unreal" and "unnatural." Foster mothers are often seen as being motivated by financial gain, as exploiters who use children for domestic chores and labor, or, alternatively, as seeking to adopt the children through the back door (Molin, 1994). Adoptive mothers are thought to be damaged women whose infertility symbolizes a deficit in their sexuality and identity as women (Hajal, 1996; Kaiser, 1996). Grandmothers are considered old, poor, and incompetent, incapable of proper parenting (Burnette, 1997; Courtney, 1994; Nisivoccia, 1996). Stepmothers are often portrayed as wicked and malicious (Erera, 1996; Ganong & Coleman, 1994).

The non–birth fathers are generally subject to less stigma than that experienced by non–birth mothers. In the case of foster and adoptive fathers, it is their wives who are judged the "guilty parties" that forced them into involuntary fathering. Stepfathers, especially, are subject to conflicting attitudes. On the one hand, they are viewed as noble and kind for providing for their stepchildren. On the other hand, they are also viewed with suspicion. The negative stepfather stereotypes deem them to be harsh disciplinarians towards their stepsons, and incestuous toward their stepdaughters. The most stigmatized non–birth fathers are gay men who raise children (DiLapi, 1989; Hargaden & Llewellin, 1996).

Insofar as the only appropriate mothering is considered to be that performed by heterosexual, married birth mothers, mothers in nontraditional families are regarded as less competent, and their children are thought to be more prone to problem behaviors or pathology. Adopted children are thought to be subject to adopted child syndrome, characterized by provocative, antisocial behavior and associated personality disturbances (Kirschner, 1996; Wegar, 1998). Lesbian and gay parents are viewed as unnatural and immoral (DePoy & Noble, 1992; Gallagher,

1993; Hargaden & Llewellin, 1996), and their children are considered likely to be harmed emotionally, molested, or impaired in their sex-role development (Falk, 1989; Victor & Fish, 1995). Children raised in stepfamilies have been judged to have inferior psychological well-being compared with children of intact traditional marriages (Bray & Berger, 1993; Ganong & Coleman, 1984). Foster mothers and grandmothers who raise their children are blamed for creating, or at least contributing to, the children's problems (Burnette, 1997; Courtney, 1994; Molin, 1994).

The tendency to focus on the problems of children in nontraditional families reflects the view that these families are less likely to provide a healthy environment for children, and that the traditional family is the social institution within which positive child adjustment is most likely to occur (Silverstein & Auerbach, 1999). This deficit view serves as an additional reinforcement for women to marry and assume traditional family life. The pressure on women to marry is supported by the myth of fathering. Mothers are assumed to be natural caregivers, yet responsible fathering is assumed to occur within the traditional family, as marriage has a "civilizing" effect on men (Blankenhorn, 1995).

The stereotypes of the natural mother and father, the biological and natural parents and children, establish a false dichotomy between what is normal and what is not. It provides a dangerous basis for stigmatizing families, and it devalues love and caring provided by choice. In considering the so-called natural mother as the sole, or at least the principal, caretaker of children, the stereotype is instrumental in domesticating mothers and upholding a gendered division of labor within the family.

In most heterosexual marriages, the domestic division of labor occurs along gendered lines (Acock & Demo, 1994). Women are primarily responsible for child care and household maintenance (Acock & Demo, 1994; Hochschild, 1989). This situation prevails regardless of whether or not both the mother and father are employed (Acock & Demo, 1994; Hochschild, 1989), or whether or not the mother is a birth mother. In stepfamilies, residential stepmothers spend more time with their children than the birth fathers (Hobart, 1988), and stepmothers assume more responsibilities toward their stepchildren than stepfathers (Ambert, 1986; Erera, 1996; Hobart, 1987). When the men work outside the home and the women do not, men maintain even more power and influence (Baxter, 1992). As Coontz (1997) states,

> Many of the problems commonly blamed on breakdown of the traditional family exist not because we've changed too much, but because we haven't

changed enough. . . . Because couples believe that their stresses come from
how much gender roles have already changed, they don't realize how much
more they still need to change. (p. 109)

Parenting and Its Implications for Children

Diverse families challenge existing family theories about gender-
based parenting responsibilities and division of labor (Demo & Allen,
1996). Most of the daily parenting and caretaking in traditional families
is performed by women (Acock & Demo, 1994). This is supported by the
common belief that the biologically different reproductive functions of
men and women automatically construct essential differences in parenting behaviors, and that women are better suited to caregiving roles than
men (Silverstein & Auerbach, 1999). The claim that mothers are more
natural caregivers than fathers has been proven wrong (Silverstein &
Auerbach, 1999). When fathers assume the primary caretaking role, they
are as competent and as sensitive as mothers (Lamb, 1997). Based on
research with gay men's fathering, and divorced, never-married, and
remarried fathers, Silverstein and Auerbach (1999) have found parenting
roles to be interchangeable. What is most important for the children is the
stability of the emotional connection between parent and child, and the
predictability of the caretaking relationship (Acock & Demo, 1994;
Benkov, 1995).

Neither the biological relationship to the child nor the gender of the
parents predicts positive child development (Acock & Demo; 1994;
Silverstein & Auerbach, 1999). Caregiving functions can be performed
by parenting figures of either sex, whether or not they are biologically
related to the child, and a wide variety of family structures can generate
positive child outcomes. Children need at least one responsible, caregiving adult who has a positive emotional connection to them and with
whom they have a consistent relationship. Because of the physical, financial, and emotional stress involved in raising children, a family that
includes more than one such adult is more likely to contribute to positive
child outcomes.

Blood Ties and Kinship

Much of the concern about nontraditional families is based on beliefs
about the supremacy of blood ties. It is generally assumed that people

related by blood are bound together in ways that others can never be. According to this belief, biological ties are, by nature, loyal, nurturing, caring, supporting, and loving. Therefore, families related by blood are considered essential for raising children (Laird, 1993), whereas others are thought to be inferior (Hayden, 1995). In traditional families, this glorification of blood ties acts as a powerful reinforcement of the bond between parents and children. For families that include non–birth children, this stereotype denigrates the family's structure and its core relationships.

The essentialist notion of natural caring, support, and love accorded to birth children is contradicted by the evidence of much-too-common parental abuse. Studies show that birth parents are more likely to engage in serious physical abuse of children than stepparents (Malkin & Lamb, 1994). One study found that the majority (78%) of children who suffered neglect and abuse were maltreated by a birth parent (Sedlak & Broadhurst, 1996). Parent substitutes (foster, adoptive, and stepparents) were responsible for abuse in only 14% of the cases. Furthermore, birth parents were about as likely to abuse their children sexually (29%) as were parent substitutes (25%).

The bias in favor of families based on blood ties is reflected in the terms *natural parent, real parent,* and *biological parent* (Hayden, 1995). They imply that parenting is a biological, natural phenomenon, whereas non–birth parents are artificial, fictive (literally "imaginary"), substitute, or unnatural (Laird, 1993). This both reflects and sustains a stigmatic view of non–biological children, parents, and families not based on blood relations (i.e., adoptive families, foster families, and many gay and lesbian families). However, from an anthropological point of view, all kinship, including that based on genes and blood, can be viewed as fictional, as symbols "implicated in one culturally specific way of demarcating and calculating relationships" (Weston, 1997, p. 105).

Most of the diverse families in this book raise non–birth children. Their experience demonstrates that we do not need biology or blood to create strong, loving, permanent relationships among adults and children (Biddle, Kaplan, & Silverstein, 1998; Hayden, 1995). Heterosexual, lesbian and gay, adoptive, foster, and stepfamilies, as well as families created through donor insemination, show that kinship must be viewed broadly. The essence of kinship is connection. We must therefore honor ties based on mutual caring, as well as those based on blood or marriage.

FAMILY DIVERSITY:
IMPLICATIONS FOR FAMILY THEORY

The experience of diverse families sheds new light on conventional norms and assumptions about family. These families have much to teach us about family life (Demo & Allen, 1996; Fine, Demo, & Allen, 2000; Laird, 1994). For example, Laird's (1993) comments about the innovating role of lesbian and gay families apply as well to other nontraditional families:

> [Lesbian and gay] families are generating new ideas not only about the formation and structure of families, but also about how couples and families may operate, as they pioneer new ways to conceptualize and practice parenting, couple relationship, and role and task divisions. With their fluid boundaries and varied memberships, their patterns of non-hierarchical decision-making, their innovative divisions of labor, and the relative weight given to friendship as well as blood relatedness, such families offer further challenge to dominant notions of family structure and functions, and present an opportunity for mental health professionals to assess the limitations in current definitions of family and kinship. (p. 296)

In contrast, as Blumstein and Schwartz (1983) observe, traditional families, though also providing stability and certainty, "inhibit change, innovation, and choice regarding roles and tasks" (p. 324).

The experience of diverse families calls into question some of the common assumptions about family structure, dynamics, and relationships. Here, I consider issues of intimacy, gender roles, and boundaries.

Intimacy and Couple Relationship

Family systems theory stresses that families, and especially the couple, need to establish a balance between closeness and fusion, and between differentiation and disengagement. Family systems theory however, lacks clarity about where to draw the line between positive closeness versus pathological fusion, and between differentiation and negative disengagement for couples (Green, Bettinger, & Zachs, 1996; Laird, 1993; Pearlman, 1988).

Fusion has been defined as a state in which the ego boundaries of two individuals are undifferentiated and experienced as oneness (Laird, 1993). Based on this definition, lesbian couples are frequently described as fused and enmeshed. However, research shows that although lesbian couples usually place high value on intimacy, sharing, and emotional connection, this is indicative neither of fusion nor of pathology (Greene, Causby, & Miller, 1997). The prevailing view of fusion as pathological reflects a gendered bias in favor of autonomy (Laird, 1993). The "perfect" degree of separateness and autonomy is based on heterosexual male norms that pathologize the relationships of women (Laird, 1993; Slater & Mencher, 1991). Women tend to value intimacy, and intimate relationships between women are often characterized by emotional intensity. Rather than indicative of codependency, fusion, or enmeshment, this emotional intensity is normative for women—lesbian or nonlesbian (Blumstein & Schwartz, 1983; Greene et al., 1997; Laird, 1993; Slater & Mencher, 1991). The relationships of coupled women also show that attachment and autonomy are not necessarily dichotomous, but may coexist. This calls into question conceptualizations of the polarity between differentiation and fusion, separateness and attachment, autonomy and interdependence (Blumstein & Schwartz, 1983).

Another family theory truism, that monogamy is essential for intimacy and commitment, is contravened by research on gay couples. Those not sexually exclusive have nevertheless been found to be content, committed, and satisfied in their long-lasting relations (Blumstein & Schwartz, 1983; Green et al., 1996; Kurdek, 1995; Laird, 1993). As this suggests, monogamy needs to be examined from the standpoint of the couple rather than being defined for them (Blumstein & Schwartz, 1983).

Family diversity also gives us cause to reexamine our views about parenting roles, caregiving, and couple relations. Once the family has children, members of traditional families, and especially women, have been consistently found to experience a decrease of marital satisfaction (see, for example, White & Booth, 1985). In contrast, research on lesbian and gay families suggests that having children increases the couple's satisfaction (Koepke, Hare, & Moran, 1992). These divergent findings may be due to the tendency of traditional heterosexual families to become more patriarchal following the birth of a child (Acock & Demo, 1994; LaRossa & LaRossa, 1981), whereas gay and lesbian families maintain their egalitarian division of labor following the addition of children to the family (Bigner, 1996; Hare & Richards, 1993; Kurdek, 1995; Mitchell, 1996; Patterson & Chan, 1997; Sullivan, 1996). Both lesbian parents and their children are more satisfied when child care responsibilities are evenly distributed between both parents (Chan, Raboy, & Patterson, 1998; Patterson, 1995; Sullivan, 1996). Furthermore, compared with heterosexual couples, lesbian and gay couples tend to relate to each other more as friends who are assumed to be equal in power and status (Demo & Allen, 1996; Kurdek, 1995). This equity is highly valued and regarded as an important source of intimacy and family satisfaction.

Family Boundaries

The limitation of the one-size-fits-all stereotype is also illustrated in the case of family boundaries. Family boundaries distinguish the family system from other social groups while defining who belongs in the family and what functions they will perform (Boss & Greenberg, 1984; Pasley, 1987; Pasley & Ihinger-Tallman, 1989). Lack of boundary clarity is recognized as a source of stress and dysfunction (Boss & Greenberg, 1984; Rodgers & Conrad, 1986). Nuclear families that are uncertain whether a member does or does not belong, who is "in" and who is "out," are indeed experiencing family boundary ambiguity.

Family system theorists agree that family boundaries need to be flexible enough to permit interchange with the environment and firm enough to engender a sense of a family, defining clearly who is or is not a family member. It is generally assumed that the physical boundaries of the family (i.e., residence) are coterminous with the psychological boundaries (i.e., the family members' perception of who belongs to the family). However, this understanding of family boundaries is much too narrow when applied to the families in this book. All of them—step-, single-parent, foster, grandparent-headed, lesbian and gay, and adoptive families—are composed of both residential and nonresidential members. For these families, physical and psychological boundaries are quite different. To include the family members living in separate households, these families need to maintain much more open boundaries than traditional families.

On the other hand, lesbian and gay families need to maintain much more rigid boundaries than traditional families in order to ensure the family's survival in the face of homophobia, stigma, and discrimination (Slater & Mencher, 1991). The greater the level of perceived threat and rejection, the more the couple attempts to keep the social hostility at bay and "fortify the bonds of love" (McVinney, 1988, p. 216). Although this kind of closed family system may put considerable pressure on the family members to feel responsible for fulfilling one another's needs, this closeness is adaptive.

Poor, African American families are also instructive in their adaptability to adverse situations and to changing circumstances (Littlejohn-

Blake & Darling, 1993). Compared with middle-class, white families, many African American families, especially poor ones, have more fluid caregiving roles and norms supporting interdependence, communal cooperation, and mutual support (Billingsley, 1992; Hill, 1998; Littlejohn-Blake & Darling, 1993). They define caregiving roles functionally rather than biologically (Allen & James, 1998; Goldberg, Sands, Cole, & Christofalo, 1998; Hill, 1998), and are more willing and better able to successfully absorb relatives and friends in need into their families (Fine, Schwebel, & James-Myers, 1987; Littlejohn-Blake & Darling, 1993). Shifting caregiving roles across generations from parent to grandparent, grandmother-headed families of any race exemplify flexibility, a fluidity of family roles, and mutual support (Goldberg et al., 1998).

IMPLICATIONS FOR RESEARCH

We have learned a great deal about diverse families over the past 20 years or so. Yet, as with public policy, the research has not kept pace with the rapid increase in family diversity, and, with some exceptions, is still influenced by the traditional family paradigm. There has been insufficient research on how diverse families function from their own standpoint, as opposed to comparing them with traditional families. This leaves us in relative ignorance about diverse families, which makes them seem more threatening.

Far too few studies examine diverse families as social systems in their own right. Furthermore, there is far too much emphasis on the supposed deficits and problems with diverse families, and insufficient attention to their strengths. Those who have examined these families from their own standpoint have found strengths and abilities. Instead of declaring some family structures better than others, we should focus on how well families function (Coontz, 1997). Moreover, though most researchers acknowledge the inadequacy of traditional definitions of family, they nevertheless tend to confine their studies to families that fit the old, narrow definitions (VanEvery, 1999). "We need a sociology that allows us to argue for changing family values in the face of the attack on the lack of family values in contemporary society" (VanEvery, 1999, p. 180).

Much of the literature is conceptual rather than empirical, and many of the empirical studies are beset with methodological shortcomings that limit the degree of confidence we can place in the findings. Many of the studies are based on small, nonrandom samples and cross-sectional data.

A common problem is the reliance on samples of preponderantly white families. More research is needed on families of culturally diverse backgrounds. We need more longitudinal studies to chart the experience of families over time, especially at key stages of family life cycles, and with samples more representative of the diversity and variability among families. Such studies are expensive and will require a greater commitment of funds from both government and private sources. The research agenda should also include more studies of the internal dynamics of diverse families.

For many diverse families, there is an important economic dimension that should be kept in the forefront of both research studies and policy discourse. This economic component is especially apparent with respect to single-parent families, grandmother-headed families, foster families, and adoptive families. However, having an adequate income is important for all families, irrespective of family structure. Continuing examination of the relationships between poverty, child development, and family functioning is of critical importance, especially in view of the tendency of some to attribute to family structure problems that are really due to family and child poverty.

Another crucial issue, one with implications for all families, is the gendered division of caregiving and family responsibilities. Insofar as women's caregiving is taken for granted, research on the implications of caregiving, how to accommodate caregiving and employment, how to support and compensate caregivers, is all the more important.

Federal and state legislative changes can have profound implications for families. Research is needed to track and assess the consequences, both intended and unintended, of new legislation pertinent to families. Although legislation is often driven by ideology and self-interest, empirical findings can help bring a measure of rationality to policy debates. Legislative change offers researchers a kind of natural experiment where the impact of specific policies on families can be assessed. A case in point is welfare reform. Though not viewed as family legislation per se, the Personal Responsibility and Work Opportunity Reconciliation Act of 1996 (PRWORA, Public Law 104-193) affects poor families, and especially single-parent families, in major ways. We need to look beyond the numbers of families removed from the welfare rolls to examine the impact on the well-being of children and families. Similarly, we need research to document the impact of the various laws governing foster care, adoption, grandparent and other kinship care, and gay and lesbian families.

Though having fallen out of favor in an era of limited government, the practice of funding research and demonstration projects to test alternative programs and interventions to assist diverse families needs to be revived. Research and demonstration projects, once popular in a time of social activism, hold promise for identifying and disseminating exemplary practices. They can, for example, provide answers to such questions as the best ways to support foster families, prevent placement, bring about reunification, or help older foster children make a successful transition to adulthood.

The policy debates about families in the United States tend to be highly parochial in their failure to take into account relevant experience of other countries, especially those with much more advanced family support policies. Such policies include subsidized child care, liberal family leave, income support for poor families, and universal health care. Family researchers should be familiar with these family friendly policies, and policy researchers should maintain a cross-national perspective in their research. By doing so, they will help to open the policy discussions to a wider range of options.

IMPLICATIONS FOR POLICY

We need to stop blaming families for what are, in truth, failures of public policy. The United States is a traditional society when it comes to the division of labor in the family and the lack of public policies helping working parents (Haas, 1995). The United States lags well behind other industrial countries in public subsidies for child care and maternity and parental leave. More egalitarian societies place a higher value on the welfare of children, mothers' participation in the labor force, access of women to positions of power, and trust in the government's benevolence in supporting families (Haas, 1995).

We should work to bring families to where they should be, not back to what they used to be. Instead of emphasizing divisions between so-called good and bad families, we should "start bringing as many of them as possible into our sphere of social support" (Coontz, 1997, p. 177). Support systems for all families include family friendly work policies, high-quality and affordable child care, better tax breaks for families with children, job training, more effective child support enforcement, national health insurance, high school programs in child development and community service, and a combination of income support and job programs for single mothers (Coontz, 1997).

If the well-being of children really mattered, public policy and business practices would demonstrate support for children and their families (Biddle et al., 1998; Coontz, 1997). Most other countries and many groups within the United States, including African Americans, Latin Americans, and Native Americans, have a more child-centered social ethic (Coontz, 1997). However, as long as public policy assumes a reliance on women fulfilling traditional caretaking and homemaking roles even while employed, and men are considered the breadwinners, the nation's family policy will remain undeveloped and out of step with current social and economic realities. Parents, and especially women, bear the brunt of performing and paying for caretaking that is much more adequately supported in other countries. This amounts to a privatization of caretaking responsibilities, in contrast to the greater public sharing of these responsibilities that is common elsewhere. To put it another way, women and other caretakers in the United States are privately subsidizing what ought to be provided by government—and, collectively, by all of us as taxpayers—to help reproduce the labor force and the citizenry.

Women need to be acknowledged as full-time workers along with men, and to be supported by a full range of policies and services to facilitate family life. These include generous family benefits; high-quality, publicly funded day care; universal health care; and flexible work policies to accommodate family responsibilities and reduce the tension between work and family (Rodger, 1995). We need to enact comparable worth standards of pay equity to enable women, as well as men, of all races to earn a family wage. We also need to safeguard reproductive rights to make it possible to choose to parent with responsibility. These measures, far from being utopian, are standard features of other developed countries.

We cannot alleviate family problems until we stop attributing those problems solely to the behavior of family members themselves. As Coontz (1997) writes,

We cannot help contemporary families if we accept a one-dimensional analysis of where their problems originate, insist there is only one blueprint for how all families should look and act, or offer . . . charity in place of concrete reforms to relieve the stresses on working parents and offer positive alternatives to youth. (p. 7)

A FRAMEWORK FOR
UNDERSTANDING FAMILIES

It is my belief, as expressed throughout this book, that the following points are essential in understanding family diversity:

- Family life is important to most of us, and most of us choose to live in families at least part of our lives. Rather than posing a threat to the family, the creation of different family styles is an affirmation of family life, an expression of our desire to live in families that fit our needs and our choices.

- To fully understand diverse families, we need to leave behind the assumption that one size fits all, that one family structure is good for all. This assumption is neither valid nor possible. We are too diverse, our needs and lifestyles too different to be able to fit into one single family model. To enthrone one family as the ideal is a denial of human diversity.

- There is no one family style that is universal or best. Each family style has unique strengths, advantages, and resilience, and each family style faces its own challenges. Once we consider diverse families from their respective standpoints, we have much to learn that can enhance our family lives, in whatever form they may take.

- Many of the problems experienced by diverse families are due to factors outside the family itself, including discrimination, poverty, and inadequate societal support systems for families and children. We need subsidized housing and health care, work environments that incorporate family friendly policies, and legal and social institutions that support families. There is nothing wrong with any of the families addressed in this book, or with other diverse families. The pressures, tensions, and problems they experience are, almost without exception, imposed by a social environment that does not accept or support them.

- Viewing family life through a traditional family lens reinforces this lack of acceptance and support. It renders all other families second best, problematic, and deviant. It denies us the opportunity to accept and appreciate other families. As others have said—and I concur—it is both wrong and harmful to equate family structure with family functioning (Acock & Demo, 1994; Dowd, 1997; Hill, 1998; Silverstein & Auerbach, 1999).

- Although we do need to examine the problems experienced by diverse families, it is also important that we pay attention to their strengths, achievements, and contributions. Focusing on problems alone gives a distorted perspective.

- To appreciate the unique strengths of diverse families, we need to examine their structure and dynamics. However, we cannot limit our focus to family and individual factors alone. We must consider each family holistically, assessing systematically the contribution of societal factors. This means considering the historical, economic, and social context, as well as the pertinent laws and policies. Most often, the societal context includes issues of race, ethnicity, and gender, and their derivatives—namely, bigotry, racism, homophobia, xenophobia, patriarchy, and other forms of oppression. As Hill (1998), addressing African American families, states: "The deficit perspective usually attributes the dysfunctioning of black families to their internal structure or to the 'underclass' values of family members, and de-emphasizes the impact of external factors, such as racism, sexism, economic forces, or social policies" (p. 15).

- To understand and appreciate diverse families, we need to examine them from the standpoint of their own experience rather than imposing criteria that are not relevant. The "experts" should be the family members who, as in an ethnographic study, teach and educate us from the experience of their daily lives.

- Finally, in our quest to understand diverse families, we need to keep in mind the diversity within each family style. Just as traditional families differ from one another, so do diverse families. They vary in age, social class, culture, ethnicity, race, and on many other dimensions. Though all families resemble one another in some respects, each individual family is unique and extraordinary.

DISCUSSION QUESTIONS

1. At several points in the book, I have referred to the family as a social construct. Yet we know that families are real. What does it mean to say that families are socially constructed? What are the social and political implications?

2. What do you believe is the basis for a gendered division of caretaking responsibilities? Is there a biological basis? If not, how do you explain its durability?

3. What do you think it would take to bring about a more equitable division of family caretaking responsibilities? Is this a desirable policy goal? Is it something in which government should have a role? Or is it simply up to the individuals themselves to work out?

4. I have suggested that family caretaking has been overly privatized, and that it should be made more a collective responsibility. If there were more of a public role in family caretaking, what forms might it take? What would be the impact on families? On society?

5. Why do you believe it is that the United States is so far out of step with other countries with respect to family friendly policies?

6. How has reading about the families in this book changed your thinking about families?

SUGGESTIONS FOR FURTHER READING

Acock, A. C., & Demo, D. H. (1994). *Family diversity and well-being.* Thousand Oaks, CA: Sage.

Baber, K. M., & Allen, K. R. (1992). *Women and families: Feminist reconstructions.* New York: Guilford.

Lamb, M. E. (Ed.). (1999). *Parenting and child development in "nontraditional" families.* Mahwah, NJ: Lawrence Erlbaum.

Littlejohn-Blake, S. M., & Darling, C. A. (1993). Understanding the strengths of African American families. *Journal of Black Studies, 23*(4), 460–471.

Silverstein, L. B., & Auerbach, C. F. (1999). Deconstructing the essential father. *American Psychologist, 54*(6), 397–407.

Thorne, B., & Yalom, M. (Eds.). (1982). *Rethinking the family: Some feminist questions.* New York: Longman.

REFERENCES

Abdullah, S. B. (1996). Transracial adoption is not the solution to America's problems of child welfare. *Journal of Black Psychology, 22*(2), 254–261.

Abramovitz, M. (1994). Challenging the myths of welfare reform from a woman's perspective. *Social Justice, 21, 1*(55), 17–21.

Acock, A. C., & Demo, D. H. (1994). *Family diversity and well-being.* Thousand Oaks, CA: Sage.

Adams, B. N., & Steinmetz, S. K. (1993). Family theory and methods in the classics. In P. G. Boss & W. J. Doherty (Eds.), *Sourcebook of family theories and methods: A contextual approach* (pp. 71–94). New York: Plenum.

Ahrons, C. R. (1980). Redefining the divorced family: A conceptual framework. *Social Work, 25*(6), 437–441.

Ahrons, C. R. (1981). The continuing coparental relationship between divorced spouses. *American Journal of Orthopsychiatry, 51*(3), 415–428.

Ahrons, C. R., & Rodgers, R. H. (1987). *Divorced families: A multidisciplinary developmental view.* New York: Norton.

Ahrons, C. R., & Wallisch, L. (1987). Parenting in the binuclear family: Relationships between biological and stepparents. In K. Pasley & M. Ihinger-Tallman (Eds.), *Remarriage and stepparenting: Current research and theory* (pp. 225–256). New York: Guilford.

Ainslie, J., & Feltey, K. M. (1991). Definitions and dynamics of motherhood and family in lesbian communities. *Marriage and Family Review, 17*(1–2), 63–86.

Alexander, R., Jr., & Alexander, C. L. (1995). The impact of *Suter v. Artist M.* on foster care policy. *Social Work, 40*(4), 543–548.

Alexander, R., Jr., & Curtis, C. M. (1996). A review of empirical research involving the transracial adoption of African American children. *Journal of Black Psychology, 22*(2), 223–235.

Alford-Cooper, F. (1993). Women as family caregivers: An American social problem. *Journal of Women and Aging, 5*(1), 43–57.

Allen, K. R. (1997). Lesbian and gay families. In T. Arendell (Ed.), *Contemporary parenting: Challenges and issues* (pp. 196–218). Thousand Oaks, CA: Sage.

Allen, K. R., & Baber, K. M. (1992). Starting the revolution in family life education: A feminist vision. *Family Relations, 41,* 378–384.

Allen, K. R., & Demo, D. H. (1995). The families of lesbians and gay men: A new frontier in family research. *Journal of Marriage and the Family, 57*(1), 111–127.

Allen, W. R., & James, A. D. (1998). Comparative perspectives on black family life: Uncommon explorations of a common subject. *Journal of Comparative Family Studies, 29*(1), 1–12.

Alternatives to Marriage Project. (2000, May). *Gays and lesbian "marriage" in France.* Available at: http://www.unmarried.org.

Alty, C., & Cameron, S. (1995). Open adoption: The way forward? *International Journal of Sociology and Social Policy, 15*(4–5), 40–58.

Amato, P. R. (1988). Long term implications of parental divorce for adult self-concept. *Journal of Family Issues, 9*(2), 201–213.

Amato, P. R. (1994a). The implications of research findings on children in stepfamilies. In A. Booth & J. Dunn (Eds.), *Stepfamilies: Who benefits? Who does not?* (pp. 81–87). Hillsdale, NJ: Lawrence Erlbaum.

Amato, P. R. (1994b). Life-span adjustment of children to their parents' divorce. *Future of Children, 4*(1), 143–164.

Amato, P. R. (1999). Children of divorced parents as young adults. In E. M. Hetherington (Ed.), *Coping with divorce, single parenting, and remarriage: A risk and resiliency perspective* (pp. 147–163). Mahwah, NJ: Lawrence Erlbaum.

Amato, P. R. (2000). Diversity within single-parent families. In D. H. Demo, K. R. Allen, & M. A. Fine (Eds.), *Handbook of family diversity* (pp. 149–172). New York: Oxford University Press.

Amato, P. R., & Booth, A. (1991). Consequences of parental divorce and marital unhappiness for adult well-being. *Social Forces, 69*(3), 895–914.

Amato, P. R., & Booth, A. (1996). A prospective study of divorce and parent-child relationships. *Journal of Marriage and the Family, 58*(2), 356–365.

Amato, P. R., & Keith, B. (1991). Parental divorce and well being of children: A meta-analysis. *Psychological Bulletin, 110*(1), 26–40.

Amato, P. R., Loomis, L. S., & Booth, A. (1995). Parental divorce, marital conflict, and offspring well-being during early adulthood. *Social Forces, 73*(3), 895–915.

Amato, P. R., & Rezac, S. J. (1994). Contact with nonresidential parents, interparental conflict, and children's behavior. *Journal of Family Issues, 15*(2), 191–207.

Ambert, A. M. (1982). Differences in children's behavior toward custodial mothers and custodial fathers. *Journal of Marriage and the Family, 44*(1), 73–86.

Ambert, A. M. (1986). Being a stepparent: Live-in and visiting step-children. *Journal of Marriage and the Family, 48,* 795–804.

Anderson, G. R. (1997). Introduction: Achieving permanency for all children in the child welfare system. *Journal of Multicultural Social Work, 5*(1–2), 1–8.

Anderson, J. Z., & White, G. D. (1986). An empirical investigation of interaction and relationship patterns in functional and dysfunctional nuclear families and stepfamilies. *Family Process, 25,* 407–422.

Anderson, S., Piantanida, M., & Anderson, C. (1993). Normal processes in adoptive families. In F. Walsh (Ed.), *Normal family processes* (2nd ed., pp. 254–281). New York: Guilford.

Aniels-Mohring, D., & Berger, M. (1984). Social network changes and the adjustment to divorce. *Journal of Divorce, 8*(1), 17–32.

Apfel, N. H., & Seitz, V. (1991). Four models of adolescent mother-grandmother relationships in black inner-city families. *Family Relations, 40*(10), 421–429.

Aquilino, W. S. (1991). Family structure and home-leaving: A further specification of the relationship. *Journal of Marriage and the Family, 53*(4), 999–1010.

Arditti, J. A. (1999). Rethinking relationships between divorced mothers and their children: Capitalizing on family strengths. *Family Relations, 48*(2), 109–119.

Arendell, T. J. (1993). The economic impact of divorce on American women. In L. Tepperman, S. J. Wilson, & S. Badin (Eds.), *Next of kin: An international reader on changing families* (pp. 306–311). Englewood Cliffs, NJ: Prentice Hall.

Aronson, A. (1996). Potties, pride and PC: Scenes from a lesbian mothers' group. *Frontiers, 17*(1), 58–72.

Asher, S. J., & Bloom, B. L. (1983). Geographic mobility as a factor in adjustment to divorce. *Journal of Divorce, 6*(4), 69–84.

Aumend, S. A., & Barrett, M. C. (1984). Self-concept and attitudes toward adoption: A comparison of searching and nonsearching adult adoptees. *Child Welfare, 63*(3), 251–259.

Austin, J. F. (1993). The impact of school policies on noncustodial parents. *Journal of Divorce and Remarriage, 20*(3–4), 153–171.

Austinson, K. (1995). [Comment on the article Infant relinquishment through adoption]. *IMAGE: Journal of Nursing Scholarship, 2*(2), 92.

Avery, R. J. (1998). Information disclosure and openness in adoption: State policy and empirical evidence. *Children and Youth Services Review, 20*(1–2), 57–85.

Bachrach, C. A., London, K. A., & Maza, P. L. (1991). On the path to adoption: Adoption seeking in the United States, 1988. *Journal of Marriage and the Family, 53*(3), 705–718.

Bagley, C. (1993). Transracial adoption in Britain: A follow-up study with policy considerations. *Child Welfare, 72*(3), 285–299.

Bakeis, C. D. (1996). The Indian Child Welfare Act of 1978: Violating personal rights for the sake of the tribe. *Notre Dame Journal of Law, Ethics and Public Policy, 10*(2), 543–586.

Bank, L., Forgatch, M. S., Patterson, G. R., & Fetrow, R. A. (1993). Parenting practices of single mothers: Mediators of negative contextual factors. *Journal of Marriage and the Family, 55,* 371–384.

Baran, A., & Panor, R. (1990). Open adoption. In D. M. Brodzinsky & M. D. Schneider (Eds.), *The psychology of adoption* (pp. 316–331). New York: Oxford University Press.

Barber, B. L., & Lyons, J. M. (1994). Family processes and adolescent adjustment in intact and remarried families. *Journal of Youth and Adolescence, 23*(4), 421–436.

Barker, K. (2000, July 16). DSHS faces suit from foster kids. *Seattle Times,* pp. A1, A18.

Barth, R. P. (1992). Adoption. In P. J. Pecora, J. K. Whittaker, & A. N. Maluccio (Eds.), *The child welfare challenge: Policy, practice, and research* (pp. 361–398). Hawthorne, NY: Aldine.

Barth, R. P. (1994). Adoption research: Building blocks for the next decade. *Child Welfare, 73*(5), 625–638.

Barth, R. P. (1995). Adoption. In *Encyclopedia of Social Work* (19th ed., pp. 48–59). Washington, DC: National Association of Social Workers.

Barth, R. P. (1997). Effects of age and race on the odds of adoption versus remaining in long-term out-of-home care. *Child Welfare, 76*(2), 285–308.

Barth, R. P., & Berry, M. (1988). *Adoption and disruption: Risks, rates, and responses.* Hawthorne, NY: Aldine.

Barth, R. P., Courtney, M., Berrick, J. D., & Albert, V. (1994). *From child abuse to permanency planning: Child welfare services pathways and placements.* Hawthorne, NY: Aldine.

Bartholet, E. (1993). *Family bonds: Adoption and the politics of parenting.* Boston: Houghton Mifflin.

Bartholet, E. (1994). Adoption rights and reproductive wrongs. In G. Sen & R. C. Snow (Eds.), *Power and decision: The social control of reproduction* (pp. 177–203). Boston: Harvard School of Public Health.

Barusch, A. S. (1994). *Older women in poverty: Private lives and public policies.* New York: Springer.

Bass, S. A., & Caro, F. G. (1996). The economic value of grandparent assistance. *Generations, 20*(1), 29–33.

Bassuk, E. L. (1990). Who are the homeless families? Characteristics of sheltered mothers and children. *Community Mental Health Journal, 26,* 425–434.

Bausch, R. S., & Serpe, R. T. (1997). Negative outcomes of interethnic adoption of Mexican American children. *Social Work, 42*(2), 136–143.

Baxter, J. (1992). Power attitudes and time: The domestic division of labour. *Journal of Comparative Family Studies, 23*(2), 165–182.

Beca Zinn, M. B. (1997). Family, race, and poverty. In A. S. Skolnick & J. H. Skolnick (Eds.), *Family in transition* (9th ed., pp. 316–329). New York: HarperCollins.

Becvar, R. J., Ray, W. A., & Becvar, D. S. (1996). A modest/immodest proposal: Reciprocal foster families. *Contemporary Family Therapy, 18*(2), 257–265.

Begun, A. L. (1995). Sibling relationships and foster care placements for young children. *Early Child Development and Care, 106,* 237–250.

Belcastro, P. A., Gramlich, T., Nicholson, T., Price, J., & Wilson, R. (1993). A review of data based studies addressing the affects of homosexual parenting on children's sexual and social functioning. *Journal of Divorce and Remarriage, 20*(1–2), 105–123.

Benedict, M. I., Zuravin, S., & Stallings, R. Y. (1996). Adult functioning of children who lived in kin versus nonrelative family foster homes. *Child Welfare, 75*(5), 529–549.

Benkov, L. (1994). *Reinventing the family: The emerging story of lesbian and gay parents.* New York: Crown.

Benkov, L. (1995). Lesbian and gay parents: From margin to center. *Journal of Feminist Family Therapy, 7*(1–2), 49–64.

Benkov, L. (1997). Reinventing the family. In A. S. Skolnick & J. H. Skolnick (Eds.), *Family in transition* (9th ed., pp. 354–379). New York: HarperCollins.

Berger, R. (1988). *Stepfamilies: A multi-dimensional perspective.* New York: Haworth.

Berger, R. (1995). Three types of stepfamilies. *Journal of Divorce and Remarriage, 24*(1–2), 35–49.

Bernstein, A. C. (1994). Women in stepfamilies: The fairy godmother, the wicked witch, and Cinderella reconstructed. In M. Pravder Mirkin (Ed.), *Women in context: Toward a feminist reconstruction of psychotherapy* (pp. 188–213). New York: Guilford.

Bernstein, A. C. (1997). Stepfamilies from siblings' perspectives. *Marriage and Family Review, 26*(1–2), 153–175.

Bernstein, B. E., & Haberman, B. G. (1981). Lawyer and counselor as an interdisciplinary team: Problem awareness in the blended family. *Child Welfare, 60*(4), 211–219.

Berrick, J. D., & Barth, R. P. (1994). Research on kinship foster care: What do we know? Where do we go from here? *Children and Youth Services Review, 16*(1–2), 1–5.

Berrick, J. D., Barth, R. P., & Needell, B. (1994). A comparison of kinship foster homes and foster family homes: Implications for kinship foster care as family preservation. *Children and Youth Services Review, 16*(1–2), 35–63.

Berrick, J. D., & Lawrence, K. R. (1995). Emerging issues in child welfare. *Public Welfare, 53*(4), 4–11, 50.

Berry, M. (1993). Risks and benefits of open adoption. *Future of Children, 3*(1), 125–138.

Berry, M., Barth, R. P., & Needell, B. (1996). Preparation, support, satisfaction of adoptive families in agency and independent adoptions. *Child and Adolescent Social Work Journal, 13*(2), 157–183.

Berry, M., Dylla, D. J. C., Barth, R. P., & Needell, B. (1998). The role of open adoption in the adjustment of adopted children and their families. *Children and Youth Services Review, 20*(1–2), 151–171.

Bianchi, S. M. (1995). The changing demographic and socioeconomic characteristics of single parent families. *Marriage and Family Review, 20*(1–2), 71–97.

Biddle, C., Kaplan, S. R., & Silverstein, D. (1998). *Kinship: Ties that bind.* Available at: http://www.adopting.org/silveroze/html/kinship.html.

Biehal, N., & Wade, J. (1996). Looking back, looking forward: Care leavers, families and change. *Children and Youth Services Review, 18*(4–5), 425–445.

Bigner, J. J. (1996). Working with gay fathers: Developmental, postdivorce parenting, and therapeutic issues. In J. Laird & R. J. Green (Eds.), *Lesbians and gays in couples and families: A handbook for therapists* (pp. 370–403). San Francisco: Jossey-Bass.

Bigner, J. J. (1999). Raising our sons: Gay men as fathers. *Journal of Gay and Lesbian Social Services, 10*(1), 61–77.

Bigner, J. J., & Jacobson, R. B. (1989). The value of children to gay and heterosexual fathers. *Journal of Homosexuality, 18,* 163–172.

Billingsley, A. (1992). *Climbing Jacob's ladder: The enduring legacy of African American families.* New York: Simon & Schuster.

Blankenhorn, D. (1995). *Fatherless America: Confronting our most urgent social problem.* New York: Basic Books.

Blau, Z. S. (1973). *Old age in a changing society.* New York: New Viewpoints.

Block, J. H., Block, J., & Gjerde, P. F. (1986). The personality of children prior to divorce: A prospective study. *Child Development, 57,* 827–840.

Block, J. H., Block, J., & Gjerde, P. F. (1988). Parental functioning and the home environment in families of divorce: Prospective and concurrent analyses. *Journal of the American Academy of Child and Adolescent Psychiatry, 27,* 207–213.

Blome, W. W. (1997). What happens to foster kids: Educational experiences of a random sample of foster care youth and a matched group of non-foster care youth. *Child and Adolescent Social Work Journal, 14*(1), 41–53.

Blumstein, P., & Schwartz, P. (1983). *American couples.* New York: William Morrow.

Bograd, M. (1988). Power, gender, and the family: Feminist perspectives on family systems theory. In M. A. Dutton-Douglas & L. E. A. Walker (Eds.), *Feminist psychotherapies: Integration of therapeutic and feminist systems* (Developments in Clinical Psychology, pp. 118–133). Norwood, NJ: Ablex.

Bohannan, P. (1970). Divorce chains, households of remarriage, and multiple divorces, In P. Bohannan (Ed.), *Divorce and after* (pp. 113–123). Garden City, NY: Doubleday.

Bohannan, P. (1997). Divorce. In Grolier Multimedia Encyclopedia. Available at: http://gi.grolier.com/gi/products/reference/99gme/index.htm

Books-Gunn, J. (1994). Research on stepparenting families: Integrating disciplinary approaches and informing policy. In A. Booth & J. Dunn (Eds.), *Stepfamilies: Who benefits? Who does not?* (pp. 167–189). Hillsdale, NJ: Lawrence Erlbaum.

Booth, A., & Edwards, J. N. (1992). Starting over: Why remarriages are more unstable. *Journal of Family Issues, 13*(2), 179–195.

Borgman, R. (1985). The influence of family visiting upon boys' behavior in a juvenile correctional institution. *Child Welfare, 64*(6), 629–638.

Boss, P. (1987). Family stress. In M. B. Sussman & S. K. Steinmetz (Eds.), *Handbook of marriage and the family* (pp. 695–724). New York: Plenum.

Boss, P., & Greenberg, J. (1984). Family boundary ambiguity: A new variable in family stress theory. *Family Process, 23,* 535–546.

Bowen, G. L., Desimone, L. M., & McKay, J. K. (1995). Poverty and the single mother family: A macroeconomic perspective. *Marriage and Family Review, 20*(1–2), 115–142.

Bowlby, J. (1982). *Attachment and loss. Vol. 1: Attachment* (2nd ed.). New York: Basic Books.

Bozett, F. W. (1980). Gay fathers: How and why do they disclose their homosexuality to their children. *Family Relations, 29,* 173–179.

Bozett, F. W. (1987). Gay fathers. In F. W. Bozett (Ed.), *Gay and lesbian parents* (pp. 3–22). New York: Praeger.

Brand, E., & Clingempeel, W. G. (1987). Interdependencies of marital and stepparent-stepchild relationships and children's psychological adjustment: Research findings and clinical implications. *Family Relations, 36,* 140–145.

Brandon, P. D. (2000). Did the AFDC program succeed in keeping mothers and young children living together? *Social Service Review, 74*(2), 214–230.

Bray, J. H. (1992). Family relationships and children's adjustment in clinical and nonclinical stepfather families. *Journal of Family Psychology, 6*(1), 60–68.

Bray, J. H. (1995). Children in stepfamilies: Assessment and treatment issues. In D. K. Huntley (Ed.), *Understanding stepfamilies: Implications for assessment and treatment* (pp. 59–71). Alexandria, VA: American Counseling Association.

Bray, J. H., & Berger, S. H. (1990). Noncustodial father and paternal grandparent relationships in stepfamilies. *Family Relations, 39*(4), 414–419.

Bray, J. H., & Berger, S. H. (1993). Developmental issues in stepfamilies research project: Family relationships and parent-child interactions. *Journal of Family Psychology, 7*(1), 76–90.

Bray, J. H., Berger, S. H., & Boethel, C. L. (1995). Role integration and marital adjustment in stepfather families. In K. Pasley & M. Ihinger-Tallman (Eds.), *Stepparenting: Issues in theory, research, and practice* (pp. 69–86). Westport, CT: Praeger.

Bray, J. H., Berger, S. H., Siverblatt, A. H., & Hollier, A. (1987). Family process and organization during early remarriage: A preliminary analysis. In J. P. Vincent (Ed.), *Advances in family intervention, assessment, and theory* (pp. 253–279). Westport, CT: Praeger.

Bray, J. H., & Kelly, J. (1998). *Stepfamilies: Love, marriage, and parenting in the first decade.* New York: Broadway Books.

Brewer, R. M. (1995). Gender, poverty, culture, and economy: Theorizing female-led families. In B. J. Dickerson (Ed.), *African American single mothers: Understanding their lives and families* (pp. 164–178). Thousand Oaks, CA: Sage.

Brienza, J. (1996). Convicted killer, not lesbian mother, awarded custody of girl. *Trial, 32*(5), 16–18.

Brody, G. H., & Flor, D. L. (1997). Maternal psychological functioning, family processes, and child adjustment in rural, single-parent, African American families. *Developmental Psychology, 33*(6), 1000–1011.

Brodzinsky, D. M. (1997). Infertility and adoption adjustment: Considerations and clinical issues. In S. R. Leiblum (Ed.), *Infertility: Psychological issues and counseling strategies* (pp. 246–262). New York: John Wiley.

Brodzinsky, D. M., Lang, R., & Smith, D. W. (1995). Parenting adopted children. In M. H. Bornstein (Ed.), *Handbook of parenting. Vol. 3: Status and social conditions of parenting* (pp. 209–232). Mahwah, NJ: Lawrence Erlbaum.

Buehler, C. (1988). The social and emotional well-being of divorced residential parents. *Sex Roles, 18*(5–6), 247–257.

Bumpass, L., Castro, M. T., & Sweet, J. A. (1991). The impact of family background and early marital factors on marital disruption. *Journal of Family Issues, 12*(1), 22–42.

Burgess, J. K. (1995). Widowers as single fathers. *Marriage and Family Review, 20*(3–4), 447–461.

Burgess, N. J. (1995). Female-headed households in sociohistorical perspective. In B. J. Dickerson (Ed.), *African American single mothers: Understanding their lives and families* (pp. 21–36). Thousand Oaks, CA: Sage.

Burke, K. (1996, Spring). The case for open adoption records. *Decree, 13*(1). Available at: http://www.txcare.org/stats/kate.html.

Burnette, D. (1997). Grandparents raising grandchildren in the inner city. *Families in Society, 78*(5), 489–499.

Burton, D., & Showell, P. W. (1997). Partnership parenting in foster care. *Families in Society, 78*(5), 520–521.

Burton, L. M. (1992). Black grandparents rearing children of drug-addicted parents: Stressors, outcomes, and social service needs. *Gerontologist, 32*(6), 744–751.

Burton, L. M. (1996). Age norms, the timing of family role transitions, and intergenerational caregiving among aging African American women. *Gerontologist, 36*(2), 199–208.

Burton, L. M., Dilworth-Anderson, P., & Merriwether-deVries, C. (1995). Context and surrogate parenting among contemporary grandparents. In S. M. H. Hansen (Ed.), *Single parent families: Diversity, myths and realities* (pp. 349–366). New York: Haworth.

Bynum, M. K., & Durm, M. W. (1996). Children of divorce and its effect on their self-esteem. *Psychological Reports, 79*(2), 447–450.

Cabaj, R. P. (1998). History of gay acceptance and relationships. In R. P. Cabaj & D. W. Purcell (Eds.), *On the road to same-sex marriage: A supportive guide to psychological, political, and legal issues* (pp. 1–28). San Francisco: Jossey-Bass.

Campbell, F. A., Breitmayer, B., & Ramey, C. T. (1986). Disadvantaged single teenage mothers and their children: Consequences of free educational day care. *Family Relations, 35*, 63–68.

Cantos, A. L., Gries, L. T., & Slis, V. (1997). Behavioral correlates of parental visiting during family foster care. *Child Welfare, 76*(2), 309–329.

Carbino, R. (1992). Policy and practice for response to foster families when child abuse or neglect is reported. *Child Welfare, 71*(6), 497–509.

Carp, E. W. (1998). *Family matters: Secrecy and disclosure in the history of adoption.* Cambridge, MA: Harvard University Press.

Carrier, J. M. (1992). Miguel: Sexual life history of a gay Mexican American. In G. Herdt (Ed.), *Gay culture in America: Essays from the field* (pp. 202–224). Boston: Beacon.

Carrieri, J. R. (1991). *Child custody, foster care, and adoptions.* New York: Lexington Books.

Chalfie, D. (1994). *Going it alone: A closer look at grandparents parenting grandchildren.* Washington, DC: AARP Women's Initiative.

Chambers, D. L. (1990). Stepparents, biological parents, and the law's perception of "family" after divorce. In S. D. Sugarman & H. Hill Kay (Eds.), *Divorce reform at the crossroads* (pp. 102–129). New Haven, CT: Yale University Press.

Chan, R. W., Brooks, R. C., Raboy, B., & Patterson, C. J. (1998). Division of labor among lesbian and heterosexual parents: Associations with children's adjustment. *Journal of Family Psychology, 12*(3), 402–419.

Chan, R. W., Raboy, B., & Patterson, C. J. (1998). Psychosocial adjustment among children conceived via donor insemination by lesbian and heterosexual mothers. *Child Development, 69*(2), 443–457.

Cherlin, A. (1992). *Marriage, divorce, remarriage: Social trends in the U.S.* Cambridge, MA: Harvard University Press.

Cherlin, A., & Furstenberg, F. F., Jr. (1986). *The new American grandparent.* New York: Basic Books.

Cherlin, A., & Furstenberg, F. F., Jr. (1994). Stepfamilies in the United States: A reconsideration. *Annual Review of Sociology, 20,* 359–381.

Cherlin, A. J., Furstenberg, F. F., Jr., Chase-Lansdale, P. L., Kiernan, K. E., Robins, P. K., Morrison, D. R. T., & Julien, O. (1991). Longitudinal studies of effects of divorce on children in Great Britain and the United States. *Science, 252,* 5011, 1386–1389.

Child Welfare League of America. (1994). *Kinship care: A national bridge.* Washington, DC: Author.

Child Welfare League of America. (1995). *Child abuse and neglect: A look at the states.* Washington, DC: Author.

Chima, F. O. (1996). Transracial adoption revisited: African American college students' perspective. *Free Inquiry in Creative Sociology, 24*(1), 43–49.

Christopher, F. S. (1995). Adolescent pregnancy prevention. *Family Relations, 44*(4), 384–391.

Churchman, D. (1986). The debate over open adoption. *Public Welfare, 44,* 11–14.

Clarke, S. C., & Wilson, D. F. (1994). The relative stability of remarriages: A cohort approach using vital statistics. *Family Relations, 43*(3), 305–311.

Clegg, P., & Toll, K. (1996). Videotape and the memory visit: A living life book for adopted children. *Child Welfare, 75*(4), 311–319.

Clingempeel, W. G., Brand, E., & Levoli, R. (1984). Stepparent-stepchild relationships in stepmother and stepfather families: A multimethod study. *Family Relations, 33,* 465–474.

Clingempeel, W. G., Brand, E., & Segal, S. (1987). A multivariable-developmental perspective for future research on stepfamilies. In K. Pasley & M. Ihinger-Tallman (Eds.), *Remarriage and stepfamilies: Current research and theory* (pp. 65–93). New York: Guilford.

Clingempeel, W. G., & Segal, S. (1986). Stepparent-stepchild relationships and the psychological adjustment of children in stepmother and stepfather families. *Child Development, 57,* 474–484.

Cohen, N. J., Coyne, J. C., & Duvall, J. D. (1996). Parents' sense of "entitlement" in adoptive and nonadoptive families. *Family Process, 35*(4), 441–456.

Coleman, M., & Ganong, L. H. (1997). Stepfamilies from the stepfamily's perspective. *Marriage and Family Review, 26*(1–2), 107–121.

Collishaw, S., Maughan, B., & Pickles, A. (1998). Infant adoption: Psychosocial outcomes in adulthood. *Social Psychiatry and Psychiatric Epidemiology, 33*(2), 57–65.

Colton, M. J., Heath, A., & Aldgate, J. (1995). Factors which influence the educational attainment of children in foster family care. *Community Alternatives, 7*(1), 15–36.

Cook, J. F. (1995). A history of placing-out: The orphan trains. *Child Welfare, 74*(1), 181–197.

Cook, L. W. (1992). Open adoption: Can visitation with natural family members be in the child's best interest? *Journal of Family Law, 30,* 471–492.

Cook, R., Golombok, S., Bish, A., & Murray, C. (1995). Disclosure of donor insemination: Parental attitudes. *American Journal of Orthopsychiatry, 65*(4), 549–559.

Coontz, S. (1997). *The way we really are: Coming to terms with America's changing families.* New York: Basic Books.

Council on Families in America. (1996). Marriage in America: A report to the nation. In D. Popenoe, J. Bethke Elshtain, & D. Blankenhorn (Eds.), *Promises to keep: Decline and renewal of marriage in America* (pp. 293–317). Lanham, MD: Rowman & Littlefield.

Courtney, M. E. (1994). Factors associated with the reunification of foster children with their families. *Social Service Review, 68*(1), 81–109.

Courtney, M. E., & Barth, R. P. (1996). Pathways of older adolescents out of foster care: Implications for independent living services. *Social Work, 41*(1), 75–83.

Courtney, M. E., Barth, R. P., Berrick, J. D., Brooks, D., Needell, B., & Park, L. (1996). Race and child welfare services: Past research and future directions. *Child Welfare, 75*(2), 99–137.

Craig, C. (1995). "What I need is a mom": The welfare state denies homes to thousands of foster children. *Policy Review, 73,* 41–49.

Crosbie-Burnett, M. (1984). The centrality of the step relationship: A challenge to family theory and practice. *Family Relations, 33,* 459–463.

Crosbie-Burnett, M., & Helmbrecht, L. (1993). A descriptive empirical study of gay male stepfamilies. *Family Relations, 42,* 256–262.

Crosbie-Burnett, M., & Lewis, E. A. (1993). Use of African American family structures and functioning to address the challenges of European American postdivorce families. *Family Relations, 42,* 243–248.

Csikszentmihalyi, M. (1997). *Finding flow: The psychology of engagement with everyday life.* New York: Basic Books.

Cummings, E., & Henry, W. E. (1961). *Growing old: The process of disengagement.* New York: Basic Books.

Curtis, C. M. (1996). The adoption of African American children by whites: A renewed conflict. *Families in Society, 77*(3), 156–165.

Curtis, C. M., & Alexander, R., Jr. (1996). The Multiethnic Placement Act: Implications for social work practice. *Child and Adolescent Social Work Journal, 13*(5), 401–410.

Cushman, L. F., Kalmuss, D. A., & Namerow, P. B. (1997). Openness in adoption: Experiences and social psychological outcomes among birth mothers. *Marriage and Family Review, 25*(1–2), 7–18.

Dahl, A. S., Cowgill, K. M., & Asmundsson, R. (1987). Life in remarriage families. *Social Work, 32*(1), 40–44.

Daly, K. J., & Sobol, M. P. (1997). Key issues in adoption legislation: A call for research. *Marriage and Family Review, 25*(3–4), 145–158.

Danziger, S. K., & Farber, N. B. (1990). Keeping inner-city youths in school: Critical experiences of young black women. *Social Work Research and Abstracts, 26*(4), 32–39.

Davidson, B. (1997). Service needs of relative caregivers: A qualitative analysis. *Families in Society, 78*(5), 502–510.

Davis, I. P., Landsverk, J., Newton, R., & Ganger, W. (1996). Parental visiting and foster care reunification. *Children and Youth Services Review, 18*(4–5), 363–382.

Deacon, S. A. (1997). Intercountry adoption and the family life cycle. *American Journal of Family Therapy, 25*(3), 245–260.

DeMaris, A., & Greif, G. L. (1997). Single custodial fathers and their children: When things go well. In A. J. Hawkins & D. C. Dollahite (Eds.), *Generative fathering: Beyond deficit perspectives* (pp. 134–146). Thousand Oaks, CA: Sage.

Demo, D. H., & Acock, A. C. (1988). The impact of divorce on children. *Journal of Marriage and the Family, 50*(3), 619–648.

Demo, D. H., & Acock, A. C. (1996). Family structure, family process, and adolescent well-being. *Journal of Research on Adolescence, 6*(4), 457–488.

Demo, D. H., & Allen, K. R. (1996). Diversity within lesbian and gay families: Challenges and implications for family theory and research. *Journal of Social and Personal Relationships, 13*(3), 415–434.

Denby, R., & Rindfleisch, N. (1996). African Americans' foster parenting experiences: Research findings and implications for policy and practice. *Children and Youth Services Review, 18*(6), 523–552.

DePoy, E., & Noble, S. (1992). The structure of lesbian relationships in response to oppression. *Affilia, 7*(4), 49–65.

DeSimone, M. (1996). Birth mother loss: Contributing factors to unresolved grief. *Clinical Social Work Journal, 24*(1), 65–76.

deToledo, S., & Brown, D. E. (1995). *Grandparents as parents: A survival guide for raising a second family.* New York: Guilford.

DiLapi, E. M. (1989). Lesbian mothers and the motherhood hierarchy. *Journal of Homosexuality, 18*(1–2), 101–122.

Dilworth-Anderson, P., & McAdoo, H. P. (1988). The study of ethnic minority families: Implications for practitioners and policymakers. *Family Relations, 37*(3), 265–267.

Dilworth-Anderson, P., & Williams, S. W. (1996). African American elderly. In S. J. Price & T. Brubaker (Eds.), *Vision 2010: Families and aging* (pp. 32–33). Minneapolis, MN: National Council on Family Relations.

DiPlacido, J. (1998). Minority stress among lesbians, gay men, and bisexuals: A consequence of heterosexism, homophobia, and stigmatization. In G. M. Herek (Ed.), *Stigma and sexual orientation: Understanding prejudice against lesbians, gay men, and bisexuals* (pp. 138–159). Thousand Oaks, CA: Sage.

Doress-Worters, P. B. (1994). Adding elder care to women's multiple roles: A critical review of the caregiver stress and multiple roles literature. *Sex Roles, 31*(9–10), 597–616.

Doucette-Dudman, D., & LaCure, J. R. (1996). *Raising our children's children.* Minneapolis, MN: Fairview Press.

Dowd, N. E. (1997). *In defense of single-parent families.* New York: New York University Press.

Downey, D. B., Ainsworth-Darnell, J. W., & Dufur, M. J. (1998). Sex of parent and children's well-being in single-parent households. *Journal of Marriage and the Family, 60*(4), 878–893.

Dressel, P. L. (1994). . . . And we keep on building prisons: Racism, poverty, and challenges to the welfare state. *Journal of Sociology and Social Welfare, 21*(3), 7–30.

Dressel, P. L., & Barnhill, S. K. (1994). Reframing gerontological thought and practice: The case of grandmothers with daughters in prison. *Gerontologist, 34*(5), 685–691.

Dubowitz, H., Feigelman, S., Harrington, D., Starr, R., Zuravin, S., & Sawyer, R. (1994). Children in kinship care: How do they fare? *Children and Youth Services Review, 16* (1–2), 85–106.

Dudley, J. R. (1991). Increasing our understanding of divorced fathers who have infrequent contact with their children. *Family Relations, 40*(3), 279–285.

Dumaret, A. C., Coppel-Batsch, M., & Couraud, S. (1997). Adult outcome of children reared for long-term periods in foster families. *Child Abuse and Neglect, 21*(10), 911–927.

Dunn, J., Deater-Deckard, K., Pickering, K., O'Connor, T. G., & Golding, J. (1998). Children's adjustment and prosocial behaviour in step-, single-parent, and non-stepfamily settings: Findings from a community study. *Journal of Child Psychology and Psychiatry and Allied Disciplines, 39*(8), 1083–1095.

Duran-Aydintug, C. (1997). Adult children of divorce revisited: When they speak up. *Journal of Divorce and Remarriage, 27*(1–2), 71– 83.

Duran-Aydintug, C., & Causey, K. A. (1996). Child custody determination: Implications for lesbian mothers. *Journal of Divorce and Remarriage, 25*(1–2), 55–75.

Duran-Aydintug, C., & Ihinger-Tallman, M. (1995). Law and stepfamilies. *Marriage and Family Review, 21*(3–4), 169–192.

Dwyer, J. W., & Seccombe, K. (1991). Elder care as family labor: The influence of gender and family position. *Journal of Family Issues, 12*(2), 229–247.

East, P. L. (1999). The first teenage pregnancy in the family: Does it affect mothers' parenting, attitudes, or mother-adolescent communication? *Journal of Marriage and the Family, 61*(2), 306–319.

Eastman, K. S. (1979). The foster family in a systems theory perspective. *Child Welfare, 58*(8), 564–570.

Eastman, K. S. (1982). Foster parenthood: A nonnormative parenting arrangement. *Child Welfare, 61*(2), 95–120.

Eckstein, M. A. (1995). Foster family clusters: Continuum advocate network. In L. Combrinck-Graham (Ed.), *Children in families at risk: Maintaining the connections* (pp. 275–298). New York: Guilford.

Eggebeen, D. J., Snyder, A. R., & Manning, W. D. (1996). Children in single-father families in demographic perspective. *Journal of Family Issues, 17*(4), 441–465.

Eheart, B. K., & Power, M. B. (1995). Adoption: Understanding the past, present, and future through stories. *Sociological Quarterly, 36*(1), 197–216.

Erera, P. I. (1994). Sources of stress, ambiguity and conflict among the remarried in Israel. *Society and Welfare, 14*(3–4), 291–311.

Erera, P. I. (1996). On becoming a stepparent: Factors associated with the adoption of alternative stepparenting style. *Journal of Divorce and Remarriage, 25*(3–4), 155–174.

Erera, P. I. (1997a). Foster parents' attitudes toward birth parents and caseworkers: Implications for visitation. *Families in Society, 78*(5), 511–519.

Erera, P. I. (1997b). Step- and foster families: A comparison. *Marriage and Family Review, 26*(3–4), 301–315.

Erera, P. I., & Fredricksen, K. (1999). Lesbian stepfamilies: A unique family structure. *Families in Society, 80*(3), 263–270.

Erlichman, K. L. (1988). Lesbian mothers: Ethical issues in social work practice. *Women and Therapy, 8*(1–2), 207–224.

Etter, J. (1993). Levels of cooperation and satisfaction in 56 open adoptions. *Child Welfare, 72*(3), 257–267.

Falk, P. J. (1989). Lesbian mothers: Psychosocial assumptions in family law. *American Psychologist, 44*(6), 941–947.

Fanshel, D. (1982). *On the road to permanency: An expanded data base for service to children in foster care.* New York: Child Welfare League of America.

Fanshel, D., Finch, S. J., & Grundy, J. F. (1989). Foster children in life-course perspective: The Casey Family program experience. *Child Welfare, 68*(5), 467–478.

Fanshel, D., & Shinn, E. B. (1978). *Children in foster care: A longitudinal investigation.* New York: Columbia University Press.

Fassinger, P. A. (1989). Becoming the breadwinner: Single mothers' reactions to changes in their paid work lives. *Family Relations, 38*(4), 404–411.

Feigelman, W. (1997). Adopted adults: Comparisons with persons raised in conventional families. *Marriage and Family Review, 25*(3–4), 199–223.

Fein, E. (1991). Issues in foster family care: Where do we stand? *American Journal of Orthopsychiatry, 61*(4), 578–583.

Fein, E., & Maluccio, A. N. (1992). Permanency planning: Another remedy in jeopardy. *Social Service Review, 66*(3), 335–348.

Fein, E., Maluccio, A. N., Hamilton, J. V., & Ward, D. E. (1983). After foster care: Outcomes of permanency planning for children. *Child Welfare, 62*(6), 485–550.

Fein, E., & Staff, I. (1992). Together or separate: A study of siblings in foster care. *Child Welfare, 71*(3), 257–270.

Fenster, J. (1997). The case for permanent foster care. *Journal of Sociology and Social Welfare, 24*(2), 117–126.

Festinger, T. (1983). *No one ever asked us: A postscript to foster care.* New York: Columbia University Press.

Fine, M. A., Coleman, M., & Ganong, L. H. (1998). Consistency in perceptions of the step-parent role among step-parents, parents and step-children. *Journal of Social and Personal Relationships, 15*(6), 810–828.

Fine, M. A., Demo, D. H., & Allen, K. R. (2000). Family diversity in the 21st century: Implications for research, theory, and practice. In D. H. Demo, K. R. Allen, & M. A. Fine (Eds.), *Handbook of family diversity* (pp. 440–448). New York: Oxford University Press.

Fine, M. A., & Kurdek, L. A. (1995). Relation between marital quality and (step)parent-child relationship quality for parents and stepparents in stepfamilies. *Journal of Family Psychology, 9*(2), 216–223.

Fine, M. A., Schwebel, A. I., & James-Myers, L. (1987). Family stability in black families: Values underlying three different perspectives. *Journal of Comparative Studies, 18*(1), 1–23.

Finn, J. D., & Owings, M. F. (1994). Family structure and school performance in eighth grade. *Journal of Research and Development in Education, 27*(3), 176–187.

Fitchen, J. M. (1995). "The single-parent family," child poverty, and welfare reform. *Human Organization, 54*(4), 355–362.

Flaks, D. K., Ficher, I., Masterpasqua, F., & Joseph, G. (1995). Lesbians choosing motherhood: A comparative study of lesbian and heterosexual parents and their children. *Developmental Psychology, 31*(1), 105–125.

Folaron, G. (1993). Preparing children for reunification. In B. A. Pine, R. Warsh, & A. N. Maluccio (Eds.), *Together again: Family reunification in foster care* (pp. 141–154). Washington, DC: Child Welfare League of America.

Folberg, J. (Ed.). (1991). *Joint custody and shared parenting* (2nd ed.). New York: Guilford.

Foster, S. E., & Brizius, J. A. (1993). Caring too much? American women and the nation's caregiving crisis. In J. Allen & A. Pifer (Eds.), *Women on the front lines: Meeting the challenge of an aging America* (pp. 47–73). Washington, DC: Urban Institute.

Foulke, S. R., Alford-Cooper, F., & Butler, S. (1993). Intergenerational issues in long term planning. *Marriage and Family Review, 18*(3–4), 73–95.

Friedemann, M. L., & Andrews, M. (1990). Family support and child adjustment in single-parent families. *Issues in Comprehensive Pediatric Nursing, 13*(4), 289–301.

Fuller-Thomson, E., Minkler, M., & Driver, D. (1997). A profile of grandparents raising grandchildren in the United States. *Gerontologist, 37*(3), 406–411.

Furstenberg, F. F., Jr. (1980). Reflections on remarriage. *Journal of Family Issues, 1,* 443–453.

Furstenberg, F. F., Jr. (1981). Remarriage and intergenerational relations. In R. W. Fogel, E. Hatfield, S. B. Kiesler, & E. Shanas (Eds.), *Aging: Stability and change in the family* (pp. 115–142). New York: Academic Press.

Furstenberg, F. F., Jr. (1987). The new extended family: The experience of parents and children after remarriage. In K. Pasley & M. Ihinger-Tallman (Eds.), *Remarriage and stepfamilies: Current research and theory* (pp. 42–61). New York: Guilford.

Furstenberg, F. F., Jr., & Cherlin, A. J. (1991). *Divided families: What happens to children when parents part.* Cambridge, MA: Harvard University Press.

Furstenberg, F. F., Jr., & Spanier, G. B. (1984). *Recycling the family: Remarriage after divorce.* Beverly Hills, CA: Sage.

Furstenberg, F. F., Jr., & Teitlev, J. O. (1994). Reconsidering the effects of marital disruption: What happens to children of divorce in early adulthood? *Journal of Family Issues, 15*(2), 173–190.

Gallagher, J. (1993, November). Raw deal (Agenda). *Advocate, 641,* 24–26.

Galvin, K. M., & Brommel, B. J. (1982). *Family communication: Cohesion and change.* Glenview, IL: Scott, Foresman.

Gambrill, E. D., & Stein, T. J. (1985). Permanency planning for children. *Children and Youth Services Review, 7,* 243–257.

Ganong, L. H., & Coleman, M. (1984). Effects of remarriage on children: A review of the empirical literature. *Family Relations, 33,* 389–406.

Ganong, L. H., & Coleman, M. (1988). Do mutual children cement bonds in stepfamilies? *Journal of Marriage and the Family, 50*(3), 687–698.

Ganong, L. H., & Coleman, M. (1992). Financial responsibility for children following divorce and remarriage. *Journal of Family and Economic Issues, 13*(4), 445–455.

Ganong, L. H., & Coleman, M. (1993a). An exploratory study of stepsibling subsystems. *Journal of Divorce and Remarriage, 19*(3–4), 125–141.

Ganong, L. H., & Coleman, M. (1993b). A meta-analytic comparison of the self-esteem and behavior problems of stepchildren to children in other family structures. *Journal of Divorce and Remarriage, 19*(3–4), 143–163.

Ganong, L. H., & Coleman, M. (1994). *Remarried family relationships.* Thousand Oaks, CA: Sage.

Ganong, L. H., & Coleman, M. (1997). How society views stepfamilies. *Marriage and Family Review, 26*(1–2), 85–106.

Gardner, H. (1998). The concept of family: Perceptions of adults who were in long-term out-of-home care as children. *Child Welfare, 77*(6), 681–700.

Garfinkel, I., & McLanahan, S. S. (1986). *Single mothers and their children: A new American dilemma.* Washington, DC: Urban Institute.

Garland, A. F., & Besinger, B. A. (1997). Racial/ethnic differences in court referred pathways to mental health services for children in foster care. *Children and Youth Services Review, 19*(8), 651–666.

Garnefski, N., & Diekstra, R. F. W. (1997). Adolescents from one parent, stepparent and intact families: Emotional problems and suicide attempts. *Journal of Adolescence, 20*(2), 201–208.

Garrett, S. C., & Tidwell, R. (1999). Differences between adolescent mothers and nonmothers: An interview study. *Adolescence, 34*(133), 91–105.

Gattai, F. B., & Musatti, T. (1999). Grandmothers' involvement in grandchildren's care: Attitudes, feelings, and emotions. *Family Relations, 48*(1), 35–42.

Gaudin, J. M., Jr., & Sutphen, R. (1993). Foster care vs. extended family care for children of incarcerated mothers. *Journal of Offender Rehabilitation, 19*(3–4), 129–147.

Gean, M. P., Gillmore, J. L., & Dowler, J. K. (1985). Infants and toddlers in supervised custody: A pilot study of visitation. *Journal of the American Academy of Child Psychiatry, 24*(5), 608–612.

Gebel, T. J. (1996). Kinship care and nonrelative family foster care: A comparison of caregiver attributes and attitudes. *Child Welfare, 75*(1), 5–18.

George, L. J. (1997). Why the need for the Indian Child Welfare Act? *Journal of Multicultural Social Work, 5*(3–4), 165–175.

Gerstel, N. (1988). Divorce, gender, and social integration. *Gender and Society, 2*(3), 343–367.

Giarrusso, R., Silverstein, M., & Bengston, V. L. (1996). Family complexity and the grandparent role: New opportunities, new stresses. *Generations, 20*(1), 17–23.

Gibbs, E. D. (1988). Psychosocial development of children raised by lesbian mothers: A review of research. *Women and Therapy, 8*(1–2), 65–75.

Giles-Sims, J., & Finkelhor, D. (1984). Child abuse in stepfamilies. *Family Relations, 33*(3), 407–413.

Gleeson, J. P., & Craig, L. C. (1994). Kinship care in child welfare: An analysis of states' policies. *Children and Youth Services Review, 16*(1–2), 7–31.

Glick, P. C. (1989). Remarried families, stepfamilies, and stepchildren: A brief demographic analysis. *Family Relations, 38,* 24–27.

Glick, P. C. (1997). Demographic pictures of African American families. In H. P. McAdoo (Ed.), *Black families* (3rd ed., pp. 118–138). Thousand Oaks, CA: Sage.

Glick, P. C., & Lin, S. L. (1987). Remarriage after divorce: Recent changes and demographic variation. *Sociological Perspectives, 30*(2), 162–167.

Glover, R. J., & Steele, C. (1989). Comparing the effects on the child of post-divorce parenting arrangements. In C. A. Everett (Ed.), *Children of divorce: Developmental and clinical issues* (pp. 185–201). New York: Haworth.

Gluhoski, V. L., Fishman, B., & Perry, S. W. (1997). The impact of multiple bereavement in a gay male sample. *AIDS Education and Prevention, 9*(6), 521–531.

Goddard, L. L. (1996). Transracial adoption: Unanswered theoretical and conceptual issues. *Journal of Black Psychology, 22*(2), 273–281.

Goerge, R. M. (1990). The reunification process in substitute care. *Social Service Review, 64*(3), 422–457.

Goerge, V. (1970). *Foster care: Theory and practice.* London: Routledge & Kegan Paul.

Goetting, A. (1983). The relative strength of the husband-wife and parent-child dyads in re-marriage: A test of the Hsu model. *Journal of Comparative Family Studies, 14,* 117–128.

Gold, J. M., Bubenzer, D. L., & West, J. D. (1993). Differentiation from ex-spouses and stepfamily marital intimacy. *Journal of Divorce and Remarriage, 19*(3–4), 83–96.

Goldberg, G. R., Sands, R. G., Cole, R. D., & Cristofalo, C. (1998). Multigenerational pat-terns and internal structures in families in which grandparents raise grandchildren. *Families in Society, 79*(5), 477–489.

Goldstein, J. A., Freud, A., & Solnit, A. J. (1973). *Beyond the best interests of the child.* New York: Free Press.

Goldstein, J. A., Freud, A., & Solnit, A. J. (1979). *Before the best interests of the child.* New York: Free Press.

Golombok, S., & Tasker, F. (1996). Do parents influence the sexual orientation of their chil-dren? Findings from a longitudinal study of lesbian families. *Developmental Psychol-ogy, 32*(1), 3–12.

Gonzalez, K. P., Field, T. M., Lasko, D., & Harding, J. (1995). Adolescents from divorced and intact families. *Journal of Divorce and Remarriage, 23*(3–4), 165–175.

Goransson, L. (1998). International trends in same-sex marriage. In R. P. Cabaj & D. W. Purcell (Eds.), *On the road to same-sex marriage: A supportive guide to psychological, political, and legal issues* (pp. 165–189). San Francisco: Jossey-Bass.

Gordon, L., & McLanahan, S. S. (1991). Single parenthood in 1900. *Journal of Family His-tory, 16*(2), 97–117.

Green, G. D., & Bozett, F. W. (1991). Lesbian mothers and gay fathers. In J. C. Gonsiorek & J. D. Weinrich (Eds.), *Homosexuality: Research implications for public policy* (pp. 197–214). Newbury Park, CA: Sage.

Green, G. D. (1987, August). *Lesbian mothers.* Paper presented at the 95th Annual Conven-tion of the American Psychological Association, New York, NY.

Green, R. (1982). The best interests of the child with a lesbian mother. *Bulletin of the Amer-ican Academy of Psychiatry and the Law, 10*(1), 7–15.

Green, R., Mandel, J. B., Hotvedt, M. E., Gray, J., & Smith, L. (1986). Lesbian mothers and their children: A comparison with solo parent heterosexual mothers and their children. *Archives of Sexual Behavior, 15*(2), 167–184.

Green, R. J., Bettinger, M., & Zacks, E. (1996). Are lesbian couples fused and gay male couples disengaged? Questioning gender straightjackets. In J. Laird & R. J. Green (Eds.), *Lesbians and gays in couples and families: A handbook for therapists* (pp. 185–230). San Francisco: Jossey-Bass.

Greene, K., Causby, V., & Miller, D. H. (1997). The nature and function of fusion in the dy-namics of lesbian relationships. *Affilia, 14*(1), 78–97.

Greif, G. L. (1995). Single fathers with custody following separation and divorce. *Marriage and Family Review, 20*(1–2), 213–231.

Griffith, E. E. H. (1995). Culture and the debate on adoption of black children by white fam-ilies. *American Psychiatric Press Review of Psychiatry, 14,* 543–564.

Grigsby, R. K. (1994). Maintaining attachment relationships among children in foster care. *Families in Society, 75*(5), 269–277.

Grinwald, S., & Shabat, T. (1997). The "invisible" figure of the deceased spouse in a remar-riage. *Journal of Divorce and Remarriage, 26*(3–4), 105–113.

Gross, E. R. (1992). Are families deteriorating or changing? *Affilia, 7*(2), 7–33.

Gross, H. E. (1993). Open adoption: A research-based literature review and new data. *Child Welfare, 72*(3), 269–284.

Gross, H. E. (1997). Variants of open adoptions: The early years. *Marriage and Family Review, 25*(1–2), 19–42.

Grotevant, H. D. (1997). Family processes, identity development, and behavioral outcomes for adopted adolescents. *Journal of Adolescent Research, 12*(1), 139–161.

Groze, V. (1997). Adoption: International. In *Encyclopedia of Social Work, 1997 Supplement* (19th ed., pp. 1–14). Washington, DC: National Association of Social Workers.

Groze, V. (1996a). A 1- and 2-year follow-up study of adoptive families and special needs children. *Children and Youth Services Review, 18*(1–2), 57–82.

Groze, V. (1996b). *Successful adoptive families: A longitudinal study of special needs adoption.* Westport, CT: Praeger.

Groze, V., & Ileana, D. (1996). A follow-up study of adopted children from Romania. *Child and Adolescent Social Work Journal, 13*(6), 541–565.

Groze, V., & Rosenthal, J. A. (1991). Single parents and their adopted children: A psychosocial analysis. *Families in Society, 72*(2), 67–77.

Guberman, N., Maheu, P., & Maille, C. (1992). Women as family caregivers: Why do they care? *Gerontologist, 32*(5), 607–617.

Guidubaldi, J., Cleminshaw, H. K., Perry, J. D., & McLoughlin, C. S. (1983). The impact of parental divorce on children: Report of the nationwide NASP study. *School Psychology Review, 12,* 300–323.

Guisinger, S., Cowan, P. A., & Schuldberg, D. (1989). Changing parent and spouse relations in the first years of remarriage of divorced fathers. *Journal of Marriage and the Family, 51*(2), 445–456.

Gustafson, N. S., & MacEachron, A. E. (1997). Poverty and child placement: A new/old idea. *Journal of Poverty, 1*(2), 81–93.

Haas, L. L. (1995). Household division of labor in industrial societies. In B. B. Ingoldsby & S. D. Smith (Eds.), *Families in multicultural perspective* (pp. 268–296). New York: Guilford.

Hajal, F. (1996). Adoption: Its benefits and problems. In C. R. Pfeffer (Ed.), *Severe stress and mental disturbance in children* (pp. 533–557). Washington, DC: American Psychiatric Press.

Hajal, F., & Rosenberg, E. B. (1991). The family life cycle in adoptive families. *American Journal of Orthopsychiatry, 61*(1), 78–86.

Haldeman, D. C. (1998). Ceremonies and religion in same-sex marriage. In R. P. Cabaj & D. W. Purcell (Eds.), *On the road to same-sex marriage: A supportive guide to psychological, political, and legal issues* (pp. 141–164). San Francisco: Jossey-Bass.

Hanson, S. M. H., Heims, M. L., Julian, K. J., & Sussman, M. B. (1995). Single parent families: Present and future perspectives. *Marriage and Family Review, 20*(1–2), 1–26.

Hanson, T. L., McLanahan, S. S., & Thomson, E. (1996). Double jeopardy: Parental conflict and stepfamily outcomes for children. *Journal of Marriage and the Family, 58*(1), 141–154.

Hare, J. (1994). Concerns and issues faced by families headed by a lesbian couple. *Families in Society, 75*(1), 27–36.

Hare, J., & Richards, L. (1993). Children raised by lesbian couples: Does context of birth affect father and partner involvement? *Family Relations, 42*(3), 249–256.

Hargaden, H., & Llewellin, S. (1996). Lesbian and gay parenting issues. In D. Davies & C. Neal (Eds.), *Pink therapy: A guide for counselors and therapists working with lesbian, gay and bisexual clients* (pp. 116–130). Buckingham, England: Open University Press.

Harrison, A. O. (1996). Comments on transracial adoption. *Journal of Black Psychology,* 22(2), 236–239.

Hartman, A. (1985). Practice in adoption. In J. Laird & A. Hartman (Eds.), *A handbook of child welfare* (pp. 667–692). New York: Free Press.

Hartman, A. (1990). Aging as a feminist issue. *Social Work, 35*(5), 387–388.

Hartman, A. (1993). Family preservation under attack [Editorial]. *Social Work, 38*(5), 509–512.

Hartman, A. (1996). Social policy as a context for lesbian and gay families: The political is personal. In J. Laird & R. J. Green (Eds.), *Lesbians and gays in couples and families: A handbook for therapists* (pp. 69–85). San Francisco: Jossey-Bass.

Haugaard, J. J. (1998). Is adoption a risk factor for the development of adjustment problems? *Clinical Psychology Review, 18*(1), 47–69.

Hayden, C. P. (1995). Gender, genetics, and generation: Reformulating biology in lesbian kinship. *Cultural Anthropology, 10*(1), 41–63.

Heath, A. F., Colton, M. J., & Aldgate, J. (1994). Failure to escape: A longitudinal study of foster children's educational attainment. *British Journal of Social Work, 24*(3), 241–260.

Hegar, R. L. (1993). Assessing attachment, permanence, and kinship in choosing permanent homes. *Child Welfare, 72*(4), 367–378.

Heiss, J. (1997). Values regarding marriage and the family from a woman's perspective. In H. P. McAdoo (Ed.), *Black families* (3rd ed., pp. 284–300). Thousand Oaks, CA: Sage.

Henry, W. A., III. (1993, September 20). Gay parents: Under fire and on the rise. *Time,* 66–69.

Hess, P. (1988). Case and context: Determinants of planned visit frequency in foster family care. *Child Welfare, 67*(4), 311–325.

Hess, P., & Folaron, G. (1991). Ambivalence: A challenge to permanency for children. *Child Welfare, 70*(4), 403–424.

Hess, P., & Proch, K. (1993). Visiting: The heart of reunification. In B. A. Pine, R. Warsh, & A. N. Maluccio (Eds.), *Together again: Family reunification in foster care* (pp. 119–139). Washington, DC: Child Welfare League of America.

Hetherington, E. M. (1989). Coping with family transitions: Winners, losers, and survivors. *Child Development, 60*(1), 1–14.

Hetherington, E. M. (1991). The role of individual differences and family relationships in children's coping with divorce and remarriage. In P. Cowan & E. M. Hetherington (Eds.), *Family transitions* (pp. 165–194). Hillsdale, NJ: Lawrence Erlbaum.

Hetherington, E. M. (1997). Teenaged childbearing and divorce. In S. S. Luthar & J. A. Burack (Eds.), *Developmental psychopathology: Perspectives on adjustment, risk, and disorder* (pp. 350–373). New York: Cambridge University Press.

Hetherington, E. M., & Clingempeel, W. G. (1992). Coping with marital transitions: A family systems perspective. *Monographs of the Society for Research in Child Development, 57*(2–3, Serial No. 227).

Hetherington, E. M., Cox, M., & Cox, R. (1982). Effects of divorce on parents and children. In M. E. Lamb (Ed.), *Non-traditional families* (pp. 223–288). Hillsdale, NJ: Lawrence Erlbaum.

Hetherington, E. M., & Hagan, M. S. (1995). Parenting in divorced and remarried families. In M. H. Bornstein (Ed.), *Handbook of parenting, Vol. 3: Status and social conditions of parenting* (pp. 233–254). Mahwah, NJ: Lawrence Erlbaum.

Hetherington, E. M., & Jodl, K. M. (1994). Stepfamilies as settings for child development. In A. Booth & J. Dunn (Eds.), *Stepfamilies: Who benefits? Who does not?* (pp. 55–79). Hillsdale, NJ: Lawrence Erlbaum.

Hetherington, E. M., & Stanley-Hagan, M. (2000). Diversity among stepfamilies. In D. H. Demo, K. R. Allen, & M. A. Fine (Eds.), *Handbook of family diversity* (pp. 173–196). New York: Oxford University Press.

Hildreth, G. J., & Williams, N. (1996). Older Hispanic families. In S. J. Price & T. Brubaker (Eds.), *Vision 2010: Families and aging* (pp. 34–35). Minneapolis, MN: National Council on Family Relations.

Hill, M. S. (1995). When is a family a family? Evidence from survey data and implications for family policy. *Journal of Family and Economic Issues, 16*(1), 35–64.

Hill, R. B. (1998). Understanding black family functioning: A holistic perspective. *Journal of Comparative Family Studies, 29*(1), 15–26.

Hobart, C. (1987). Parent-child relations in remarried families. *Journal of Family Issues, 8,* 259–277.

Hobart, C. (1988). The family system in remarriage: An exploratory study. *Journal of Marriage and the Family, 50*(3), 649–661.

Hochschild, A. R. (1989). *The second shift: Working parents and the revolution at home.* New York: Viking.

Hoksbergen, R. A. C. (1997). Turmoil for adoptees during their adolescence? *International Journal of Behavioral Development, 20*(1), 33–46.

Hollinger, J. H. (1998). *Adoption law and practice: Vol. 1: Supplement.* New York: Matthew Bender.

Hollingsworth, L. D. (1998). Promoting same-race adoption for children of color. *Social Work, 43*(2), 104–116.

Hoopes, J. L., Alexander, L. B., Silver, P., Ober, G., & Kirby, N. (1997). Formal adoption of the developmentally vulnerable African-American child: Ten-year outcomes. *Marriage and Family Review, 25*(3–4), 131–144.

Horowitz, J. A. (1995). A conceptualization of parenting: Examining the single parent family. *Marriage and Family Review, 20*(1–2), 43–70.

Howe, D. (1997). Parent-reported problems in 211 adopted children: Some risk and protective factors. *Journal of Child Psychology and Psychiatry and Allied Disciplines, 38*(4), 401–411.

Hubbell, R. (1981). *Foster care and families: Conflicting values and policies.* Philadelphia: Temple University Press.

Hudson, J., & Galaway, B. (1989). Specialist foster family care: A normalizing experience [Special issue]. *Child and Youth Services, 12*(1–2).

Hudson, J., Nutter, R., & Galaway, B. (1994). Treatment foster care programs: A review of evaluation research and suggested directions. *Social Work Research, 18*(4), 198–210.

Huggins, S. L. (1989). A comparative study of self-esteem of adolescent children of divorced heterosexual mothers. *Journal of Homosexuality, 18*(1–2), 123–135.

Hunter, J., & Mallon, G. P. (1998). Social work practice with gay men and lesbians within communities. In G. P. Mallon (Ed.), *Foundations of social work practice with lesbian and gay persons* (pp. 229–248). New York: Haworth.

Hunter, J. E., & Schuman, N. (1980). Chronic reconstitution as a family style. *Social Work, 25,* 446–451.

Icard, L. (1986). Black gay men and conflicting social identities: Sexual orientation versus racial identity. *Journal of Social Work and Human Sexuality, 4*(1–2), 89–93.

Iglehart, A. P. (1995). Readiness for independence: Comparison of foster care, kinship care, and non-foster care adolescents. *Children and Youth Services Review, 17*(3), 417–432.

Ihinger-Tallman, M., & Pasley, K. (1987). *Remarriage.* Newbury Park, CA: Sage.

Ihinger-Tallman, M., & Pasley, K. (1997). Stepfamilies in 1984 and today: A scholarly perspective. *Marriage and Family Review, 26*(1–2), 19–40.

Jackson-White, G., Dozier, C., Davenport, O. J. T., & Gardner, L. B. (1997). Why African American adoption agencies succeed: A new perspective on self-help. *Child Welfare, 76*(1), 239–254.

Jacobs, J. L. (1994). Gender, race, class, and the trend toward early motherhood: A feminist analysis of teen mothers in contemporary society. *Journal of Contemporary Ethnography, 22*(4), 442–462.

Jagger, G., & Wright, C. (1999). Introduction: Changing family values. In G. Jagger & C. Wright (Eds.), *Changing family values* (pp. 1–16). London: Routledge.

Jarrett, R. L. (1994). Living poor: Family life among single parent, African-American women. *Social Problems, 41*(1), 30–49.

Jendrek, M. P. (1993). Grandparents who parent their grandchildren: Effects on lifestyle. *Journal of Marriage and the Family, 55,* 609–621.

Jendrek, M. P. (1994). Grandparents who parent their grandchildren: Circumstances and decisions. *Gerontologist, 34*(2), 206–216.

Johnson, C. L. (1985). Grandparenting options in divorcing families: An anthropological perspective. In V. L. Bengston & J. F. Robertson (Eds.), *Grandparenthood* (pp. 81–96). Beverly Hills, CA: Sage.

Johnson, D., & Fein, E. (1991). The concept of attachment: Applications to adoption. *Children and Youth Services Review, 13*(5–6), 397–412.

Johnson, P. R., Yoken, C., & Voss, R. (1995). Family foster care placement: The child's perspective. *Child Welfare, 74*(5), 959–974.

Juffer, F., & Rosenboom, L. G. (1997). Infant-mother attachment of internationally adopted children in the Netherlands. *International Journal of Behavioral Development, 20*(1), 93–107.

Kaden, J., & McDaniel, S. A. (1990). Caregiving and care-receiving: A double bind for women in Canada's aging society. *Journal of Women and Aging, 2*(3), 3–26.

Kadushin, A., & Martin, J. A. (1988). *Child welfare services* (4th ed.). New York: Macmillan.

Kagan, R. (1996). *Turmoil to turning points: Building hope for children in crisis placements.* New York: Norton.

Kaiser, P. (1996). Relationships in the extended family and diverse family forms. In A. E. Auhagen & M. von Salisch (Eds.), *The diversity of human relationships* (pp. 141–170). New York: Cambridge University Press.

Kamerman, S. B., & Kahn, A. J. (1988). *Mothers alone: Strategies for a time of change.* Dover, MA: Auburn House.

Kamerman, S. B., & Kahn, A. J. (1995). *Starting right: How America neglects its youngest children and what we can do about it.* New York: Oxford University Press.

Kaplan, E. B. (1997). *Not our kind of girl: Unraveling the myths of black teenage motherhood.* Berkeley, CA: University of California Press.

Kaplan, Z., & Fein, E. (1989). Foster care: Last resort or treatment of choice? *Child and Youth Services, 12*(1–2), 187–194.

Karp, N. (1996). Legal problems of grandparents and other kinship caregivers. *Generations, 20*(1), 57–60.

Kaye, S. H. (1989). The impact of divorce on children's academic performance. In C. A. Everett (Ed.), *Children of divorce: Developmental and clinical issues* (pp. 283–298). New York: Haworth.

Kelley, S. J. (1993). Caregiver stress in grandparents raising grandchildren. *IMAGE: Journal of Nursing Scholarship, 25*(4), 331–337.

Kelly, J. B., Emery, R. E., Kressel, K., Kurdek, L. A., & Sprenkle, D. H. (1988). Longer-term adjustment in children of divorce: Converging findings and implications for practice. *Journal of Family Psychology, 2*(2), 119–140.

Kheshgi, G. Z., & Genovese, T. A. (1997). Developing the spousal relationship within stepfamilies. *Families in Society, 78*(3), 255–264.

Kiernan, K. E. (1992). The impact of family disruption in childhood on transitions made in young adult life. *Population Studies, 46*(2), 213–234.

King, V. (1994). Nonresident father involvement and child well-being: Can dads make a difference? *Journal of Family Issues, 15*(1), 78–96.

Kingson, E. R., & O'Grady-LeShane, R. (1993). The effects of caregiving on women's social security benefits. *Gerontologist, 33*(2), 230–239.

Kirk, H. D. (1964). *Shared fate*. New York: Free Press.

Kirkpatrick, M. (1987). Clinical implications of lesbian mother studies. *Journal of Homosexuality, 14*(1–2), 201–211.

Kirschner, D. (1996). *Adoption psychopathology and the "adopted child syndrome": The Hatherleigh guide to child and adolescent therapy* (Hatherleigh Guides series, Vol. 5). New York: Hatherleigh Press.

Klee, L., Kronstadt, D., & Zlotnick, C. (1997). Foster care's youngest: A preliminary report. *American Journal of Orthopsychiatry, 67*(2), 290–299.

Klee, L., Schmidt, C., & Johnson, C. (1989). Children's definitions of family following divorce of their parents. In C. A. Everett (Ed.), *Children of divorce: Developmental and clinical issues* (pp. 109–127). New York: Haworth.

Kleinmann, M., Kuptsch, C., & Koeller, O. (1996). Parenting stepchildren and biological children: The effects of stepparents' gender and new biological children. *Journal of Family Issues, 17*(1), 5–25.

Koepke, L., Hare, J., & Moran, B. (1992). Relationship quality in a sample of lesbian couples with children and child-free lesbian couples. *Family Relations, 41*(2), 224–230.

Kompara, D. R. (1980). Difficulties in the socialization process of step parenting. *Family Relations, 29*, 69–73.

Kopels, S. (1995). Wrongful adoption: Litigation and liability. *Families in Society, 76*(1), 20–29.

Kosonen, M. (1996). Maintaining sibling relationships—Neglected dimension in child care practice. *British Journal of Social Work, 26*(6), 809–822.

Kposowa, A. J. (1998). The impact of race on divorce in the United States. *Journal of Comparative Family Studies, 29*(3), 529–548.

Kraft, A., Palombo, J., Woods, P., Mitchell, D., & Schmidt, A. (1985). Some theoretical considerations on confidential adoptions, Part II: The adoptive parent. *Child and Adolescent Social Work Journal, 2*, 69–82.

Kressierer, D. K., & Bryant, C. D. (1996). Adoption as deviance: Socially constructed parent-child kinship as a stigmatized and legally burdened relationship. *Deviant Behavior, 17*(4), 391–415.

Krueger, M. J. J., & Hanna, F. J. (1997). Why adoptees search: An existential treatment perspective. *Journal of Counseling and Development, 75*(3), 195–202.

Kurdek, L. A. (1995). Lesbian and gay couples. In A. R. D'Augelli & C. J. Patterson (Eds.), *Lesbian, gay, and bisexual identities over the lifespan: Psychological perspectives* (pp. 243–261). New York: Oxford University Press.

Kurdek, L. A. (1997). Adjustment to relationship dissolution in gay, lesbian, and hetero-sexual partners. *Personal Relationships, 4*(2), 145–161.

Kurdek, L. A. (1998). Relationship outcomes and their predictors: Longitudinal evidence from heterosexual married, gay cohabiting, and lesbian cohabiting couples. *Journal of Marriage and the Family, 60*(3), 553–568.

Kurdek, L. A., & Blisk, D. (1983). Dimensions and correlates of mothers' divorce experiences. *Journal of Divorce, 6*(4), 1–24.

Lai, D. W. L., & Yuan, S. F. (1994). *Grandparenting in Cuyahoga County: A report of survey findings*. Cleveland, OH: Cuyahoga County Community Office on Aging.

Laird, J. (1993). Lesbian and gay families. In F. Walsh (Ed.), *Normal family processes* (2nd ed., pp. 282–328). New York: Guilford.

Laird, J. (1994). Lesbian families: A cultural perspective. *Smith College Studies in Social Work, 64*(3), 263–296.

Lamb, M. E. (1987). The emergent American father. In M. E. Lamb (Ed.), *The father's role: Cross-cultural perspectives* (pp. 3–25). Hillsdale, NJ: Lawrence Erlbaum.

Lamb, M. E. (1997). Fathers and child development: An introductory overview and guide. In M. E. Lamb (Ed.), *The role of the father in child development* (3rd ed., pp. 1–18). New York: John Wiley & Sons.

LaRossa, R., & LaRossa, M. M. (1981). *Transition to parenthood: How infants change families*. Beverly Hills, CA: Sage.

Larson, J. H. (1992). Understanding stepfamilies. *American Demographics, 14,* 360–376.

Larson, J. H., & Allgood, S. M. (1987). A comparison of intimacy in first married and re-married couples. *Journal of Family Issues, 8*(3), 319–331.

LaSala, M. C. (1998). Coupled gay men, parents, and in-laws: Intergenerational disap-proval and the need for a thick skin. *Families in Society, 79*(6), 585–595.

Lee, J. S., & Twaite, J. A. (1997). Open adoption and adoptive mothers: Attitudes toward birthmothers, adopted children, and parenting. *American Journal of Orthopsychiatry, 67*(4), 576–584.

Lee, M. Y. (1997). Post-divorce interparental conflict, children's contact with both parents, children's emotional processes, and children's behavioral adjustment. *Journal of Divorce and Remarriage, 27*(3–4), 61–82.

Lee, V. E., Burkan, D. T., Zimiles, H., & Ladewski, B. (1994). Family structure and its effects on behavioral and emotional problems in young adolescents. *Journal of Research on Adolescence, 4,* 405–437.

Le Prohn, N. S. (1994). The role of the kinship foster parent: A comparison of the role conceptions of relative and non-relative foster parents. *Children and Youth Services Review, 16*(1–2), 65–84.

Lesbian ex-partners to share custody. (1998, November 4). *Seattle Times,* p. A9.

Levin, I. (1997). The stepparent role from a gender perspective. *Marriage and Family Review, 26*(1–2), 177–190.

Levy, E. F. (1992). Strengthening the coping resources of lesbian families. *Families in Society, 73*(1), 23–32.

Lewin, E. (1993). Lesbian mothers: Accounts of gender in American culture. Ithaca, NY: Cornell University Press.

Lichter, D. T., & McLaughlin, D. K. (1997). Poverty and marital behavior of young women. *Journal of Marriage and the Family, 59*(3), 582–595.

Lifton, B. J. (1996). The adopted self. In C. B. Strozier & M. Flynn (Eds.), *Trauma and self* (pp. 19–28). Lanham, MD: Rowman & Littlefield.

Lightburn, A., & Pine, B. A. (1996). Supporting and enhancing the adoption of children with developmental disabilities. *Children and Youth Services Review, 18*(1–2), 139–162.

Lindner, M. S., Stanley, M. H., & Cavanaugh, J. B. (1992). The adjustment of children in nondivorced, divorced single mother, and remarried families. *Monographs of the Society for Research in Child Development, 57*(2–3), 35–72.

Lino, M. (1995). The economics of single-parenthood: Past research and future directions. *Marriage and Family Review, 20*(1–2), 99–114.

Littlejohn-Blake, S. M., & Darling, C. A. (1993). Understanding the strengths of African American families. *Journal of Black Studies, 23*(4), 460–471.

Logan, J. (1996). Birth mothers and their mental health: Uncharted territory. *British Journal of Social Work, 26*(5), 609–625.

Longino, C. F., & Earle, J. R. (1996). Who are the grandparents at century's end? *Generations, 20*(1), 13–16.

Lott-Whitehead, L., & Tully, C. T. (1993). The family lives of lesbian mothers. *Smith College Studies in Social Work, 63*(3), 265–280.

Louv, R. (1993). *Father love.* New York: Pocket Books.

Lovett-Tisdale, M., & Purnell, B. A. (1996). It takes an entire village. *Journal of Black Psychology, 22*(2), 266–269.

Maccoby, E. E. (1995). The legal rights and obligations of parents and children. In G. B. Melton (Ed.), *The individual, the family, and social good: Personal fulfillment in times of change* (pp. 135–172). Lincoln, NE: University of Nebraska Press.

MacDonald, W. L., & DeMaris, A. (1994, November). *Stepparents' perceptions of the relative difficulty of parenting stepchildren versus biological children.* Paper presented at the National Council on Family Relations Conference, Minneapolis, MN.

MacEachron, A. E., Gustavsson, N. S., Cross, S., & Lewis, A. (1996). The effectiveness of the Indian Child Welfare Act of 1978. *Social Service Review, 70*(3), 451–463.

Macey, M. (1995). "Same race" adoption policy: Anti-racism or racism? *Journal of Social Policy, 24*(4), 473–491.

Mackey, R. A., O'Brien, B. A., & Mackey, E. F. (1997). *Gay and lesbian couples: Voices from lasting relationships.* Westport, CT: Praeger.

Madon, S. (1997). What do people believe about gay males? A study of stereotype content and strength. *Sex Roles, 37*(9–10), 663–685.

Mahoney, M. M. (1994a). Reformulating the legal definition of the stepparent-child relationship. In A. Booth & J. Dunn (Eds.), *Stepfamilies: Who benefits? Who does not?* (pp. 191–196). Hillsdale, NJ: Lawrence Erlbaum.

Mahoney, M. M. (1994b). *Stepfamilies and the law.* Ann Arbor, MI: University of Michigan Press.

Mainemer, H., Gilman, L. C., & Ames, E. W. (1998). Parenting stress in families adopting children from Romanian orphanages. *Journal of Family Issues, 19*(2), 164–180.

Malinowski, B. (1966). Parenthood: The basis of social structure. In R. W. Roberts (Ed.), *The unwed mother* (pp. 25–41). New York: Harper & Row.

Malkin, C. M., & Lamb, M. E. (1994). Child maltreatment: A test of sociobiological theory. *Journal of Comparative Family Studies, 25,* 121–134.

Maluccio, A. N., Abramczyk, L. W., & Thomlison, B. (1996). Family reunification of children in out-of-home care: Research perspectives. *Children and Youth Services Review, 18*(4–5), 287–305.

Maluccio, A. N., & Fein, E. (1983). Permanency planning: A redefinition. *Child Welfare, 62,* 95–201.

Maluccio, A. N., Fein, E., Hamilton, J. V., Klier, J., & Ward, D. (1980). Beyond permanency planning. *Child Welfare, 59*(9), 515–530.

Maluccio, A. N., Fein, E., & Olmstead, K. A. (1986). *Permanency planning for children.* New York: Tavistock.

Maluccio, A. N., Warsh, R., & Pine, B. A. (1993). Family reunification: An overview. In B. A. Pine, R. Warsh, & A. N. Maluccio (Eds.), *Together again: Family reunification in foster care* (pp. 3–19). Washington, DC: Child Welfare League of America.

Mann, K., & Roseneil, S. (1999). Poor choices? Gender, agency and the underclass debate. In G. Jagger & C. Wright (Eds.), *Changing family values* (pp. 98–118). London: Routledge.

March, K. (1995). Perception of adoption as social stigma: Motivation for search and reunion. *Journal of Marriage and the Family, 57*(3), 653–660.

Marcovitch, S., Cesaroni, L., Roberts, W., & Swanson, C. (1995). Romanian adoption: Parents' dreams, nightmares, and realities. *Child Welfare, 74*(5), 993–1017.

Marcovitch, S., Goldberg, S., Gold, A., Washington, J., Wasson, C., Krekewich, K., & Handley-Derry, M. (1997). Determinants of behavioural problems in Romanian children adopted in Ontario. *International Journal of Behavioral Development, 20*(1), 17–31.

Marsiglio, W. (1992). Stepfathers with minor children living at home: Parenting perceptions and relationship quality. *Journal of Family Issues, 13*(2), 195–215.

Masheter, C. (1998). Friendships between former spouses: Lessons in doing case-study research. *Journal of Divorce and Remarriage, 28*(3–4), 73–96.

Mass, M. (1994). Adoption in the bondage of the Oedipal myth. *Journal of Psychiatry and Law, 22*(2), 263–277.

McAdoo, H. P. (1998). African-American families: Strengths and realities. In H. I. McCubbin, E. A. Thompson, A. I. Thompson, & J. A. Futrell (Eds.), *Resiliency in African-American families* (pp. 17–30). Thousand Oaks, CA: Sage.

McCabe, K. M. (1997). Sex differences in the long term effects of divorce on children: Depression and heterosexual relationship difficulties in the young adult years. *Journal of Divorce and Remarriage, 27*(1–2), 123–135.

McCoy, J. (1962). The application of the role concept to foster parenthood. *Social Casework, 43*(5), 252–256.

McDaniel, K., & Jennings, G. (1997). Therapists' choice of treatment for adoptive families. *Journal of Family Psychotherapy, 8*(4), 47–68.

McDaniel, S. A. (1988). Women's roles, reproduction, and the new reproductive technologies: A new stork rising. In N. Mandell & A. Duffy (Eds.), *Reconstructing the Canadian family: Feminist perspectives* (pp. 175–206). Toronto, Ontario: Butterworths.

McFadden, E. J. (1996). Family-centered practice with foster-parent families. *Families in Society, 77*(9), 545–557.

McFadden, E. J., & Ryan, P. (1991). Allegations of maltreatment in family foster homes. In M. Robin (Ed.), *Assessing maltreatment reports: The problem of false allegations* (pp. 209–231). New York: Haworth.

McIntyre, D. H. (1994). Gay parents and child custody: A struggle under the legal system. *Mediation Quarterly, 12*(2), 135–149.

McIvor, R. (1998). Working with step-parents. *Journal of Family Studies, 4*(1), 107–108.

McKenzie, J. K. (1993). Adoption of children with special needs. *Future of Children, 3*(1), 62–76.

McLanahan, S., & Casper, L. (1994). *The American family in 1990: Growing diversity and inequality* (Luxembourg Income Study Working Paper 115). Syracuse, NY: Syracuse University, Maxwell School of Citizenship and Public Affairs.

McLean, B., & Thomas, R. (1996). Informal and formal kinship care populations: A study in contrasts. *Child Welfare, 75*(5), 489–505.

McMahon, M. (1995). *Engendering motherhood.* New York: Guilford.

McRoy, R. G. (1996). Racial identity issues for black children in foster care. In S. L. Logan (Ed.), *The black family: Strengths, self-help, and positive change* (pp. 131–143). Boulder, CO: Westview.

McRoy, R. G., Grotevant, H. D., & Zurcher, L. A. (1988). *Emotional disturbance in adopted adolescents: Origins and development.* New York: Praeger.

McRoy, R. G., & Hall, C. C. I. (1996). Transracial adoptions: In whose best interest? In M. P. P. Root (Ed.), *The multiracial experience: Racial borders as the new frontier* (pp. 63–78). Thousand Oaks, CA: Sage.

McRoy, R. G., Oglesby, Z., & Grape, H. (1997). Achieving same-race adoptive placements for African American children: Culturally sensitive practice approaches. *Child Welfare, 76*(1), 85–104.

McVinney, L. D. (1988). Social work practice with gay male couples. In G. P. Mallon (Ed.), *Foundations of social work practice with lesbian and gay persons* (pp. 229–248). New York: Haworth.

Mech, E. V. (1985). Parental visiting and foster placement. *Child Welfare, 64,* 67–72.

Meezan, W. (1980). *Adoption services in the states* (DHHS Publication No. OHDS 80-30288). Washington, DC: U.S. Department of Health and Human Services.

Menard, B. J. (1997). A birth father and adoption in the perinatal setting. *Social Work in Health Care, 24*(3–4), 153–163.

Messinger, L. (1984). *Remarriage: A family affair.* New York: Plenum.

Meyer, C. H. (1985). A feminist perspective on foster care: A redefinition of the categories. *Child Welfare, 54*(3), 249–257.

Meyer, M. H. (1990). Family status and poverty among older women: The gendered distribution of retirement income in the United States. *Social Problems, 37*(4), 551–563.

Miall, C. E. (1987). The stigma of adoptive parent status: Perceptions of community attitudes toward adoption and the experience of informal social sanctioning. *Family Relations, 36*(1), 34–39.

Miall, C. E. (1995). The social construction of adoption: Clinical and community perspectives. *Family Relations, 45,* 309–317.

Mica, M. D., & Vosler, N. R. (1990). Foster-adoptive programs in public social service agencies: Toward flexible family resources. *Child Welfare, 69*(5), 433–447.

Miles, D. M. (1984). A model for stepfamily development. *Family Relations, 33,* 365–372.

Miller, J. A., Jacobsen, R. B., & Bigner, J. J. (1981). The child's home environment for lesbian vs. heterosexual mothers: A neglected area of research. *Journal of Homosexuality, 7*(1), 49–56.

Milner, J. L. (1987). An ecological perspective on duration of foster care. *Child Welfare, 66*(2), 113–123.

Minkler, M., Driver, D., Roe, K. M., & Bedeian, K. (1993). Community interventions to support grandparent caregivers. *Gerontologist, 33*(6), 807–811.

Minkler, M., & Roe, K. M. (1993). *Grandmothers as caregivers: Raising children of the crack cocaine epidemic.* Newbury Park, CA: Sage.

Minkler, M., Roe, K. M., & Price, M. (1992). The physical and emotional health of grand-mothers raising grandchildren in the crack cocaine epidemic. *Gerontologist, 32*(6), 752–761.

Minkler, M., Roe, K. M., & Robertson-Beckley, R. J. (1994). Raising children from crack-cocaine households: Effects on family and friendship ties of African American women. *American Journal of Orthopsychiatry, 64*(1), 20–29.

Minkler, M., & Stone, R. (1985). The feminization of poverty and older women. *Gerontologist, 25*(4), 351–357.

Minuchin, S. (1974). *Families and family therapy.* Cambridge, MA: Harvard University Press.

Mitchell, B., Wiser, A. V., & Burch, T. K. (1989). The family environment and leaving the parental home. *Journal of Marriage and the Family, 51*(3), 605–613.

Mitchell, V. (1996). Two moms: Contribution of the planned lesbian family to the decons-truction of gendered parenting. In J. Laird & R. J. Green (Eds.), *Lesbians and gays in couples and families: A handbook for therapists* (pp. 343–357). San Francisco: Jossey-Bass.

Mizio, E. (1983). The impact of macro systems on Puerto Rican families. In G. J. Powell (Ed.), *The psychological development of Puerto Rican families* (pp. 216–236). New York: G. J. Powell.

Modell, J. (1997). "Where do we go next?" Long-term reunion relationships between adoptees and birth parents. *Marriage and Family Review, 25*(1–2), 43–66.

Moffitt, R. A. (1997). *The effects of welfare on marriage and fertility: What do we know and what do we need to know?* (Discussion Paper 1153-97). Madison, WI: Institute for Re-search on Poverty.

Molin, R. (1994). Foster families and larger systems: Image and identity. *Community Alter-natives, 6*(1), 19–31.

Moorman, J. E., & Hernandez, D. J. (1989). Married-couple families with step, adopted, and biological children. *Demography, 26*(2), 267–277.

Morales, E. (1996). Gendered roles among Latino gay and bisexual men. In J. Laird & R. J. Green (Eds.), *Lesbians and gays in couples and families: A handbook for therapists* (pp. 272–297). San Francisco: Jossey-Bass.

Moran, R. A. (1994). Stages of emotion: An adult adoptee's postreunion perspective. *Child Welfare, 73*(3), 249–260.

Morison, S. J., Ames, E. W., & Chisholm, K. (1995). The development of children adopted from Romanian orphanages. *Merrill-Palmer Quarterly, 41*(4), 411–430.

Moroz, K. J. (1996). Kids speak out on adoption: A multiage book writing group for adopted children with special needs. *Child Welfare, 75*(3), 235–251.

Morrison, N. C. (1995). Successful single-parent families. *Journal of Divorce and Remar-riage, 22*(3–4), 205–219.

Morrow, D. F. (1996). Coming-out issues for adult lesbians: A group intervention. *Social Work, 41*(6), 647–656.

Mosher, W. D., & Bachrach, C. A. (1996). Understanding U.S. fertility: Continuity and change in the National Survey of Family Growth. *Family Planning Perspectives, 28*(1), 4–12.

Murdock, G. P. (1949). *Social structure.* New York: Free Press.

Muzio, C. (1993). Lesbian co-parenting: On being/being with the invisible (m)other. *Smith College Studies in Social Work, 63*(3), 215–229.

Muzio, C. (1996). Lesbians choosing children: Creating families, creating narratives. In J. Laird & R. J. Green (Eds.), *Lesbians and gays in couples and families: A handbook for therapists* (pp. 358–369). San Francisco: Jossey-Bass.

National Center for Health Statistics (NCHS), Office of Public Affairs. (1989–1990). *Advance Report of Final Divorce Statistics* (Monthly Vital Statistics Report 43, No. 9, Supplement). Hyattsville, MD: Author.

National Center for Health Statistics (NCHS). (1997). *Fertility, family planning, and women's health: New data from the 1995 National Survey of Family Growth* (Monthly Vital Health Statistics Report 23, No. 19). Hyattsville, MD: Author.

National Commission on Children. (1991). *Speaking of kids: A national survey of children and parents.* Washington, DC: Author.

Neisen, J. H. (1990). Heterosexism: Redefining homophobia for the 1990s. *Journal of Gay and Lesbian Psychotherapy, 1*(3), 21–35.

Nelson, K. M. (1992). Fostering homeless children and their parents too: The emergence of whole-family foster care. *Child Welfare, 71*(6), 575–584.

Neugarten, B. L., & Weinstein, K. K. (1964). The changing American grandparent. *Journal of Marriage and the Family, 26*(5), 199–204.

Nickman, S. L. (1996). Retroactive loss in adopted persons. In D. Klass, P. R. Silverman, & S. L. Nickman (Eds.), *Continuing bonds: New understandings of grief* (pp. 257–272). Washington, DC: Taylor & Francis.

Nisivoccia, D. (1996). Working with kinship foster families: Principles for practice. *Community Alternatives, 8*(1), 1–21.

Nissim, R. (1997). Children living in substitute families: Historical perspectives on family placement: Patronage or partnership? *Educational and Child Psychology, 14*(2), 4–12.

Nixon, S. (1997). The limits of support in foster care. *British Journal of Social Work, 27*(6), 913–930.

Norton, A. J., & Miller, L. F. (1992). Marriage, divorce, and remarriage in the 1990s. *Current population reports* (Series P-23, No. 180). Washington, DC: Government Printing Office.

Oerton, S. (1997). "Queer housewives?": Some problems in theorising the vision of domestic labour in lesbian and gay households. *Women's Studies International Forum, 20*(3), 421–430.

Oles, T. P., Black, B. M., & Cramer, E. P. (1999). From attitude change to effective practice: Exploring the relationship. *Journal of Social Work Education, 35*(1), 87–100.

Ortiz, D. R. (1995). Feminism and the family. *Harvard Journal of Law and Public Policy, 18*(2), 523–530.

Owen, M. (1994). Single-person adoption: For and against. *Children and Society, 8*(2), 151–163.

Oyserman, D., & Benbenishty, R. (1992). Keeping in touch: Ecological factors related to foster care visitation. *Child and Adolescent Social Work Journal, 9*(6), 541–554.

Ozawa, M. N. (1995). The economic status of vulnerable older women. *Social Work, 40*(3), 323–331.

Pacheco, F., & Eme, R. (1993). An outcome study of the reunion between adoptees and biological parents. *Child Welfare, 72*(1), 53–64.

Pagani, L., Tremblay, R. E., Vitaro, F., Kerr, M., & McDuff, P. (1998). The impact of family transition on the development of delinquency in adolescent boys: A 9-year longitudinal study. *Journal of Child Psychology and Psychiatry and Allied Disciplines, 39*(4), 489–499.

Pagelow, M. D. (1980). Heterosexual and lesbian single mothers: A comparison of problems, coping, and solutions. *Journal of Homosexuality, 5*(3), 189–204.

Palmer, S. E. (1996). Placement stability and inclusive practice in foster care: An empirical study. *Children and Youth Services Review, 18*(7), 589–601.

Papernow, P. L. (1993). *Becoming a stepfamily: Patterns of development in remarried families.* San Francisco: Gardner.

Parish, T. S., & Parish, J. G. (1991). The effects of family configuration and support system failures during childhood and adolescence on college students' self-concepts and social skills. *Adolescence, 26*(102), 441–447.

Parsons, T. (1964). *Social structure and personality.* New York: Macmillan.

Pasley, K. (1987). Family boundary ambiguity: Perceptions of adult stepfamily members. In K. Pasley & M. Ihinger-Tallman (Eds.), *Remarriage and stepparenting: Current research and theory* (pp. 206–224). New York: Guilford.

Pasley, K., & Ihinger-Tallman, M. (1988). Remarriage and stepfamilies. In C. S. Chilman, E. W. Nunnally, & F. M. Cox (Eds.), *Variant family forms* (pp. 204–221). Beverly Hills, CA: Sage.

Pasley, K., & Ihinger-Tallman, M. (1989). Boundary ambiguity in remarriage: Does ambiguity differentiate degree of marital adjustment and integration? *Family Relations, 38,* 46–52.

Pasztor, E. M. (1985). Permanency planning and foster parenting. *Children and Youth Services Review, 7,* 191–205.

Patterson, C. J. (1995). Families of the lesbian baby boom: Parents' division of labor and children's adjustment. *Developmental Psychology, 31*(1), 115–124.

Patterson, C. J. (1996). Lesbian and gay parents and their children. In R. C. Savin-Williams & K. M. Cohen (Eds.), *The lives of lesbians, gays, and bisexuals: Children to adults* (pp. 274–304). Fort Worth, TX: Harcourt Brace.

Patterson, C. J., & Chan, R. W. (1997). Gay fathers. In M. E. Lamb (Ed.), *The role of the father in child development* (3rd ed., pp. 246–260). New York: John Wiley.

Patterson, C. J., & Chan, R. W. (1999). Families headed by lesbian and gay parents. In M. E. Lamb (Ed.), *Parenting and child development in "nontraditional" families* (pp. 191–219). Mahwah, NJ: Lawrence Erlbaum.

Patterson, C. J., & Redding, R. E. (1996). Lesbian and gay families with children: Implications of social science research for policy. *Journal of Social Issues, 52*(3), 29–50.

Pearlman, S. F. (1988). Distancing and connectedness: Impact on couple formation in lesbian relationships. *Women and Therapy, 8*(1–2), 77–88.

Pearson, J. L., Hunter, A. G., Ensminger, M. E., & Kellam, S. G. (1990). Black grandmothers in multigenerational households: Diversity in family structure and parenting involvement in the Woodlawn community. *Child Development, 61,* 434–442.

Pearson, J. L., & Thoennes, N. (1988). The denial of visitation rights: A preliminary look at its incidence, correlates, and consequences. *Law and Policy, 10,* 363–380.

Pecora, P. J., Le Prohn, N. S., & Nasuti, J. J. (1999). Role perceptions of kinship and other foster parents in family foster care. In R. L. Hegar & M. Scannapieco (Eds.), *Kinship foster care: Policy, practice, and research* (pp. 155–178). New York: Oxford University Press.

Pecora, P. J., Whittaker, J. K., & Maluccio, A. N. (with Plotnick, R.). (1992). *The child welfare challenge: Policy, practice and research.* Hawthorne, NY: Aldine.

Pecora, P. J., Whittaker, J. K., Maluccio, A. N., & Barth, R. P. (with Plotnick, R.). (2000). *The child welfare challenge: Policy, practice and research* (2nd ed.). Hawthorne, NY: Walter de Gruyter.

Pelton, L. H. (1989). *For reasons of poverty: A critical analysis of the public child welfare system in the United States.* New York: Praeger.

Penn, M. L., & Coverdale, C. (1996). Transracial adoption: A human rights perspective. *Journal of Black Psychology, 22*(2), 240–245.

Peplau, L. A. (1991). Lesbian and gay relationships. In J. C. Gonsiorek & J. D. Weinrich (Eds.), *Homosexuality: Research implications for public policy* (pp. 177–196). Newbury Park, CA: Sage.

Peterson, J., & Zill, N. (1986). Marital disruption, parent-child relationships, and behavior problems in children. *Journal of Marriage and the Family, 48,* 295–307.

Phillips, R. (1997). Stepfamilies from a historical perspective. *Marriage and Family Review, 26*(1–2), 5–18.

Pies, C. A. (1989). Lesbians and the choice to parent. *Marriage and Family Review, 14*(3–4), 137–154.

Pine, B. A., Warsh, R., & Maluccio, A. N. (1993). Training for competence in family reunification practice. In B. A. Pine, R. Warsh, & A. N. Maluccio (Eds.), *Together again: Family reunification in foster care* (pp. 5–50). Washington, DC: Child Welfare League of America.

Pink, J. E. T., & Wampler, K. S. (1985). Problem areas in step-families: Cohesion, adaptability, and the stepfather-adolescent relationship. *Family Relations, 34,* 327–335.

Pinson-Milburn, N. M., Fabian, E. S., Schlossberg, N. K., & Pyle, M. (1996). Grandparents raising grandchildren. *Journal of Counseling and Development, 74,* 548–554.

Polakow, V. (1993). *Lives on the edge: Single mothers and their children in the other America.* Chicago: University of Chicago Press.

Polikoff, N. (1986). Lesbian mothers, lesbian families: Legal obstacles, legal challenges. *Review of Law and Social Change, 14*(4), 907–914.

Popenoe, D. (1992). Fostering the new familism: A goal for America. *Responsive Community, 2*(4), 31–39.

Popenoe, D. (1996). *Life without father: Compelling new evidence that fatherhood and marriage are indispensable for the good of children and society.* New York: Free Press.

Poulin, J. E. (1992). Kin visiting and the biological attachment of long-term foster children. *Journal of Social Service Research, 15*(3–4), 65–79.

Powell, B., & Downey, D. B. (1997). Living in single-parent households: An investigation of the same-sex hypothesis. *American Sociological Review, 62*(4), 521–539.

Power, M. B., & Krause-Eheart, B. (1995). Adoption, myth, and emotion work: Paths to disillusionment. In M. G. Flaherty & C. Ellis (Eds.), *Social perspectives on emotion* (Vol. 3, pp. 97–120). Greenwich, CT: JAI.

Presser, H. B. (1989). Some economic complexities of child care provided by grandmothers. *Journal of Marriage and the Family, 51*(8), 581–591.

Prilik, P. K. (1998). *Becoming an adult stepchild: Adjusting to a parent's new marriage.* Washington, DC: American Psychiatric Press.

Proch, K., & Howard, J. A. (1986). Parental visiting of children in foster care. *Social Work, 31*(3), 178–181.

Purnell, M., & Bagby, B. H. (1993). Grandparents' rights: Implications for family specialists. *Family Relations, 42,* 173–178.

Quinn, P., & Allen, K. R. (1989). Facing challenges and making compromises: How single mothers endure. *Family Relations, 38*(4), 390–395.

Rae, G. (1995). Therapy with a lesbian stepfamily with an electively mute child: A comment. *Journal of Family Psychotherapy, 6*(1), 15–20.

Rainwater, L., & Smeeding, T. (1995). *Doing poorly: The real income of American children in a comparative perspective.* Luxembourg Income Study Working Paper No. 127. Syracuse, NY: Syracuse University, Maxwell School of Citizenship and Public Affairs.

Rand, C., Graham, D. L., & Rawlings, E. I. (1982). Psychological health and factors the court seeks to control in lesbian mother custody trials. *Journal of Homosexuality, 8*(1), 27–39.

Reddy, A., & Pfeiffer, S. I. (1997). Effectiveness of treatment foster care with children and adolescents: A review of outcome studies. *Journal of the American Academy of Child and Adolescent Psychiatry, 36*(5), 581–588.

Reed, J. A. (1994). We live here too: Birth children's perspectives on fostering someone with learning disabilities. *Children and Society, 8*(2), 164–173.

Reilly, T. (1996). Gay and lesbian adoptions: A theoretical examination of policy-making and organizational decision making. *Journal of Sociology and Social Welfare, 23*(4), 99–115.

Reitz, M., & Watson, K. W. (1992). *Adoption and the family system: Strategies for treatment.* New York: Guilford.

Rice, J. K. (1994). Reconsidering research on divorce, family life cycle, and the meaning of family. *Psychology of Women Quarterly, 18*(4), 559–584.

Richardson, V. E. (1993). *Women and retirement: Retirement counseling.* New York: Springer.

Riessman, C. K. (1990). *Divorce talk: Women and men make sense of personal relationships.* New Brunswick, NJ: Rutgers University Press.

Riley, N. (1997). American adoptions of Chinese girls: The socio-political matrices of individual decisions. *Women's Studies International Forum, 20*(1), 87–102.

Risman, B. J. (1998). *Gender vertigo: American families in transition.* New Haven, CT: Yale University Press.

Rivera, R. R. (1991). Sexual orientation and the law. In J. C. Gonsiorek & J. D. Weinrich (Eds.), *Homosexuality: Research implications for public policy* (pp. 81–100). Newbury Park, CA: Sage.

Robinson, L. C., Garthoeffner, J. L., & Henry, C. S. (1995). Family structure and interpersonal relationship quality in young adults. *Journal of Divorce and Remarriage, 23*(3–4), 23–43.

Robson, R. (1992). Mother: The legal domestication of lesbian existence. *Hypatia, 7*(4), 172–186.

Rodgers, J. (1995). Family policy or moral regulation? *Critical Social Policy, 15*(1), 5–25.

Rodgers, R. H., & Conrad, L. M. (1986). Courtship for remarriage: Influences on family reorganization after divorce. *Journal of Marriage and the Family, 48,* 767–775.

Rohrbaugh, J. B. (1992). Lesbian families: Clinical issues and theoretical implications. *Professional Psychology: Research and Practice, 23*(6), 467–473.

Roizblatt, A., Rivera, S., Fuchs, T., Toso, P., Ossandon, E., & Guelfand, M. (1997). Children of divorce: Academic outcome. *Journal of Divorce and Remarriage, 26*(3–4), 51–56.

Rosenberg, K. F., & Groze, V. (1997). The impact of secrecy and denial in adoption: Practice and treatment issues. *Families in Society, 78*(5), 522–530.

Rosenthal, J. A. (1993). Outcomes of adoption of children with special needs. *Future of Children, 3*(1), 77–88.

Rosenthal, J. A., & Groze, V. (1994). A longitudinal study of special-needs adoptive families. *Child Welfare, 73*(6), 689–706.

Rosenthal, J. A., Groze, V., & Morgan, J. (1996). Services for families adopting children via public child welfare agencies: Use, helpfulness, and need. *Children and Youth Services Review, 18*(1–2), 163–182.

Rosettenstein, D. S. (1995). Trans-racial adoption in the United States and the impact of considerations relating to minority population groups on international adoptions in the United States. *International Journal of Law and the Family, 9*(2), 131–154.

Rothblum, E. D. (1985, November). *Lesbianism: Affirming non-traditional roles.* Paper presented at the Annual Meeting of the Association for Advancement of Behavior Therapy, Houston, TX.

Rothstein, A., & Erera. P. I. (1994, May–June). *Remarriage among the elderly.* Paper presented at the meeting of the Family on the Threshold of the 21st Century: Trends and Implications, Jerusalem.

Rubenfeld, A. R. (1994). Sexual orientation and custody. *Human Rights, 21*(1), 14–18.

Rubenstein, J. L., Halton, A., Kasten, L., Rubin, C., & Stechler, G. (1998). Suicidal behavior in adolescents: Stress and protection in different family contexts. *American Journal of Orthopsychiatry, 68*(2), 274–284.

Rushton, A., & Minnis, H. (1997). Annotation: Transracial family placements. *Journal of Child Psychology and Psychiatry and Allied Disciplines, 38*(2), 147–159.

Ryan, P., McFadden, E. J., Rice, D., & Warren, B. L. (1988). The role of foster parents in helping young people develop emancipation skills. *Child Welfare, 67*(6), 563–572.

Ryan, P., McFadden, E. J., & Warren, B. L. (1981). Foster families: A resource for helping parents. In A. N. Maluccio & P. A. Sinanoglu (Eds.), *The challenge of partnership: Working with parents of children in foster care* (pp. 189–199). Washington, DC: Child Welfare League of America.

Ryburn, M. (1996). A study of post-adoption contact in compulsory adoptions. *British Journal of Social Work, 26*(5), 627–646.

Ryburn, M. (1997). The effects on adopters of adoption without parental consent. *Early Child Development and Care, 134,* 103–119.

Sack, L. (1992). Women and children first: A feminist analysis of the primary caretaker standard in child custody cases. *Yale Journal of Law and Feminism, 4,* 291–328.

Saluter, A. F. (1992). *Marital status and living arrangements: Current population reports, population characteristics* (Series P-20, No. 461). Washington, DC: Government Printing Office.

Sands, R. G., & Goldberg-Glen, R. S. (2000). Factors associated with stress among grandparents raising their grandchildren. *Family Relations, 49*(1), 97–105.

Sands, R. G., & Nuccio, K. E. (1989). Mother-headed single-parent families: A feminist perspective. *Affilia, 4*(3), 25–41.

Santrock, J. W., & Sitterle, K. A. (1987). Parent-child relationships in stepmother families. In K. Pasley & M. Ihinger-Tallman (Eds.), *Remarriage and stepfamilies: Current research and theory* (pp. 273–299). New York: Guilford.

Santrock, J. W., Warshak, R., Lindbergh, C., & Meadows, L. (1982). Children and parents' observed social behavior in stepfather families. *Child Development, 53,* 472–480.

Sawyer, R. J., & Dubowitz, H. (1994). School performance of children in kinship care. *Child Abuse and Neglect, 18*(7), 587–597.

Scannapieco, M., Hegar, R. L., & McAlpine, C. (1997). Kinship care and foster care: A comparison of characteristics and outcomes. *Families in Society, 78*(5), 480–488.

Scaramella, L. V., Conger, R. D., Simons, R. L., & Whitbeck, L. B. (1988). Predicting risk for pregnancy by late adolescence: A social contextual perspective. *Developmental Psychology, 34*(6), 1233–1245.

Schnayer, R., & Orr, R. R. (1989). Comparison of children living in single-mother and single-father families. In C. A. Everett (Ed.), *Children of divorce: Developmental and clinical issues* (pp. 171–184). New York: Haworth.

Schwebel, A. I., Fine, M. A., & Renner, M. A. (1991). A study of perceptions of the stepparent role. *Journal of Family Issues, 12*(1), 43–58.

Seaberg, J. R. (1981). Foster parents as aides to parents. In A. N. Maluccio & P. A. Sinanoglu (Eds.), *The challenge of partnership: Working with parents in foster care* (pp. 209–220). Washington, DC: Child Welfare League of America.

Seaberg, J. R., & Harrigan, M. P. (1997). Family functioning in foster care. *Families in Society, 78*(5), 463–470.

Seaberg, J. R., & Tolley, E. S. (1986). Predictors of the length of stay in foster care. *Social Work Research and Abstracts, 22*(3), 11–19.

Sears, B. (1994). Winning arguments/losing themselves: The (dys)functional approach. *Harvard Civil Rights Civil Liberties Law Review, 29*(2), 559–580.

Sedlak, A. J., & Broadhurst, D. D. (1996). *Third national incidence study of child abuse and neglect.* Washington, DC: National Center on Child Abuse and Neglect.

Seltzer, J. A. (1991). Relationships between fathers and children who live apart: The father's role after separation. *Journal of Marriage and the Family, 53*(1), 79–101.

Seltzer, J. A. (1994). Consequences of marital dissolution for children. *Annual Review of Sociology, 20,* 235–266.

Seltzer, J. A., & Bianchi, S. M. (1988). Children's contact with absent parents. *Journal of Marriage and the Family, 50,* 663–677.

Serbin, L. A. (1997). Research on international adoption: Implications for developmental theory and social policy. *International Journal of Behavioral Development, 20*(1), 83–92.

Sharma, A. R., McGue, M. K., & Benson, P. L. (1996a). The emotional and behavioral adjustment of United States adopted adolescents, Part I: An overview. *Children and Youth Services Review, 18*(1–2), 83–100.

Sharma, A. R., McGue, M. K., & Benson, P. L. (1996b). The emotional and behavioral adjustment of United States adopted adolescents, Part II: Age at adoption. *Children and Youth Services Review, 18*(1–2), 101–114.

Shaw, M., & Hipgrave, T. (1983). *Specialist fostering.* London: Batsford.

Sheets, V. L., & Braver, S. L. (1996). Gender differences in satisfaction with divorce settlements. *Family Relations, 45*(3), 336–342.

Shireman, J. F. (1995). Adoptions by single parents. *Marriage and Family Review, 20*(3–4), 367–388.

Silin, M. W. (1996). The vicissitudes of adoption for parents and children. *Child and Adolescent Social Work Journal, 13*(3), 255–269.

Silverman, P. R., Campbell, L., & Patti, P. (1994). Reunions between adoptees and birth parents: The adoptive parents' view. *Social Work, 39*(5), 542–549.

Silverstein, D. R., & Demick, J. (1994). Toward an organizational-relational model of open adoption. *Family Process, 33*(2), 111–124.

Silverstein, L. B., & Auerbach, C. F. (1999). Deconstructing the essential father. *American Psychologist, 54*(6), 397–407.

Simms, M. D., & Bolden, B. J. (1991). The family reunification project: Facilitating regular contact among foster children, biological families, and foster families. *Child Welfare, 70*(6), 679–690.

Simms, M. D., & Horwitz, S. M. (1996). Foster home environments: A preliminary report. *Journal of Developmental and Behavioral Pediatrics, 17*(3), 170–175.

Simon, R. J., & Alstein, H. (1987). *Transracial adoptees and their families: A study of identity and commitment.* New York: Praeger.

Simon, R. J., & Altstein, H. (1996). The case for transracial adoption. *Children and Youth Services Review, 18*(1–2), 5–22.

Simon, R. J., Altstein, H., & Melli, M. S. (1994). *The case for transracial adoption.* Washington, DC: American University Press.

Simons, R. L. (1996). Theoretical and policy implications of the findings. In R. L. Simons et al. (Eds.), *Understanding differences between divorced and intact families: Stress, interaction, and child outcome* (pp. 195–225). Thousand Oaks, CA: Sage.

Simons, R. L., Whitbeck, L. B., Beamn, J., & Conger, R. D. (1994). The impact of mothers' parenting, involvement by nonresidential fathers, and parental conflict on the adjustment of adolescent children. *Journal of Marriage and the Family, 56*(2), 356–374.

Skopin, A. R., Newman, B. M., & McKenry, P. C. (1992). Influences on the quality of stepfather-adolescent relationships: Views of both family members. *Journal of Divorce and Remarriage, 19*(3–4), 181–197.

Slater, S., & Mencher, J. (1991). The lesbian family life cycle: A contextual approach. *American Journal of Orthopsychiatry, 61*(3), 372–382.

Smith, B., & Smith, T. (1990). For love and money: Women as foster mothers. *Affilia, 5*(1), 66–80.

Smith, E. P., & Merkel-Holguin, L. A. (1995). Introduction. *Child Welfare, 74*(1), 13–18.

Smith, M. (1997). Psychology's under-valuation of single motherhood. *Feminism and Psychology, 7*(4), 529–532.

Smith, T. E. (1995). What a difference a measure makes: Parental-separation effect on school grades, not academic achievement. *Journal of Divorce and Remarriage, 23*(3–4), 151–164.

Sobol, M. P., & Daly, K. J. (1992). The adoption alternative for pregnant adolescents: Decision making, consequences, and policy implications. *Journal of Social Issues, 48,* 143–161.

South, S. J., Crowder, K. D., & Trent, K. (1998). Children's residential mobility and neighborhood environment following parental divorce and remarriage. *Social Forces, 77*(2), 667–693.

Spanier, G. B., & Furstenberg, F. F. (1982). Remarriage after divorce: A longitudinal analysis of well-being. *Journal of Marriage and the Family, 44,* 709–720.

Sprey, J. (1969). On the institutionalization of sexuality. *Journal of Marriage and the Family, 31*(3), 432–440.

Sprey, J. (1988). Current theorizing on the family: An appraisal. *Journal of Marriage and the Family, 50*(4), 875–890.

Springer, C. (1995). Lessons of divorce: The intersection of private dilemmas and public issues. *Smith College Studies in Social Work, 65*(2), 167–179.

Stacey, J. (1996). *In the name of the family: Rethinking family values in the postmodern age.* Boston: Beacon.

Stacey, J. (1998). *Brave new families: Stories of domestic upheaval in late twentieth century America* (Rev. ed.). New York: Basic Books.

Stacey, J. (2000). The handbook's tail: Toward revels or a requiem for family diversity? In D. H. Demo, K. R. Allen, & M. A. Fine (Eds.), *Handbook of family diversity* (pp. 424–439). New York: Oxford University Press.

Steinbock, M. R. (1995). Homeless female-headed families: Relationships at risk. *Marriage and Family Review, 20*(1–2), 143–159.

Stern, P. J. (1989). The impact of divorce on children at various stages of the family life cycle. In C. A. Everett (Ed.), *Children of divorce: Developmental and clinical issues* (pp. 81–106). New York: Haworth.

Stiffman, A. R., Jung, K. G., & Feldman, R. A. (1987–1988). Parental mental illness, family living arrangements, and child behavior. *Journal of Social Service Research, 11*(2–3), 21–34.

Stokes, J. C., & Strothman, L. J. (1996). The use of bonding studies in child welfare permanency planning. *Child and Adolescent Social Work Journal, 13*(4), 347–367.

Stolley, K. S. (1993). Statistics on adoption in the United States. The future of children. *Adoption, 3*(1), 26–42.

Strand, V. C. (1995). Single parents. In *Encyclopedia of Social Work* (19th ed., pp. 2157–2163). Washington, DC: National Association of Social Workers.

Strom, R. D., & Strom, S. K. (1993). Grandparents raising grandchildren: Goals and support groups. *Educational Gerontology, 19*(8), 705–715.

Strover, A. (1997). How foster parents experience social work with particular reference to placement endings. *Adoption and Fostering, 20*(4), 29–35.

Sullivan, M. (1996). Rozzie and Harriet? Gender and family patterns of lesbian coparents. *Gender and Society, 10*(6), 747–767.

Szinovacz, M. E. (1988). Grandparents today: A demographic profile. *Gerontologist, 38*(1), 37–52.

Szinovacz, M. E., DeViney, S., & Atkinson, M. P. (1999). Effects of surrogate parenting on grandparents' well-being. *Journals of Gerontology, Series B, 54*(6), 376–389.

Tasker, F., & Golombok, S. (1995). Adults raised as children in lesbian families. *American Journal of Orthopsychiatry, 65*(2), 203–216.

Tasker, F., & Golombok, S. (1997). *Growing up in a lesbian family.* New York: Guilford.

Taylor, R. J., & Thornton, M. C. (1996). Child welfare and transracial adoption. *Journal of Black Psychology, 22*(2), 282–291.

Thomas, S. L. (1994). From the culture of poverty to the culture of single motherhood: The new poverty paradigm. *Women and Politics, 14*(2), 65–97.

Thorne, B. (1982). Feminist rethinking of the family: An overview. In B. Thorne & M. Yalom (Eds.), *Rethinking the family: Some feminist questions* (pp. 1–24). New York: Longman.

Tilly, C., & Albelda, R. (1994). It's not working: Why single mothers can't work their way out of poverty. *Dollars and Sense, 196,* 8–10.

Townsend, M. (1998). Mental health issues and same-sex marriage. In R. P. Cabaj & D. W. Purcell (Eds.), *On the road to same-sex marriage: A supportive guide to psychological, political, and legal issues* (pp. 89–107). San Francisco: Jossey-Bass.

Trent, K., & Harlan, S. L. (1994). Teenage mothers in nuclear and extended households: Differences by marital status and race/ethnicity. *Journal of Family Issues, 15*(2), 309–337.

Trolley, B. C., Wallin, J., & Hansen, J. (1995). International adoption: Issues of acknowledgement of adoption and birth culture. *Child and Adolescent Social Work Journal, 12*(6), 465–479.

Tronto, J. C. (1993). *Moral boundaries: A political statement for an ethic of care*. New York: Routledge.

Trout, M. D. (1996). The optimal adoptive launch. *Pre- and Peri-Natal Psychology Journal, 11*(2), 93–99.

Twigg, R. C. (1995). Coping with loss: How foster parents' children cope with foster care. *Community Alternatives, 7*(1), 1–12.

U.S. Bureau of Census. (1989). *Current population reports: Marital status and living arrangements* (Series P20, No. 445).Washington, DC: Government Printing Office.

U.S. Bureau of Census. (1992). *Current population reports, Special studies: Marriage, divorce, and remarriage in the 1990s* (Series P23, No.180). Washington, DC: Government Printing Office.

U.S. Bureau of Census. (1994). *Current population reports: Marital status and living arrangements* (Series P20, No. 484). Washington, DC: Government Printing Office.

U.S. Bureau of Census. (1996). *Current population reports: Marital status and living arrangements* (Series P20, No.496). Washington, DC: Government Printing Office.

U.S. Bureau of Census. (1999a). *Current population reports, Special studies: Coresident grandparents and grandchildren* (Series P23, No.198). Washington, DC: Government Printing Office.

U.S. Bureau of the Census. (1999b). *Current population reports: Marital status and living arrangements* (Series P-20, Nos. 410, 445, 450, 461, and 468). Washington, DC: Government Printing Office.

U.S. Department of Health, Health and Human Services, Administration for Children, Adminsitration on Children, youth and families, Children's Bureau. (2000, October). *The AFCARS report*. Available at: http://www.acf.dhhs.gov/programs/cb/publications/afcars/ar1000.htm.

University of Chicago National Opinion Research Center. (1999, November 24). *The emerging 21st century American family*. Available at: http://www.norc.uchicago.edu/new/homepage.htm.

Urquhart, L. R. (1989). Separation and loss: Assessing the impacts on foster parent retention. *Child and Adolescent Social Work Journal, 6*(3), 193–209.

VanDulmen, M. H. (1998, November 16). *International adoption in the Netherlands*. National Council on Family Relations Conference, Milwaukee, WI.

VanEvery, Jo. (1999). From modern nuclear family households to postmodern diversity? The sociological construction of "families." In G. Jagger & C. Wright (Eds.), *Changing family values* (pp. 165–184). London: Routledge.

Vemer, E., Coleman, M., Ganong, L. H., & Cooper, H. (1989). Marital satisfaction in remarriage. *Journal of Marriage and the Family, 51,* 713–725.

Victor, S. B., & Fish, M. C. (1995). Lesbian mothers and the children: A review for school psychologists. *School Psychology Review, 24*(3), 456–479.

Visher, E. B., & Visher, J. S. (1983). Stepparenting: Blending families. In H. I. McCubbin & C. R. Figley (Eds.), *Stress and the family, Vol. 1: Coping with normative transitions* (pp. 133–146). New York: Brunner/Mazel.

Visher, E. B., & Visher, J. S. (1988). *Old loyalties, new loyalties: Therapeutic strategies with stepfamilies*. New York: Brunner/Mazel.

Visher, E. B., & Visher, J. S. (1989). Parenting coalitions after remarriage: Dynamics and therapeutic guidelines. *Family Relations, 38*(1), 65–71.

Visher, E. B., & Visher, J. S. (1990). Dynamics of successful stepfamilies. *Journal of Divorce and Remarriage, 14*(1), 3–12.

Visher, E. B., & Visher, J. S. (1993). Remarriage families and stepparenting. In F. Walsh (Ed.), *Normal family processes* (2nd ed., pp. 235–253). New York: Guilford.

Visher, E. B., Visher, J. S., & Pasley, K. (1997). Stepfamily therapy from the client's perspective. *Marriage and Family Review, 26*(1–2), 191–213.

Vobejda, B. (1994). Study alters image of "typical" family. *Seattle Times.* Available at: http://seattletimes.nwsource.com.

Voluntary Cooperative Information System (VCIS). (1996). *Characteristics of children in substitute and adoptive care.* Washington, DC: American Public Welfare Association.

Vroegh, K. S. (1997). Transracial adoptees: Developmental status after 17 years. *American Journal of Orthopsychiatry, 67*(4), 568–575.

Vuchinich, S., Hetherington, E. M., Vuchinich, R. A., & Clingempeel, W. G. (1991). Parent-child interaction and gender differences in early adolescents' adaptation to stepfamilies. *Developmental Psychology, 27*(4), 618–627.

Waggener, N. M., & Galassi, J. P. (1993). The relation of frequency, satisfaction, and type of socially supportive behaviors to psychological adjustment in marital separation. *Journal of Divorce and Remarriage, 21*(1–2), 139–160.

Walker, A. J., Pratt, C. C., & Eddy, L. (1995). Informal caregiving to aging family members: A critical review. *Family Relations, 44,* 402–411.

Wallerstein, J., & Kelly, J. (1980). *Surviving the breakup: How children and parents cope with divorce.* New York: Basic Books.

Walsh, J. A., & Walsh, R. A. (1990). Studies of the maintenance of subsidized foster placements in the Casey Family Program. *Child Welfare, 69,* 99–114.

Walters, K. L. (1988). Negotiating conflicts in allegiances among lesbians and gays of color: Reconciling divided selves and communities. In G. P. Mallon (Ed.), *Foundations of social work practice with lesbian and gay persons* (pp. 47–75). New York: Haworth.

Walters, L. H., & Abshire, C. R. (1995). Single-parenthood and the law. *Marriage and Family Review, 20*(1–2), 161–188.

Watson, K. W. (1996). Family-centered adoption practice. *Families in Society, 77*(9), 523–534.

Watson, K. W. (1997). Bonding and attachment in adoption: Towards better understanding and useful definitions. *Marriage and Family Review, 25*(3–4), 159–173.

Wegar, K. (1997). In search of bad mothers: Social constructions of birth and adoptive motherhood. *Women's Studies International Forum, 20*(1), 77–86.

Wegar, K. (1998). Adoption and kinship. In K. V. Hansen & A. I. Garey (Eds.), *Families in the U.S.: Kinship and domestic politics* (pp. 41–51). Philadelphia: Temple University Press.

Weinreb, M., & Konstam, V. (1995). Birthmothers: Silent relationships. *Affilia, 10*(3), 315–327.

Weisner, T. S., & Garnier, H. (1992). Nonconventional family life-styles and school achievement: A 12-year longitudinal study. *American Educational Research Journal, 29*(3), 605–632.

Weiss, R. S. (1994). A different kind of parenting. In G. Handel & G. G. Whitchurch (Eds.), *The psychosocial interior of the family* (4th ed., pp. 609–639). New York: Aldine.

Weitzman, L. J. (1975). To love, honor, and obey? Traditional legal marriage and alternative family forms. *Family Coordinator, 24*(4), 531–547.

Weitzman, L. J. (1985). *The divorce resolution: The unexpected social and economic consequences for women and children in America.* New York: Free Press.

Weitzman, L. J. (1988). Women and children last: The social and economic consequences of divorce law reforms. In S. M. Dornbusch & M. H. Strober (Eds.), *Feminism, children, and the new families: Perspectives on marriage and the family* (pp. 212–248). New York: Guilford.

Wells, K., & D'Angelo, L. (1994). Specialized foster care: Voices from the field. *Social Service Review, 68*(1), 127–144.

Westhues, A., & Cohen, J. S. (1998). The adjustment of intercountry adoptees in Canada. *Children and Youth Services Review, 20*(1–2), 115–134.

Weston, K. (1994). Building gay families. In G. Handel & G. G. Whitchurch (Eds.), *The psychosocial interior of the family* (4th ed., pp. 525–533). New York: Aldine.

Weston, K. (1997). *Families we choose: Lesbians, gays, kinship* (2nd ed.). New York: Columbia University Press.

White, L. K., & Booth, A. (1985). The transition to parenthood and marital equality. *Journal of Family Issues, 6,* 435–449.

Whitehead, B. D. (1993). Dan Quayle was right. *Atlantic Monthly, 271*(4), 47–84.

Wilkinson, D. (1993). Family ethnicity in America. In H. P. McAdoo (Ed.), *Family ethnicity: Strength in diversity* (pp. 15–59). Newbury Park, CA: Sage.

Willis, M. G. (1996). The real issues in transracial adoption: A response. *Journal of Black Psychology, 22*(2), 246–253.

Wineberg, H. (1992). Childbearing and dissolution of the second marriage. *Journal of Marriage and the Family, 54,* 879–887.

Woodworth, R. S. (1996). You're not alone . . . you're one in a million. *Child Welfare, 75*(5), 619–635.

Worell, J. (1988). Single mothers: From problems to policies. *Women and Therapy, 7*(4), 3–14.

Wright, C., & Jagger, G. (1999). End of century, end of family? Shifting discourses of family "crisis." In G. Jagger & C. Wright (Eds.), *Changing family values* (pp. 17–37). London: Routledge.

Wright, D. W., & Price, S. J. (1986). Court-ordered child support payment: The effect of the former spouse relationship on compliance. *Journal of Marriage and the Family, 48,* 869–874.

Wright, J. M. (1998). *Lesbian stepfamilies: An ethnography of love.* New York: Haworth.

Wu, Z. (1994). Remarriage in Canada: A social exchange perspective. *Journal of Divorce and Remarriage, 21*(3–4), 191–225.

Young, I. M. (1995). Mothers, citizenship, and independence: A critique of pure family values. *Ethics, 105*(3), 535–556.

Zeppa, A., & Norem, R. H. (1993). Stressors, manifestations of stress, and first-family/ stepfamily group membership. *Journal of Divorce and Remarriage, 19*(3–4), 3–24.

Ziegler, D. (1995). Single parenting: A visual analysis. In B. J. Dickerson (Ed.), *African American single mothers: Understanding their lives and families* (pp. 80–93). Thousand Oaks, CA: Sage.

Zuravin, S., Benedict, M., & Somerfield, P. (1993). Child maltreatment in family foster care. *American Journal of Orthopsychiatry, 63*(4), 589–596.

INDEX

ABOUT THE AUTHOR

Pauline Irit Erera is Associate Professor at the University of Washington School of Social Work. She has a BSW and MSW in social work from the University of Haifa, Israel, and a PhD in human service studies from Cornell University. She has researched and written extensively about family diversity, focusing mainly on step-, foster, and lesbian families, and on noncustodial fathers. In addition to family diversity, her interests include feminism, multiculturalism, and qualitative research methods.